THE STUDIO RECORDINGS OF THE MILES
DAVIS QUINTET, 1965–68

OXFORD STUDIES IN RECORDED JAZZ
Series Editor   JEREMY BARHAM

Louis Armstrong's Hot Five and Hot Seven Recordings
Brian Harker

The Studio Recordings of the Miles Davis Quintet, 1965–68
Keith Waters

THE STUDIO RECORDINGS OF THE MILES DAVIS QUINTET, 1965–68

KEITH WATERS

OXFORD
UNIVERSITY PRESS

OXFORD

UNIVERSITY PRESS

Oxford University Press, Inc., publishes works that further
Oxford University's objective of excellence
in research, scholarship, and education.

Oxford   New York
Auckland   Cape Town   Dar es Salaam   Hong Kong   Karachi
Kuala Lumpur   Madrid   Melbourne   Mexico City   Nairobi
New Delhi   Shanghai   Taipei   Toronto

with offices in
Argentina   Austria   Brazil   Chile   Czech Republic   France   Greece
Guatemala   Hungary   Italy   Japan   Poland   Portugal   Singapore
South Korea   Switzerland   Thailand   Turkey   Ukraine   Vietnam

Copyright © 2011 by Oxford University Press, Inc.

Published by Oxford University Press, Inc.
198 Madison Avenue, New York, New York 10016

www.oup.com

Oxford is a registered trademark of Oxford University Press.

Library of Congress Cataloging-in-Publication Data
Waters, Keith, 1958–
The studio recordings of the Miles Davis Quintet, 1965–68 / Keith Waters.
   p.   cm.—(Oxford studies in recorded jazz)
Includes bibliographical references, discography, and index.
ISBN 978-0-19-539383-5; 978-0-19-539384-2 (pbk.)
   1. Davis, Miles—Criticism and interpretation.
   2. Jazz—1961–1970—History and criticism.
   3. Miles Davis Quintet—Discography. I. Title.
ML419.D39W38 2011
785'.35195165—dc22   2010020252

Printed in the United States of America on acid-free paper

SERIES PREFACE

THE OXFORD STUDIES IN Recorded Jazz series offers detailed historical, cultural, and technical analysis of jazz recordings across a broad spectrum of styles, periods, performing media, and nationalities. Each volume, authored by a leading scholar in the field, addresses either a single jazz album or a set of related recordings by one artist/group, placing the recordings fully in their historical and musical context, and thereby enriching our understanding of their cultural and creative significance.

With access to the latest scholarship and with an innovative and balanced approach to its subject matter, the series offers fresh perspectives on both well-known and neglected jazz repertoire. It sets out to renew musical debate in jazz scholarship, and to develop the subtle critical languages and vocabularies necessary to do full justice to the complex expressive, structural, and cultural dimensions of recorded jazz performance.

JEREMY BARHAM
SERIES EDITOR

PREFACE

THERE ARE MANY VIEWS of Miles Davis. There is Davis the innovator, shaping the prominent jazz directions of postwar America, Davis the collaborator, relying on other musicians for creative tensions and foils, Davis the representative of a St. Louis trumpet tradition, Davis a constructor of racial identity and black masculinity in the 1950s, Davis the "most brilliant sellout in the history of jazz," Davis the aloof and irascible, Davis the trumpeter engaged in "signifyin'," the propagandist for musical organization based on scales, the heroin addict, the champion over heroin addiction, the boxer, the searing melodist, the abstractionist, the owner of sports cars and expensive suits. And there are many others.

The inventory draws attention to a significant musician and complex cultural figure. It also highlights the plurality of views on Davis and his music. The intent for this book is not to examine all those facets, but to concentrate on those that relate to a specific set of studio recordings that Davis made with a specific group of musicians, his so-called second quintet, with Wayne Shorter, Herbie Hancock, Tony Williams, and Ron Carter. The book uses transcriptions and description, calling attention to details of the music in order for them to be heard. It relies on a view of musical analysis that offers further ways to hear or think about those recordings.

Musical analysis—and discourse on music more generally—is selective and provisional. It atomizes the music in particular ways, presenting some elements while ignoring others. The analyses presented here are no exception. They merely explore ideas that may be of particular interest to jazz musicians, listeners, writers, historians, and analysts, present features of the music that I think are audible but may not be immediately apparent, and consider ways in which these recordings broached or broke with jazz traditions.

Jazz studies has profited considerably by recent intersections with cultural studies. Such enterprises focus on jazz as a process that emerges from larger musical, social, and cultural relationships, and celebrates jazz as a collective endeavor. I am eager to acknowledge the influence of many recent writers in regard to collective processes, ensemble interaction, and the methods in which the players relied on one another in improvisational settings.

Yet occasionally such studies critique other approaches that allow more detailed views of musical organization, structure, and theorizing about them. The discomfort becomes especially acute when the focus remains on individual improvisations rather than on collective processes. The criticisms flow from several sources: that these analyses valorize the music by calling attention to features shared with Western classical music repertory (particularly features of coherence, continuity, or organicism), that they ignore larger collaborative processes and therefore favor "product" over "process," or that they represent dominant academic institutional ideologies.

Yet jazz musicians as a general community are often keenly interested in and focused on details of musical organization and structure, are quick to theorize about these ideas, and frequently are savvy, passionate, and omnivorous in seeking out and using such details to facilitate musical development and growth. Further, published transcriptions related to individual improvisations by particular players, with or without commentary, have been an ancillary part of the jazz tradition at least since the 1927 publication of *Louis Armstrong's 50 Hot Choruses for Cornet*. It is not my intention to suggest that musical analysis arising from notated transcriptions plays a more fundamental role for musicians than other methods that they may cultivate. And it is certainly true that some analytical studies do privilege criteria such as organicism and coherence. (Andre Hodeir and Gunther Schuller are typically held as the culprits for unquestioningly establishing aesthetic values that mirror those of Western European music.) Yet jazz transcription and analysis—both of ensemble processes as well as individual improvisations—often answer questions asked by communities of listeners, musicians, analysts, and writers, and form part of a long-standing tradition. It may be that those interested in jazz as seen through a cultural lens are interested in asking questions different from those with a more analytical focus. However, it seems that allowing for a plurality of views about music acknowledges more richly the breadth of its traditions.

In addition to discussions of improvisation, many of the analyses in this book also present details of the compositions more generally—that is, the head statements with melody, harmony, rhythm, and accompaniment. I am aware of problems of ontology that arise from the idea of "the composition," that the notion of "the composition" itself suggests a fixed or idealized entity at odds with the ways in which players freely and flexibly construct head statements. Rather than tend to those particular and interesting philosophical problems, I will use the term *composition* (or, as jazz musicians typically say, the *head* or *tune*) in the way that jazz musicians generally do—that the head relies on flexibly constructed statements of melody, harmony, bass, and rhythm, and subsequent statements may preserve certain contours but may alter others.

Discrete equal-tempered pitches temporally placed along a time line of equally spaced beats create convenient fictions or half-truths. Musical notation and transcriptions are at best a type of shorthand incapable of capturing or revealing every nuance of a performance. They themselves form a type of selective analysis. Here transcriptions are intended to supplement, not replace, the sound. In my transcriptions I have attended to some details but not to others. The transcriptions use symbols to pitches that indicate bent, smeared, or ghosted notes. (An "x" in place of a notehead indicates a ghosted note, the "turn" symbol indicates a lip smear.) When I have heard pitches as sharp or flat relative to equal temperament, I affix the symbols "+" or "−" to those pitches. Notated rhythm suggests an idealized fixed metrical grid or timeline, but naturally jazz players take all types of liberties with rhythm in terms of expressive microtimings, swing rhythms, and so forth. The transcriptions typically indicate swing rhythms as even eighth notes and identify pitches that are heard as late or early relative to the perception of the beat. Those particularly interested in Tony Williams will be disappointed to note limited drum transcriptions, and I readily acknowledge this omission to be a drastic one, considering the vast contributions he made to the group.

There are different conventions for indicating measure numbers in transcriptions. I have chosen to indicate them completely consecutively, rather than by using two or more labels to represent chorus number or place in the form (i.e., m. 46 instead of 2nd chorus/2nd A section/m. 6). Consecutive numbering maintains consistency since, for a number of the improvisations, the quintet does not preserve chorus structure. When the group does, I annotate the transcriptions to indicate where new choruses begin. I will refer to, say, the first measure in the second chorus of a 16-bar composition as m. 17, rather than 2/1. Discussion of particular pitches relies on the convention of middle C as C4, an octave above as C5, and so forth.

I frequently rely on shorthand by providing chord symbols in place of transcribing the piano voicings. It would be instructive to consistently transcribe the piano voicings, but for space considerations I use chord symbols most of the time, which provide a convenient way of generalizing the underlying harmonic framework in a way with which most jazz musicians are familiar. (Transcriptions of piano solos, however, include both left hand and right hand.) Yet chord symbols can be notoriously inconsistent or individual, and there is frequently in performance wide latitude for multiple interpretations, extensions, and alterations. The idea of the "correct" chord changes does not comport very well with jazz practice, and it is likely that others may prefer different harmonic labels at times. I use current conventions that are not in evidence in the quintet players' lead sheets, such as the use of the term "alt" to refer to extensions that may include flatted ninth, raised ninth, raised eleventh, and flatted thirteenth. I have heard objections to this since "alt" is taken to refer to a scale, rather than a harmony. But this is true also of most thirteenth chords (C-13; Cmaj13/#11): their extensions can be collapsed in a seven-pitch scale. Further, some of the players' lead sheets do rely on scale labels: the 1963 lead sheet copyright deposit to Herbie Hancock's "King Cobra" uses "F# phrygian" as a chord designation. I have attempted to provide chord symbols that I think are most accurate and provide the most information.

In addition to transcriptions, the following chapters make use of other materials. The copyright deposits of lead sheets to Shorter's second quintet compositions are located at the Library of Congress. They are part of a larger set of Shorter compositions that include those recorded with Blakey 1959–63 as well as those recorded under Shorter's own name as leader for a series of Blue Note recordings during the 1960s. The second quintet compositions each bear Library of Congress dates that range between 1965 and 1968 and are written in Shorter's own hand. Likely Shorter submitted all the lead sheets to the Library of Congress at least in part to ensure that he would receive mechanical royalties for record sales. The lead sheets are instructive in several ways. As copyright deposits, they suggest that Shorter considered them as providing a somewhat definitive version in terms of melody and harmony. While it is not certain that the players used precisely those versions in the studio, there are nevertheless changes to form, melody, or harmony on the studio recordings relative to the lead sheets, which suggest to me that the group altered them. If so, Shorter's lead sheets perhaps reveal something of the working studio processes of the quintet, who frequently made such alterations to other compositions while in the recording studio. Shorter's lead sheets also show ongoing issues and problems with harmonic labels (chord symbols), which tell us something about inconsistencies of chord symbols during the 1960s, inconsistencies that still linger.

Reception history takes many forms. One type comes from the jazz trade press in journals such as *Down Beat*, which offer record reviews and interviews. But there are others. Jazz fake books offer a different type of reception history, particularly for the studio recordings of the Davis second quintet. By including particular compositions, fake books participate in establishing one type of jazz canon. In the past several decades, sources (such as, for example, *The Real Book*) have had a remarkable transmission, and they include a number of second quintet compositions, including "E.S.P.," "Eighty-One," "Iris," "Orbits," "Dolores," "Freedom Jazz Dance," "Footprints," "The Sorcerer," "Prince of Darkness," "Pee Wee," "Nefertiti," "Fall," "Pinocchio," and "Stuff." But while these sources have enhanced the visibility of these compositions among jazz musicians, they can also be flawed and problematic, particularly when the melodies and harmonies do not align with those heard on the recordings. Yet even in these instances such lead sheet discrepancies with the recordings may be instructive since they may call attention to theoretical tenets and biases that have arisen in jazz pedagogy since the 1970s. The analyses of "Pee Wee" and "Pinocchio" show that errors in the lead sheets likely arose in order either to avoid situations that the transcribers would have considered problematic (such as "avoid tones"), or to replace the progressions from the recordings with more conventional functional harmonic progressions.

Ideas of form in improvisation loom large throughout the book. I am particularly interested in the relationship of these recordings to the larger jazz tradition of chorus structure, and thinking specifically about the ways in which the quintet relied on or abandoned chorus structure. I also consider ideas related to "hypermeter," which suggests that larger metrical groupings (of, say, 4, 8, 16, or 32 bars) operate more or less analogously to meter. Some of the following commentary on the second quintet compositions demonstrates how larger metrical organization plays into form, and considers departures from 4-, 8-, or 16-bar organization. I am not proposing that 4-, 8-, 16-, or 32-bar organization is necessarily better, but it is useful to acknowledge that those groupings are part of the larger jazz tradition from which the players emerged, and many if not most of the compositions performed by those players earlier—either jazz standards or original compositions—relied on such organization. Departures from those metrical structures need not be heard as working against the backdrop of that tradition, but it is interesting to hear the music in that way and it is likely one way that the players and other musicians heard it.

Further, the analyses point out the use of ongoing musical motives, particularly during the improvisations. The use of motivic labels is not intended to suggest that ongoing motives make the music more organic, more continuous, or more coherent. Rather, such discussions are meant merely to provide ways to help hear how these players worked out individual ideas during the flow of improvisation. I rely on a rather general and loose notion of motive, based on subsequent melodic ideas that retain some aspect of pitch, interval, rhythm, or contour. I am less interested in providing a rigorous definition of motive than I am in calling attention to those recurring features that I think are generally audible.

The organization of the book is as follows. In chapter 1, I discuss the formation of the quintet, their output in terms of compositions and recordings, and their working methods in the studio, followed by a consideration of the earlier careers of each of the members, particularly in relation to what they brought to the quintet. Chapter 2 provides some analytical avenues that I use in the book, and considers issues related to modal jazz, motivic organization, phrase overlap, meter and hypermeter, group interactions, circular tunes, and form in improvisation. Each of the following chapters then regards the studio recordings, individually for *E.S.P.* (chapter 3), *Miles Smiles* (chapter 4), *Sorcerer* (chapter 5), *Nefertiti* (chapter 6), and collectively for the final two recordings, *Miles in the Sky* and *Filles de Kilimanjaro* (chapter 7). The final chapter engages the legacy of the quintet, in terms of its repertory as well as broader repercussions in terms of jazz-rock (or jazz-funk) fusion of the late 1960s and 1970s and the "hard bop resurgence" of the 1980s and beyond.

There is a wealth of information about Miles Davis. I have relied on a number of thoughtful and sensitive biographies, particularly those by Ian Carr, Jack Chambers, and John Szwed. In the second edition of his biography *Milestones*, Chambers discusses some problems with Davis's autobiography, written in collaboration with Quincy Troupe, and he claims that Troupe derived some of the content and facts from Chambers's own *Milestones*, rather than from Troupe's interviews with Davis. As a result, I have avoided using the Davis autobiography as a source since I suspect that passages that seem troublesome to me (such as comments about modal jazz and Davis's composition "Milestones") may have been drawn from Chambers's biography. (Cassette tapes of the Troupe/Davis interviews are at the Schomburg Library in New York City, but their audio fidelity is problematic.) Bassist Todd Coolman's New York University dissertation, "The Miles Davis Quintet of the Mid-1960s: Synthesis of

Improvisational and Compositional Elements" includes the contents of substantive interviews with the quintet members and offers any number of intriguing ways to hear the quintet compositions.

I suppose in many ways I have been working on this book since I was a teenager. As an aspiring jazz musician, I found these recordings immensely valuable for providing me with models for performance. At different times in my performing and academic career, I have transcribed portions of these recordings. Nevertheless, most of the work for this book began in earnest while on sabbatical from the University of Colorado during the year 2003–4, during which I undertook many of the transcriptions. Several of the ideas and analyses included here formed parts of earlier papers or publications, particularly the discussions of "Iris," "Orbits," "Pinocchio," and "Madness." I received a research grant from the Graduate Commission on Arts and Humanities (of the University of Colorado at Boulder) in order to visit the Library of Congress spring 2008, and was awarded the University's Kayden Research Grant in autumn 2009 in order to help with subvention costs.

I owe a debt of gratitude to many individuals for their help with this book. Many made detailed suggestions for improvement, or provided ideas through correspondence or through thought-provoking discussions. Ben Givan, Larry Kart, Barry Kernfeld, Steve Larson, Henry Martin, Keith Salley, Steve Strunk, and Carl Woideck provided comments on drafts of portions of chapters or—in some cases—multiple chapters. Many of the ideas about circular tunes arose as the result of a joint paper given with Martin, Strunk, and Larson; other ideas through informal conversation with them. Due to her extensive knowledge of Wayne Shorter's music, Patricia Julien was an invaluable resource, and she patiently responded to my many inquiries. Many of the ideas within the book were sparked by conversations with pianists Harold Danko, Andy LaVerne, Marc Copland, and Fred Hersch, trumpeters Brad Goode and Jim Ketch, saxophonists John Gunther and Kurtis Adams, bassists Tommy Cecil and Johannes Weidenmüller, drummers David Via, Tony Martucci, Graeme Boone, and Kent Williams, as well as my brother Robert Waters. Bertrand Ueberall provided me with access to the Shorter lead sheets at the Library of Congress. Patricia Julien, Tom Myer, and Daphne Leong offered helpful suggestions to improve the transcriptions. Lewis Porter aided me in numerous ways, and I would especially like to acknowledge Bob Belden and Hyland Harris for providing me with access to other lead sheets and rare recordings not generally available. Special thanks are also due Gene Hayworth, who compiled the index.

As series editor, Jeremy Barham provided me with excellent editorial support and suggestions for content. Suzanne Ryan, senior editor for Oxford, was staunchly enthusiastic in her support for this project and the overall series. Production editor Liz Smith was delightful to work with throughout the project. Greg Simon participated in the latter stages of creating Finale files of the transcriptions, and Lezlie Botkin proofread a later draft. Michael Conklin compiled the book's discography. Naturally, any factual errors or problems with the transcriptions or analyses are entirely my own.

CONTENTS

THE STUDIO RECORDINGS OF THE MILES
DAVIS QUINTET, 1965–68

CHAPTER 1

THE QUINTET

IN THE 30TH ST. COLUMBIA recording studio the five musicians begin to rehearse Eddie Harris's composition "Freedom Jazz Dance." The studio, a former Presbyterian Church on the east side of Manhattan, has high arched ceilings, lath and plaster walls, and an unvarnished wood floor, all contributing to its celebrated warm and rich acoustic ambience.[1] Miles Davis begins with bassist Ron Carter, providing Carter with suggestions as he tries different bass accompanimental figures. Carter comes up with a figure that sounds like a funky jazz cliché—Davis dismisses it: "No, that's too common. Come on." He sings through some different rhythms. Several minutes later pianist Herbie Hancock starts to work

---

1   Meyer Berger, "About New York," *New York Times* (April 22, 1953): 31; David Simons, *Studio Stories: How the Great New York Records Were Made: From Miles to Madonna, Sinatra to the Ramones* (San Francisco: Backbeat Books, 2004); Greg Milner, *Perfecting Sound Forever: An Aural History of Recorded Music* (New York: Faber and Faber: 2009), 149.

out a melodic idea in the lower register of the piano to harmonize with Carter's bass. Davis says, "Herbie, hit a chord, hit a chord." Davis walks over to the piano, and voices a B♭♮9(♯11) chord. Hancock plays a denser chord, consisting of a C♯ diminished seventh chord above a D diminished seventh chord. Davis responds: "Yeah, OK."

The group runs through the head a couple of times. There are a few problems in executing the melody. To saxophonist Wayne Shorter, Davis rasps: "We need to divide this up, brother," suggesting that each play separately a portion of the second half of the melody. Hancock: "It's getting there, it's getting there." Following the next take, Davis says, "You know, Wayne, what we can do," and he sings the melody, but adds two bars of silence between each of the three phrases. They try it with the additional bars without melody. To producer Teo Macero in the control room, Davis says, "Hey, Teo. Play that back." Regarding his own suggestion for the bars of silence added within Harris's melody, Davis adds, "That's a nice idea, through. *Brilliant* idea." The group runs through the head several more times. To drummer Tony Williams, Davis suggests that he play eighth note triplets. The group tries the head in another recorded take, the tenth. Finally, despite a false start—Davis comes in early at the beginning—Take 11 continues with solos. It becomes the master take released on the recording.

"Freedom Jazz Dance" would appear on the quintet's studio album *Miles Smiles*. The above dialogue, taken from the October 24, 1966, session reels, shows the collaborative workshop aspect to the group's preparations. Many of the decisions for rhythm section accompaniment and for alterations to Harris's melody arise from Davis's suggestions, but the other players also offer comments and contributions. Not all of Davis's suggestions were used in the final take—early on, Davis has Williams play woodblocks, and elsewhere suggests that Hancock lay out during the head statements—but the reels suggest an ongoing brainstorming process, one that allows revision, avoids cliché, and considers additional ideas to emerge while the group records, then listens to earlier takes.

Miles Smiles was the second of six studio recordings that this quintet would release during their time together. These recordings form the focus of this study:

E.S.P. (January 1965)
Miles Smiles (October 1966)
Sorcerer (May 1967)
Nefertiti (June 1967)
Miles in the Sky (January and May 1968)
Filles de Kilimanjaro (June 1968)

Davis's "second classic quintet," coinciding on the one side with the election of Lyndon Johnson in the fall of 1964, and on the other with the death of Martin Luther King in the spring of 1968, was to have a profound impact on the development of postbop jazz. Critics and musicians view the quintet as the touchstone for innovative small-group jazz improvisation. It was, saxophonist Dave Liebman noted, "one of the most influential groups in jazz history."[2] The personnel of the quintet included Davis (1926–91) on trumpet, tenor saxophonist Wayne Shorter (b. 1933), pianist Herbie Hancock (b. 1940), bassist Ron Carter (b. 1937), and drummer Tony Williams (1945–97).

Davis hired the rhythm section of Hancock, Carter, and Williams in 1963, but the personnel stabilized with the addition of Shorter in September 1964. The group provided a formative workshop for the creative young innovators to develop individually and collectively. The players developed paths for extended improvisation and group interaction on an astonishingly high level.

Bassist Ron Carter called attention to the quintet members' substantial freelance and recording experiences that took place before they joined Davis's quintet. The group, he noted, brought more "initial variety, a larger variety of musical views to the band than the band we replaced."[3] With the exception of Tony Williams, all of the other members recorded extensively before they joined Davis. In addition to their recordings with Davis during 1964–68, his sidemen participated on other significant recordings both as leaders and as sidemen. Shorter, Hancock, Carter, and Williams were to go on and continue to develop significant careers after departing from the quintet.

All of the performers had deeply absorbed hard bop influences. But while the group eagerly reflected many of those influences during their time with Davis, they also explored a host of improvisational and accompanimental techniques that departed from standard hard bop practice. The players redefined spontaneous small-group interaction, particularly by working through techniques of harmonic substitution and superimposition, metrical conflict, and metric modulation. In works that used repeated chorus structure during improvisation, these techniques had important implications for musical form since they could work either to delineate or disguise important formal junctures.

---

2   Todd Coolman, "The Miles Davis Quintet of the Mid-1960s: Synthesis of Improvisational and Compositional Elements" (Ph.D. diss., New York University, 1997), 9.
3   Coolman, "The Miles Davis Quintet," 15.

On some recordings, the quintet also departed from chorus structure during the improvisations. It is essential to consider the quintet's
accomplishments—the group's creativity, spontaneity, and interaction—
against the backdrop of 1960s avant-garde jazz. By the mid-1960s, the
work of avant-garde jazz musicians (such as Ornette Coleman) was, as
pianist Mal Waldron indicated, impossible to ignore and required some
response—even if negative—from most creative musicians.[4] The players
in Davis's quintet exhibited a deft ability to merge traditional with avant-
garde approaches to improvisation. Pianist Hancock later recalled that
the group was attempting to

> take those influences that were happening to all of us at that time and
> amalgamate them, personalize them in such a way that when people
> were hearing us, they were hearing the avant-garde on the one hand,
> and they were hearing the history of jazz that led up to it on the other
> hand—because Miles was that history. He was that link. We were sort
> of walking a tightrope with the kind of experimenting we were doing
> in music, not total experimentation, but we used to call it "controlled
> freedom."[5]

Hancock's notion of controlled freedom is intriguing. It indicates a
willingness to cultivate earlier influences alongside avant-garde ones. It
also suggests that the group located intermediate spaces between traditional jazz and free jazz. As Gerald Early writes, Davis "walked a line
between freedom and tradition with his 1960s quintet that has become
the basis for virtually all small-group jazz being played now."[6] Chapter 2
considers in more detail how the group negotiated this line between freedom and tradition, particularly in response to underlying form during
improvisation.

The quintet's audio recordings and a handful of video recordings doc-
ument the accomplishments and the progress of the group. Most commentators acknowledge two aspects to the group's recordings. On the
one hand are the live recordings, which feature primarily jazz standards.
Some standards, such as "My Funny Valentine," Davis had been playing

---

4 Personal phone interview with Waldron, summer 1998.
5 Quoted from the film *Miles Ahead*, Mark Obenhaus, dir., Obenhaus Films, 1986. Cited in
   John Szwed, *So What: The Life of Miles Davis* (New York: Simon & Schuster, 2002), 255.
6 Gerald Early, "The Art of the Muscle: Miles Davis as American Knight and American
   Knave," in *Miles Davis and American Culture*, ed. Gerald Early (St. Louis: Missouri Historical Society Press, 2001), 17.

regularly since the 1950s.[7] On the other hand are the studio recordings, which feature primarily original compositions. With a few exceptions ("Agitation," "Footprints," "Ginger Bread Boy," "Riot," and "Masqualero") the quintet did not perform those studio compositions live. *Why?*

Prior to Shorter's arrival, the quintet released several live recordings made with either George Coleman or Sam Rivers on tenor saxophone (1963–64). The group made two live recordings after Shorter joined the quintet: *Miles in Berlin* (1964) and *Live at the Plugged Nickel* (1965).[8] The live recordings display remarkably innovative approaches to standard tune improvisation. Extant analytical research on the quintet focuses on the live recordings, and these publications emphasize improvisational techniques within the context of jazz standards.[9] The later portion of this chapter will address some aspects of the group's live recordings.

This study, however, regards the body of compositions contained on the studio recordings. Although Wayne Shorter wrote the majority of them, all the quintet members contributed compositions to these studio recordings. Arguably, in many ways these recordings reflect a number of very conventional jazz practices. Many rely on the typical head-solos-head format, most feature a predictable solo sequence of trumpet, tenor saxophone, and piano, and most feature standard jazz accompanimental textures: walking bass in 4/4, jazz waltzes, ballads, and straight eighth-note accompaniment.

Despite these conventional practices, the studio recordings are ground-breaking in a variety of ways. The compositions themselves represent a significant contribution to the jazz repertory, and their innovations

---

7 See Howard Brofsky, "Miles Davis and 'My Funny Valentine': The Evolution of a Solo," *Black Music Research Journal* 3 (1983): 23–45.

8 Also now available is a recording from a 1967 Paris performance, released as *No Blues* (Jazz Music Yesterday JMY 1003).

9 See Paul Berliner, *Thinking in Jazz: The Infinite Art of Improvisation* (Chicago: University of Chicago Press, 1994), esp. 527–30, 633–36, 651–52, 654–57, 709–27; Brofsky, "Miles Davis and 'My Funny Valentine,'" David DeMotta, "An Analysis of Herbie Hancock's Accompanying in the Miles Davis Quintet on the 1967 Album *No Blues*" (M.Mus. thesis, William Paterson University, 2006); Franz Krieger, "Herbie Hancock in seiner Zeit bei Miles Davis: Transkription und Analyse ausgewählter 'My Funny Valentine'-soli," *Jazzforschung* 30 (1998): 101–56; David Morgan, "Superimposition in the Improvisations of Herbie Hancock," *Annual Review of Jazz Studies* 11 (2000–2001): 69–90; Henry Martin, "The Nature of Recomposition: Miles Davis and 'Stella by Starlight,'" *Annual Review of Jazz Studies* 9 (1997–98): 77–92; Alona Sagee, "Miles Davis's Improvised Solos in Recordings of 'Walkin': 1954–67," *Annual Review of Jazz Studies* 13 (2003): 27–47; Robert Walser, " 'Out of Notes': Signification, Interpretation, and the Problem of Miles Davis," *Musical Quarterly* 77/2 (1993): 343–65.

form a cornerstone of contemporary jazz composition. Many of these original compositions recorded by the quintet have enjoyed an extended shelf life through later performances by quintet members and by others. Their availability as lead sheets in sources such as *The Real Book* has heightened their visibility, although some lead sheets contain inaccurate harmonies and melodies (such as "Orbits," "Pee Wee," "Prince of Darkness," and "Pinocchio"). The studio compositions reflect an expansion of compositional resources available to jazz composers through chord type (harmonic structure), chord-to-chord succession (harmonic progression), and through their departure from functional harmonic progressions. These compositions also provided vigorous alternatives to standard-tune formal frameworks since they largely abandoned 32-bar AABA or ABAC chorus forms. Many were single-section works without bridges and without standard harmonic turnarounds, and the absence of internal formal divisions contributed to the group's flexible and open sound. Commentators have called attention to these single-section forms, highlighting their status as novel alternatives to standard-tune compositions.[10] Yet it is important to acknowledge that a number of Shorter's earlier compositions written between 1959 and 1963 are likewise single-section forms, rather than standard-tune AABA or ABAC forms.

Herbie Hancock regarded Shorter's compositions as a powerful catalyst for the quintet: "The compositions," he said, "seemed to give rise to a whole new approach to improvising. They had a powerful influence on our collective musical direction."[11] No doubt their departure from hard bop harmonic and formal principles posed challenges and suggested new and different improvisational solutions. Melodically, too, the compositions' reliance on short, memorable motives seemed to encourage highly motivic improvisations, and the analyses contained in this book will show ways in which the soloists ranged between short compact motives and longer standard eighth-note hard bop phrasing. The melodies to a number of compositions explored the use of successive perfect fourths ("E.S.P.," "Orbits," "Freedom Jazz Dance," "Nefertiti," "Madness") operating as a recurrent token of 1960s modernism.

The studio recordings are also notable for their range of formal strategies during improvisation. Some compositions rely on chorus structure during the solos: that is, the rhythm section and soloist maintain the meter, harmonic progression, and formal design heard during the head.

---

10 Coolman, "The Miles Davis Quintet," 17; Mark Gridley, *Jazz Styles*, 10th ed. (Upper Saddle River, N.J.: Prentice Hall, 2009), 275.

11 Coolman, "The Miles Davis Quintet," 30.

Some compositions, however, do not. In particular, the group on many compositions features a technique sometimes referred to as "time, no changes." Here the rhythm section maintains the underlying meter while accompanying the improvisations, but abandons the harmonic progression and underlying formal design stated during the head. On a "time, no changes" composition such as "Orbits" (*Miles Smiles*), for example, the absence of piano comping during horn solos contributes further to the group's open sound, and the soloists frequently refer to and improvise with motives derived from the melody. On some recordings the group even omitted improvisations by the horns and piano entirely—tracks such as "Nefertiti" and the alternate take to "Pinocchio" (*Nefertiti*) consist of repeated statements of the melody. This technique then reverses the roles of horn and rhythm section, with the horns continuing the melody as a repeated obbligato throughout the track, while the rhythm section takes on the focal improvisatory role. Chapter 2 examines more completely the range of formal strategies used during improvisation.

Later CD releases of the studio recordings included alternate takes for a number of compositions. In 1998, Columbia issued the *Miles Davis Quintet 1965–68* (Columbia 4–67398), which also includes those alternate takes as well as additional rehearsal tracks for several compositions. In addition to the six studio recordings that this book examines, the quintet also recorded other material in the studio that Columbia released as three recordings between 1976 and 1981: *Water Babies* (consisting of other material recorded during the *Nefertiti* session), *Directions*, and *Circle in the Round*. (For the latter two recordings Davis brought in additional players to augment the quintet.) The group recorded *Filles de Kilimanjaro* during the group's personnel changes, and the original quintet contributed three compositions to it.

STUDIO PROCESSES

The chronology of the quintet's six studio recordings shows that they were recorded intermittently over 3½ years. Because the quintet often made the recordings with a minimum of takes and little rehearsal, they contribute to Davis's reputation as a one-take musician. John Szwed writes that the level of the quintet's interaction and Davis's "love of first takes at recording sessions were part of an aesthetic of discovery that was given priority over a finished, perfected performance."[12] And some recordings do reveal this lack of interest in polished perfection, creating some notable

12 Szwed, *So What*, 264.

clashes. For example, the horns return to the final head statements of "The Sorcerer" (*Sorcerer*), "Pinocchio," and "Riot" (*Nefertiti*) before Hancock has concluded his piano solo, forcing it into an abrupt conclusion. Other releases include false starts ("Freedom Jazz Dance," *Miles Smiles*) or ragged out-heads ("Dolores," *Miles Smiles*). Nevertheless, the quintet did not always rely on single takes and did record alternate ones. Martin Williams, present at a 1968 studio session, related that one of the compositions used at least fifteen takes.[13] "Freedom Jazz Dance" required ten takes (and additional rehearsal discussion) prior to the released master, and—as indicated at the beginning of the chapter—the studio reels reveal Davis's keen interest in establishing clear roles for the rhythm section players. Other releases spliced together different takes. The presence of rehearsal takes, alternate takes, and the use of postproduction splicing techniques show that the "warts and all" aesthetic was not total.

Various quintet members described working processes in the studio. Their descriptions highlighted Davis's role in suggesting changes to compositions brought in by the sidemen. Hancock noted: "If anybody brings a composition in to Miles, he breaks it down to a skeletal form in such a way that each person in the group can start putting the pieces back together. You still have the essence of the original composition, but you create a new composition on that essence."[14] Davis himself discussed this in an interview: "Well, Herbie, Wayne [Shorter] or Tony will write something, then I'll take and spread it out or space it, or add some more chords, or change a couple of phrases, or write a bass line to it, or change the tempo of it, and that's the way we record. If it's in 4/4 time, I might change it to 3/4, 6/8 or 5/4."[15] Hancock described how Davis applied this process to Ron Carter's composition "Eighty-One": "Miles took the first two bars of melody notes and squished them all together, and he took out other areas to leave a big space that only the rhythm section would play. To me, it sounded like getting to the essence of the composition."[16]

Todd Coolman's interviews with quintet members considerably enhance the picture of the group's working processes in the studio. The

13 Martin Williams, "Recording Miles Davis," essay in *Jazz Masters in Transition* (New York: Macmillan, 1970), 275.

14 David Baker, Lida Belt, and Herman Hudson, eds., *The Black Composer Speaks* (Bloomington, Ind.: Afro-American Arts Institute, 1978), 114.

15 Arthur Taylor, *Notes and Tones: Musician-to-Musician Interviews* (New York: Coward, McCann & Geoghegan, 1977), 13.

16 Len Lyons, *The Great Jazz Pianists: Speaking of Their Lives and Music* (New York: William Morrow, 1983), 274.

interviews further describe how all the members participated in making changes or alterations to compositions brought into the studio. "When we'd bring in tunes, we would all work on them," said Ron Carter. "Herbie would still get credit for the tune, but it would be changed by all of us to make it do what we tried to do collectively better.... Whatever it would take; maybe take out these two bars, maybe it's in the wrong key... whatever it is... like in a workshop."[17]

Coolman concludes:

> Through the course of my interviews with the members of the ensemble, it became apparent that the studio recordings they made were done in a less than formal fashion. Additionally, they took place in relatively short time spans, with some compositions requiring only one or two complete takes. Typically, the composers brought in sketches, sometimes of complete compositions and sometimes of just a few thematic fragments, a partial bass line, or some other partial harmonic framework. Frequently, Davis would encourage the ensemble to experiment and even suggest changes to the compositional elements to better serve the improvised solos. Rehearsals seldom preceded the actual recording session, and often the recordings were made after brief run-throughs. Since these new compositions were largely unknown to the ensemble prior to the recording date, the performers had to rely largely on their musical instincts, ingenuity, and combined empathy to create a musical result that would sound complete and cohesive. Of course, after all of the material was recorded, the technology of the time allowed for various amounts of editing that sometimes took place under the supervision of producer Teo Marcero [*sic*]. In short, the recordings were treated as works in progress.[18]

The later CD releases of the studio recordings also provide a glimpse into working studio processes since they contain the alternate takes alongside the originally released tracks. On some, the treatment of the composition on the alternate takes differs from that on the released track. On the alternate take to "Limbo" (*Sorcerer*), for example, the group alters the harmonic progression drastically by omitting nearly every other chord heard in the released track. The alternate take to "Pinocchio" (*Nefertiti*) differs extensively from the released track, since—unlike the released version—it contains only repeated statements of the head without improvisations by trumpet, tenor saxophone, or piano.

17 Coolman, "The Miles Davis Quintet," 23.
18 Coolman, "The Miles Davis Quintet," 86–87.

In addition to these alternate takes, *Miles Davis Quintet 1965–68* (Columbia 4-67398) contains previously unreleased rehearsal tracks for two Hancock compositions, "Speak Like a Child," and "I Have a Dream" (recorded January 1968). The Davis quintet never released completed takes of these compositions. (Hancock's own recordings *Speak Like a Child* and *The Prisoner* include later performances of these compositions with other musicians.)

The rehearsal track to Herbie Hancock's "Madness" (*Nefertiti*) likely unveils the most radical change to the original intent of a composition. On it, the group plays "Madness" as a slow impressionistic waltz consisting of a 16-bar section, which is followed by a section consisting of six distinct chords. But on the subsequent alternate take and the released tracks, the group abandoned the opening 16-bar section, using only the following section of six chords. Further, they altered the tempo and meter, performing it more rapidly, with the meter now changed from 3/4 to 4/4. Thus with "Madness," the group dismembered and reconstituted many of the original structural features of Hancock's composition.

The extent to which Davis and the other musicians made alterations to Wayne Shorter's compositions is unclear. Hancock noted that Shorter's compositions "were the only ones left completely unedited by Miles," and Shorter also indicated that his compositions remained unaltered.[19] However, as indicated above, Shorter's "Limbo" received very different treatments during the alternate and released take. Martin Williams discusses Davis's changes to Shorter's "Paraphernalia" made at the recording session.[20] Additionally, Shorter's copyright deposits of his lead sheets, such as "Iris," differ strikingly in chord progression, meter, and number of measures from the recorded version.[21] All this suggests that the group may have made alterations to some of Shorter's compositions, contradicting the view that they remained unchanged in the studio.

The idea of "sketches" arises frequently in regard to Davis's own compositions recorded in the studio, and this idea formed part of an emerging compositional aesthetic for him. This aesthetic began earlier than the 1965–68 studio recordings with the second quintet, and continued well

19 Coolman, "The Miles Davis Quintet," 24 and 30.
20 Williams, "Recording Miles Davis," 276.
21 It is not certain that Shorter's copyright deposit lead sheets represented precisely what the group used in the studio. Nevertheless, since Shorter sent these copyright lead sheets to the Library of Congress (and they are frequently dated very close to the time of the studio recordings), it is likely that Shorter considered that lead sheet version definitive in some sense. If so, the harmonic, melodic, and formal differences between the lead sheets and the recorded compositions suggest alterations to Shorter's original idea of the composition.

beyond. Interviews with the musicians who performed with Davis in 1957 for the soundtrack to *Ascenseur pour l'échafaud* (*Lift to the Scaffold*) indicate that Davis merely provided minimal verbal guidelines for chord progressions.[22] The title to "Flamenco Sketches" (*Kind of Blue*, 1959) highlights the sketch facet of the composition. Recent evidence from a studio photograph shows that for "Flamenco Sketches" the musicians were merely given a series of five notated scales with the instruction to "play in (the) sound of these scales."[23] Wayne Shorter recalled that Davis frequently brought sketches of thematic ideas to the studio and asked the players to "see what you can do with that."[24] For Davis, the likely allure of compositional sketches (rather than a more standard lead sheet) was that they provided his musicians with a germinal idea, allowing room for flexibility and substantial individual input.

In most jazz contexts, the idea of a "composition" with a single author remains highly questionable. Even given a single author's lead sheet containing harmony and melody, all the musicians participate immeasurably in shaping the direction of the composition through decisions regarding accompaniment, improvisation, phrasing, and so forth. With the Davis quintet, authorship and attribution become even more elusive since the evidence points to highly collaborative studio processes, ones that brought significant alterations to many of the original harmonic, melodic, or metric details of the composition.

In addition to these alterations made to compositional details, the recordings suggest a high degree of flexibility and spontaneity realized with *improvisational* strategies by the soloists and the rhythm section. This is especially true regarding decisions about maintaining or abandoning chorus structure during the solos. Chapter 2 examines this idea more thoroughly, and suggests the likelihood that the group frequently did not determine precisely beforehand what strategy to use. For example, on the released track to "Pinocchio" the horn players do not adhere to chorus structure during their improvisations ("time, no changes"), while Hancock's subsequent piano solo does maintain the underlying 18-bar form.

---

22 Andrea Pejrolo, "The Origins of Modal Jazz in the Music of Miles Davis: A Complete Transcription and a Linear/Harmonic Analysis of *Ascenseur pour l'échafaud* (*Lift to the Scaffold*)—1957" (Ph.D. diss., New York University, 2001), 220 and 233.
23 Ashley Kahn, *Kind of Blue: The Making of the Miles Davis Masterpiece* (New York: Da Capo, 2001), 70.
24 Coolman, "The Miles Davis Quintet," 34. See also Szwed, *So What*, 277, regarding the role of sketches for Davis's later recordings.

THE PERSONNEL ꝑeꝺꝑle

MILES DAVIS

Davis was, in Gerald Early's words, "probably one of the finest conceptualists of music in American history."[25] By the time Davis assembled the quintet between 1963 and 1964, he had already been a crucial figure in most of the postwar developments that had taken place in jazz.

Like most restless innovators, Davis was a moving target. He offered compelling stylistic and aesthetic positions, then shifted to different ones, leaving other musicians to pursue the implications of the ones left behind. Following his earliest recordings with Charlie Parker, Davis's 1949–50 nonet recordings, later released collectively as *Birth of the Cool*, became profoundly influential for the development of what critics referred to as "cool jazz" in the 1950s. *Birth of the Cool*'s posture of restraint and its balance of improvisation with arranged elements became a point of departure for jazz on the West Coast, particularly the eight- to ten-piece groups that flourished in California during the decade.

Davis's *Prestige* recordings during the first half of the 1950s and his Columbia recordings made with the other members of his "first classic" quintet—John Coltrane, Red Garland, Paul Chambers, and Philly Joe Jones—set the standard for hard bop improvisation and rhythm section accompanimental roles. These recordings also emphasized Davis's expressive and evocative ballad playing, especially after he began using the Harmon mute in 1954. On recordings such as *Milestones* (1958), the inclusion of Coltrane on tenor saxophone (as well as Cannonball Adderley on alto saxophone) revealed Davis's interest in surrounding himself with players that complemented rather than duplicated his own musical strengths.

Davis's 1957 soundtrack to the French film *Ascenseur pour l'échafaud* (*Lift to the Scaffold*), his collaborations with arranger Gil Evans, particularly *Porgy and Bess* (1958) and *Sketches of Spain* (1959–60), and Davis's landmark album *Kind of Blue* (1959), all capitalized on what one Davis sideman referred to as Davis's "ambience" sound.[26] Much of this music emphasized the use of space, slow harmonic rhythm, and—frequently—the idea of improvisations derived from scales (or modes). (Chapter 2 discusses more thoroughly issues related to modal jazz.) Davis's output

---

25 Early, "The Art of the Muscle," 15.
26 Pejrolo, "Origins of Modal Jazz," 220. The term comes from an interview with pianist Réne Urtreger.

during the late 1940s and 1950s, the recordings of the second quintet of 1964–68, as well as his move to jazz-rock fusion by the end of the 1960s secured Davis's pivotal reputation for forging the development of jazz styles during the second half of the twentieth century.

Timbral control and nuance were key features of Davis's sound. "If you don't add something to a note," he claimed, "it dies."[27] In an overview of Davis's career, Stanley Crouch writes that "Davis grasped the musical power that comes of having a sound that is itself a musical expression.... Davis's work began to reflect his affection for the resources of color and nuance heard in Armstrong, Freddy Webster, Harry Edison, Buck Clayton, Rex Stewart, Navarro, Dud Bascomb, Ray Nance."[28]

Not all commentators have regarded Davis's timbral variety uncritically. Robert Walser has written persuasively on the "problem" of Davis's playing, with its occasional "cracks, slips, and spleeahs" that do not conform to conventional standards of technical excellence. Walser responds to this problem by concluding that Davis

> constantly and consistently put himself at risk in his trumpet playing, by using a loose, flexible embouchure that helped him to produce a great variety of tone colors and articulations, by striving for dramatic gestures rather than consistent demonstration of mastery, and by experimenting with unconventional techniques.... He played closer to the edge than anyone else and simply accepted the inevitable missteps, never retreating to a safer, more consistent performing style.[29]

In order to indicate more closely the timbral variations in Davis's 1964 solo from "My Funny Valentine" (*My Funny Valentine*), Walser's transcription incorporates two distinct symbols attached to specific pitches. The first symbol indicates a half-valved note, the second symbol a "swallowed, burbled, or ornamented note." Walser's score also contains a number of written descriptive terms: splatter, squeeze, bend, waver, and slide.[30] Paul Berliner's *Thinking in Jazz* contains a key for notating timbral variations in jazz transcriptions. Among Berliner's transcriptions of different jazz artists, his Davis transcriptions are—unsurprisingly—the most liberal in their use of these alternate notations. Berliner uses

27 Leonard Feather, "Miles Davis: Miles and the Fifties," in *The Miles Davis Reader* (New York: Hal Leonard, 2007), 66. Originally publ. *Down Beat* 31/20 (July 2, 1964), 44–48.

28 Stanley Crouch, "Play the Right Thing," *The New Republic* (February 12, 1990): 30–31.

29 Walser, "Out of Notes," 344 and 356.

30 Walser, "Out of Notes," 355.

different noteheads for distinguishing among the following: pitch with half-closed sound (partially muted, slightly compressed quality), pitch with closed sound (muted, compressed, nasal quality produced by half-valve or alternate fingering technique), split attack (extraneous pitch or unpitched sound), pitch with raspy or buzzy sound, and ghosted pitch. Additionally, Berliner includes symbols to indicate expressive devices such as vibrato, shake, bend, pitch inflections (approximately quarter tone), rip, scoop, slide, bend, and fall-off.[31]

In addition to Davis's palette of timbres, his melodic ideas remain largely focused on the middle register of the trumpet, played often with minimal vibrato. His improvisations frequently made use of repeated motivic figures set off with rests. The idea of "space" became a key component in describing his aesthetic: Davis's "openness of melody, space and fleeting silence" were "aspects of haunting lyric economy."[32] Further, his searing lyricism on ballad playing combined tenderness with detachment. "In one sense, this way of playing can be called ironic," wrote Lawrence Kart of Davis in 1968. "The player refers to a mood of simplicity and romantic sentiment and places himself at an emotional distance from it."[33]

Davis had already led bands for some fifteen years by the time he formed the second quintet of 1964–68. Comments by quintet members suggest a style of bandleading that emphasized cooperative music making, careful listening and responding, operating at a high level often in response to unexpected musical challenges, spontaneity over carefully rehearsed polish, and flexibility in performance. "That's what I tell all my musicians; I tell them be ready to play what you know and play above what you know," noted Davis. "Anything might happen above what you've been used to playing—you're ready to get into that, and above that, and take that out.... You place a guy in a spot where he has to do something else, other than what he can do, so he can do *that*. He's got to have something that challenges his imagination, far above what he thinks he's going to play, and what it might lead into, then above *that*, so he won't be fighting when things change."[34] Shorter noted about Davis: "He was the only bandleader who paid his personnel not to practice at home so as to avoid the polish that makes even some improvised music sound boring. He always wanted it fresh."[35]

31 Berliner, *Thinking in Jazz*, 513.
32 Quoted in Jack Chambers, *Milestones: The Music and Times of Miles Davis* 1 (New York: Da Capo, 1998), 204. Originally publ. University of Toronto, 1983 and 1985.
33 Lawrence Kart, "Review: *Miles in the Sky*," *Down Beat* 35/20 (October 3, 1968): 24.
34 Leonard Feather, "Miles Davis/Blindfold Test Pt. 1," *Down Beat* 35/12 (June 13, 1968): 34.
35 Quoted in Chambers, *Milestones* 2, 87.

Quintet members called particular attention to Davis's ability to listen and spontaneously respond to ongoing musical situations: "Miles was the teacher, but as a master teacher, Miles was also a learner. That's something that Miles taught me. He was always *listening* to what we were playing and *responding* to what we were playing and *reacting* to what we were playing.[36] Hancock related a story that highlights this aspect of Davis:

> I remember one time we were playing a concert in Germany, I think, and we were playing this one song and we got to one chord and I played the chord too soon, way too soon; it clashed with everything that was going on. Miles played—it was during his solo—he played something on top of my chord to make it sound right. He made it fit and it blew my mind because I didn't even know where those notes came from. I'm sure he didn't think about it because it wasn't anything he could think about. He didn't hear it as a clash, he heard it as "this is what's happening right now so I'll make the most of it," and he did.[37]

Davis's role as a bandleader wielded immense influence on the quintet members by highlighting the collective role in music making, and blurring traditional distinctions between soloists and rhythm section. For Hancock, Davis influenced the pianist "in the concept of the development of music by the whole band rather than just by myself."[38] And Wayne Shorter further emphasized the idea of cooperative participation: "Playing with Miles, importance was placed on everything you did, even when you weren't soloing. There was that tendency to think that the whole evening was the composition. As far as everybody in the group thinking that way, it was up to each individual to be on his own to help create images and illusions, to sort of spread the peripheral of sight as seen by the audience."[39]

Davis himself was quite clear on the ways in which collective music making could enhance—or even rescue—material played by other members. In an interview with Art Taylor, Davis noted, "Say a guy makes a phrase and the phrase isn't exactly what he wants it to be; well, the drummer is supposed to be hip enough to sorta add to the finished phrase."[40] Davis's second quintet reflected an ongoing facet of Davis's

36 Coolman, "The Miles Davis Quintet," 28.
37 Ray Townley, "Hancock Plugs In," *Down Beat* 41 (October 24, 1974): 15.
38 Baker, *The Black Composer*, 114.
39 Tim Logan, "Wayne Shorter: Doubletake," *Down Beat* 41/12 (June 20, 1974): 17.
40 Taylor, *Notes and Tones*, 12.

collaborative bandleading strategies. By surrounding himself with inno-vative young players, Davis revealed an uncanny ability to harness, rely on, and respond to their creative participation. The analyses here will show the degree of musical communication among the players on the studio recordings, including occasions in which one or another member steps in to help clarify formal or metric discrepancies that arise during the performance.

HERBIE HANCOCK

Pianist Herbie Hancock was only 23 when he joined Davis's quintet, but he had already recorded eighteen albums, performed and toured exten-sively with trumpeter Donald Byrd and saxophonist Eric Dolphy, and recorded two albums of original compositions as a leader. Hancock began studying piano at age 7, and he performed a movement of a Mozart D major concerto at age 11 with the Chicago Symphony Orchestra. He started playing jazz in high school, transcribing and playing the solos of Oscar Peterson and George Shearing. In an interview published in 1978, Hancock identified Clare Fischer's arrangements for the vocal group the Hi-Los and Robert Farnon's orchestral arrangements of pop songs as significant influences for learning jazz harmony.[41] He attended Grinnell College beginning in 1956 at the age of 16, studying piano and composi-tion (as well as engineering), and remained at Grinnell until 1960.

Hancock moved to New York after being discovered by trumpeter Donald Byrd, and his earliest recordings are from 1961 with Donald Byrd and Pepper Adams. The repertory of Byrd's quintet recordings mingled funky jazz and hard bop. Byrd's group also dabbled in some experimen-tal playing, such as on the title composition to Byrd's album *Free Form*, which uses a four-note melodic cell and its transposition and is loosely tied to a bass pedal point. While with Byrd's quintet, Hancock made two recordings under his own name, *Takin' Off* (1962) and *My Point of View* (1963).

During 1961–63 Hancock also participated in freer styles of playing. On his recordings with Eric Dolphy, he shows a willingness to break free of harmonic constraints and a commitment to more dissonant harmo-nies. His improvisational lines become more open-ended since they are less rooted in chordal foundations than they are in the hard bop record-ings. Dolphy's *Live at the Gaslight* (1962) and *Illinois Concert* (1963) show Hancock working out ideas in more extended improvisational contexts

---

41 Baker et al., *The Black Composer*, 114.

than on his studio recordings. Describing his experiences with Dolphy, Hancock noted:

> I didn't know anything about avant-garde jazz and I had never played away from the chords....I didn't even know they played tunes. I thought they just got up and played. I got scared and said, "What do you want me to play?" He gave me some music and I said to myself, "He doesn't want me to play chord changes." So I said, "What do you want me to play?" He told me, "Play anything you want." I decided to break some rules I had been accustomed to using with rhythm, harmony, and melody. It seemed to be the right thing.[42]

The recordings Hancock made prior to joining Davis already show many features of his mature playing in embryonic form, features that ultimately contributed to Hancock's significance. His playing synthesized hard bop pianism with Bill Evans's harmonic vocabulary and touch. Evans's influence, Hancock said, "opened up a whole vista for me."[43] Hancock's early improvisations show a strong lyrical sense, a reliance on motivic improvisation rather than on melodic formulas, and a sense of dramatic pacing that frequently leads the improvisations to a culminating high point: this peak often coincides with a move from single lines to a two-handed chordal texture.

In 1995 Hancock speculated as to why his playing would have appealed to Davis, and why Davis might have hired him:

> Maybe he liked my attitude. Maybe he liked the fact that I was always exploring. He liked my touch. I think he felt I could be molded into something better than what I was. I guess he maybe thought I was "right." I wasn't too set in my ways musically about anything. I had a really good grasp of harmony and...you know...chordal textures and that kind of thing. And I was adventurous.[44]

The live recordings Hancock made with the Davis quintet in 1963–64 show further creative development in his playing, particularly through additional techniques for metric and harmonic superimposition as well as impressionistic and coloristic piano textures. Speaking of Hancock's role within the Davis rhythm section, Bill Dobbins noted: "Hancock

---

42 Townley, "Hancock Plugs In," 14–15.
43 Kahn, *Kind of Blue*, 117.
44 Coolman, "The Miles Davis Quintet," 14.

helped revolutionize traditional jazz concepts of the rhythm section and its relation to the soloists. He built on the earlier developments of such diverse groups as Bill Evans's trio and Ornette Coleman's quartet, and established a musical rapport with an extraordinary degree of freedom and interaction."[45]

The following list characterizes Hancock's playing throughout the 1960s:

- expansive and lush harmonic vocabulary
- reliance on fertile harmonic substitution and superimposition
- metric superimposition
- space in ballad playing
- dynamic shadings when phrasing individual lines
- flexible accompanimental strategies and wide range of pianistic textures
- ability to create a sense of harmonic progression over static harmony
- blues-based ideas and motives
- use of octatonic (diminished scale) collection over dominant harmonies

The notion of *overlapping* recurs in interviews with Hancock, and this principle seems to operate as an important aesthetic value: "I try to make things sound like they flow rather than sounding like I'm connecting up different chords. I try to make things sound more human and let things overlap when I'm improvising."[46] This idea of overlapping may apply both harmonically and metrically. In the harmonic dimension, overlapping creates continuity or elision through voice leading connections or common tones maintained across changes of harmony. In the metric dimension, overlapping creates continuity, elision, and elasticity across 4-bar, 8-bar, and formal divisions, and serves to camouflage significant structural boundaries. Chapter 2 examines these ideas specifically in terms of phrase overlap.

Hancock's 1961–63 compositions relied on the chord progressions and forms of hard bop and funky jazz. One of them—"Watermelon Man" (*Takin' Off*, 1962)—provided Hancock with an early funky jazz hit. Certain elements in the 1961–63 compositions prefigure those works that he

---

45 Bill Dobbins, "Herbie Hancock," in *The New Grove Dictionary of Jazz*, ed. Barry Kernfeld (New York: St. Martin's, 1988 and 1994), 478.
46 Baker et al., *The Black Composer*, 124.

later composed and recorded with Davis ("Little One," "The Sorcerer,"
"Madness"), as well as Hancock's other signature compositions of the
mid-1960s that he did not record with Davis ("Maiden Voyage" and
"Dolphin Dance"). In the 1961–63 works, three features elaborate the
underlying hard bop harmonic and melodic structures: (1) the use of
suspended fourth chords, (2) shifting harmonies over pedal points, and
(3) melodies and/or harmonies in fourths.

A few examples will demonstrate these three ideas. "Empty Pockets"
(*Takin' Off*, 1962) is a 12-bar blues, but the head choruses and the first
chorus of each use F9sus4 chords (suspended fourth chords) to express
the tonic F harmony, and this harmony itself gets embellished with a
G♭13sus4 chord a half step above. (See example 1.1.) The use of suspended
chords and the half-step elaboration provide an antecedent for techniques worked out more fully on Hancock's "Little One" (recorded on
Davis's *E.S.P.*, 1965), discussed in chapter 3.

EXAMPLE 1.1   Hancock's Harmonic Accompaniment to Opening Measures of "Empty
Pockets"

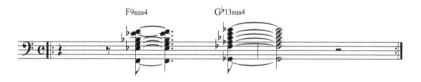

Shifting harmonies over static bass pedal points appear in a number of
Hancock's early 1961–63 compositions. (Analysts and players frequently
refer to these chords as "slash" chords, due to their visual representation,
which involves a slash that separates the upper structure harmony from
the bass pitch.) Example 1.2 shows the accompanying harmonies to the
opening of the melody of "Three Wishes" (from Byrd's *Free Form*, 1961).
The progression decorates the Fmin9 tonality by moving up a whole step
and a minor third (Gmin9/F and A♭min9/F). Likewise, the chord progression to "King Cobra" relies on pedal point harmonies: an Fsus7 chord
opening harmony is then followed by D♭Maj7/F, GMaj7/F, G♭Maj7/F,
before returning to Fsus7.[47] With these progressions, Hancock further

---

47 During the head statements, the horn voicings involve another slash chord, Etriad/F at m.
7. The lower pitches of that voicing (B3/E4) then resolve down a half step (Bb3/Eb3) the
following measure. Interestingly, Hancock's copyright deposit of the lead sheet to "King
Cobra," deposited in 1964, does not indicate *any* of the mm. 1–8 harmonies as slash chords.

EXAMPLE 1.2 Harmonic Accompaniment to Opening Measures of Melody to "Three Wishes"

works out the implications of pedal point compositions heard in earlier works such as John Coltrane's 1959 "Naima."

Additionally, other of Hancock's 1961–63 compositions, such as "The Maze" and "Empty Pockets," (*Takin' Off*, 1962), use fourth-based melodic ideas. Example 1.3 shows how in these two compositions the melodic structure does not use consecutive perfect fourths, but a harmonic inversion of them. In both, an octave frames four pitches, consisting of a perfect fourth, whole step, and another perfect fourth, either ascending or descending. ("The Maze" at mm. 1–2 ascends A–D–E–A; "Empty Pockets" at m. 10 descends with an incomplete version, F–C–B♭ before a transposition down a step to E♭–B♭–A♭–E♭.)

EXAMPLE 1.3 Perfect Fourth Melodic Construction in Hancock's "The Maze" and "Empty Pockets"

Instead, the lead sheet provides only the upper structure harmonies for this section of the composition. Elsewhere in the lead sheet, however, he does use slash chord designations for several harmonies, as well as a modal label, F♯ phrygian, for one of the chords. For further discussion of "King Cobra," see Keith Waters, "Modes, Scales, Functional Harmony, and Non-functional Harmony in the Compositions of Herbie Hancock," *Journal of Music Theory* 49/2 (2005): 333–57.

Thus in the 1961–63 works, suspended fourth chords, pedal point harmonies, and fourth-based melodic structures embellish the hard bop harmonic and melodic structures. However, Hancock's works recorded with Davis, such as "Little One," "The Sorcerer," and "Madness" (as well as Hancock's other mid-1960s compositions "Maiden Voyage" and "Dolphin Dance"), often foreground these features as principal structural elements. Chapter 2 considers more completely these features, often associated with modal jazz.

WAYNE SHORTER

Born in 1933, Shorter grew up in Newark, New Jersey. Though he attended Newark's Arts High School initially for his talent in the visual arts, he ultimately studied harmony, theory, and orchestration there, and played clarinet in the school band during his senior year. While in high school, Shorter worked with his brother, trumpeter Alan Shorter. The two of them practiced bebop and learned Lennie Tristano's formidable compositions.[48] Turning down an offer to tour with Sonny Stitt, Shorter instead opted to attend New York University, where he received a degree in music education in 1956.

Shorter displayed an intense interest in composing. According to his biographer Michelle Mercer, while attending New York University Shorter began work on an opera (*The Singing Lesson*), a project he eventually abandoned.[49] Shorter's first recording dates from 1956 (*College Jazz* with Johnny Eaton and His Princetonians). Although that recording contains no Shorter original compositions, among the jazz standards it includes a third-stream inspired "Fugue." He also worked with Horace Silver in 1956, was drafted into the army, and played briefly with pianist Josef Zawinul in Maynard Ferguson's band in 1959.

The first published review of Shorter's playing dates from 1959. In it, fellow Newark native LeRoi Jones (Amiri Baraka) provided a trenchant description of Shorter's willingness to take musical chances. "The

---

48 Shorter was remarkably conversant with the works of Tristano and the musicians associated with him, including Lee Konitz, Warne Marsh, and Billy Bauer. See Andy Hamilton, *Lee Konitz: Conversations on the Improviser's Art* (Ann Arbor: University of Michigan, 2007), esp. 60 and 159. Shorter's early exposure to their compositions—many of which featured unusual harmonic progression and required overt virtuosity—probably had an influence on his own early compositions.

49 Michelle Mercer, *Footprints: The Life and Work of Wayne Shorter* (New York: J. P. Tarcher/Penguin, 2004), 42.

playing is characterized by an almost 'literary' (in the best sense of the word) arrangement of musical relationships," he wrote. "He seems to be willing to try anything. He usually makes it."[50] The term "literary" likely addresses Shorter's dramatic tendencies for musical risks, and to avoid the expected.

These characteristics reflect a set of deliberate decisions that Shorter made from a very early age. Describing a performance with Sonny Stitt on "Donna Lee" while still an NYU student, Shorter remembered: "Stitt was playing very smoothly, all the transitions, while I was going for the originality, off to the side—I didn't play jerkily, but I had to say it and make it count, in and out of keys, till people said, 'Tricky! Cute!'"[51] At least one writer felt these attributes required some defending. "Like most of the short, painful steps that characterize artistic growth," wrote Don Heckman in the liner notes to Shorter's 1964 recording *Speak No Evil*, "Shorter's struggles do not always produce successful results. But when everything works, when the saxophone ceases to be a mechanism and becomes instead an extension of his voice (as frequently happens in this recording), the value of Shorter's goals becomes clear."[52]

The picture emerges of Shorter with an omnivorous appetite for a wide range of music, both classical and jazz. Describing their early acquaintance, Zawinul described Shorter as "a great student of the game.... Wayne was a big Miles fan and knew everything he was doing, everything Blakey was doing.... We'd talk about Ben Webster, Coleman Hawkins, about the different chords Duke Ellington used to orchestrate."[53]

As a member of Art Blakey's Jazz Messengers between 1959 and 1964, Shorter gained enhanced visibility. He became the band's musical director, writing and arranging numerous compositions for the group. The experience also provided Shorter with particular models for pacing: "The kind of timing I learned with Art was almost always consistent. Building your expressions into some sort of climax, ending your solos on something very worthy of sharing with or being remembered by everyone."[54]

There were frequent—perhaps inevitable—comparisons between Shorter and John Coltrane. Shorter spent time practicing with Coltrane, and they both shared a nearly vibrato-less passionate timbre. Shorter's

50 LeRoi Jones, "Introducing Wayne Shorter," *Jazz Review* 2/10 (November 1959): 23–24.
51 Conrad Silvert, "Wayne Shorter: Imagination Unlimited," *Down Beat* 44/13 (July 14, 1977): 16.
52 Don Heckman, Liner notes to Wayne Shorter, *Speak No Evil*, Blue Note 84194.
53 Mercer, *Footprints*, 62.
54 Mercer, *Footprints*, 67–68.

sound was, according to one reviewer, "almost exclusively colored by the pinched, ululant tenor of John Coltrane's approach."[55] Some saw beyond the similar sound, and addressed their differences more carefully. Josef Zawinul noted: "Wayne had a straight tone, and Trane did, too. . . . Wayne and Trane each came up individually, though. Trane was doing a lot of arpeggiating, running the chords. Wayne had a wonderful way of blowing chords, but he wasn't just arpeggiating. Wayne could already weave melodies as a part of the chords, and we became masters of that as time went on."[56] Shorter's recordings of 1959–64 validate Zawinul's observations. Shorter's playing is steeped in the hard bop tradition, yet much of it commits to motive and gesture in favor of patent negotiation of the harmonies. Significant, too, is how Shorter's motivic and gestural ideas sometimes range across formal boundaries of the compositions, heightening the sense of formal ambiguity.

Davis's quintet offered Shorter a dramatically different platform for improvisation. Describing his initial performance with the quintet in 1964, Shorter stated "It wasn't the bish-bash, sock-em-dead routine we had with Blakey, with every solo a climax. With Miles, I felt like a cello, I felt viola, I felt liquid, dot-dash . . . and colors started really coming."[57] While it is certainly possible to overstate the differences in Shorter's playing after he joined Davis's quintet, it did take on more space, more dramatic contrasts of articulation, more use of fragmented ideas, and he continued to pursue a style of motivic improvisation remarkably free of clichés.

Herbie Hancock addressed the motivic/thematic aspect of Shorter's playing by saying, "That's one of the things I like about Wayne's playing. He develops a theme that leads to another theme and so on. It's just great the way he can do that. It's not just clever; it makes it easier for someone to hear what you're doing. There's a thread that goes through the improvisation."[58] In a careful assessment of Shorter's work with Davis, Mark Gridley notes:

> By this time, he had evolved even further away from the bop approach to melody. His lines were formed from notes of many different durations, not primarily eighth notes. And his rhythms were not necessarily those associated with jazz. In this phase of his career, he did not

55 Pete Welding, "Review: Wayne Shorter, *Night Dreamer*," *Down Beat* 31/31 (December 3, 1964): 26.
56 Mercer, *Footprints*, 71.
57 Silvert, "Wayne Shorter," 58.
58 Lyons, *The Great Jazz Pianists*, 276.

y
THE QUINTET

25

routinely build solos from standard bop rhythmic figures that swing in obvious ways and busily fill every moment. Some of his phrases did not swing. They intentionally floated over and past the beat instead of getting down inside it. Shorter played lines of smoother contours than those of most hard bop saxophonists. His work did not have as many abrupt starts and stops, or the bobbing up and down that typified bop. His melodic approach often recalled the concise, floating themes, interspersed with long silences, that we find in music by non-jazz composers....His playing was as free of clichés as any saxophone style yet devised....He usually managed to improvise solos that were free of patterns....Wayne Shorter brought an outstanding gift for melody to his solos...he also tried to make something significant out of each kernel of melody that he invented.[59]

Shorter was an extremely prolific jazz composer, and he wielded immense influence on contemporary jazz composition. While with Blakey from 1959–63 he copyrighted fifty-three compositions, and the Library of Congress now holds these lead sheets in their collection. Shorter's sixteen compositions recorded by Davis's second quintet are in many ways responsible for the sound of the quintet studio recordings. Further, he wrote nearly all the compositions on a series of significant *Blue Note* albums made under his own name between 1964 and 1969. His compositions are noteworthy in their détente between clear memorable motives and ambiguous (and frequently nonfunctional) harmonic progressions. The following discusses aspects of harmonic progression, form, and motivic structure for Shorter's compositions written during the decade between 1959 and 1969.

HARMONIC PROGRESSION   Analysts who have examined Shorter's works focus on harmonic progression. Both Steven Strunk and Patricia Julien emphasize the manner in which bass motion establishes the tonality of the compositions, calling attention to unusual, nonfunctional harmonic progressions, unexpected chord qualities within functional progressions (such as the use of minor dominant chords), and use of stepwise bass motion within progressions.[60] Both analysts examine

---

59 Gridley, *Jazz Styles*, 277 and 283.
60 Patricia Julien, "The Structural Function of Harmonic Relations in Wayne Shorter's Early Compositions: 1959–63" (Ph.D. diss., University of Maryland, 2003); Steven Strunk, "Notes on Harmony in Wayne Shorter's Compositions, 1964–67," *Journal of Music Theory* 49/2 (Fall 2005): 301–32.

larger questions of tonality and tonal ambiguity in Shorter's compositions, particularly through those works that seem to establish more than one overall tonal center. Such works that create localized key areas but avoid a clear single overall tonic form part of a broader compositional tradition dating back at least to Dizzy Gillespie's "Con Alma," recorded in 1954.[61]

Shorter's 1959–63 compositions often rely on unusual progressions. In some works, Shorter uses unexpected resolutions (instead of more typical harmonic progressions) at the ends of compositions in order to establish the final tonic. For example, "Sakeena's Vision" moves to the final G minor tonic via Fmin7 to E7. The final progression of "Sincerely Diana" moves D♭min7 G♭7 before advancing to the final tonic of B♭ minor. This use of unusual resolutions of ii7–V7 progressions (or ii7–♭II7 progressions) becomes a recurring feature throughout Shorter's early compositions, one that provides significant (and often audible) challenges for the improvisers on the recordings. However, not all Shorter's compositions of 1959–63 completely abandon functional harmonic progressions (such as V–I; ii–V–I). Many, such as "This Is for Albert," make use of standard hard bop harmonic conventions.

FORM   "This Is for Albert" also relies on a standard 32-bar AABA form. Yet many of Shorter's early compositions use unorthodox forms. Some do host standard AABA formal designs, but without the consistent use of standard 8-bar sections. "Sakeena's Vision," for example, comprises a 40-bar AABA¹ form (10 + 10 + 8 + 12); "Ping Pong" a 36-bar AABA¹ form (10 + 10 + 8 + 8). Additionally, Shorter explored other formal solutions with irregular numbers of bars. "Sincerely Diana" is 26 bars in AA¹A² B form (10 + 8 + 4 + 4). "Sweet and Sour" uses a 38-bar AA¹B form (16 + 14 + 8) for the head while the solos employ a 34-bar AA¹B form (12 + 14 + 8).

Regarding Shorter's compositions for Davis's second quintet, commentators call attention to the novelty of the formal designs of Shorter's compositions written between 1965 and 1968, noting their formal irregularities, their absence of standard-tune AABA and ABAC forms, and their avoidance of bridge sections.[62] Most of these compositions (with the exception of "Masqualero," written as an ABA form) are single-section forms: that is, each chorus does not include repeated sections.

---

61   I am indebted to Barry Kernfeld for the comparison with Gillespie's "Con Alma."
62   Chambers, *Milestones* 2, 99; Coolman, "The Miles Davis Quintet," 17, Gridley, *Jazz Styles*, 275; Strunk, "Notes on Harmony," 301.

"E.S.P." might best be described as an AA^1 single-section form: it involves a 16-bar repeated form with a 4-bar first ending and a 4-bar second ending.[63]

Yet single-section forms were, for Shorter, anything but new by the time he joined Davis's quintet. By 1965 they provided instead a well-established template. Between 1959 and 1965 Shorter wrote numerous single-section compositions: some recorded under his own name, some with Blakey, and some with others. The following lists those single-section compositions written prior to his tenure with the quintet, and includes for each the chorus length. (The list also includes those AA^1 compositions similar to the overall form of "E.S.P." It excludes 12-bar blues compositions, typically single-section compositions in the hands of any composer.)

SHORTER'S SINGLE-SECTION COMPOSITIONS WRITTEN IN 1959–64

"Armageddon" (Shorter, *Night Dreamer*): 16 bars
"The Backsliders" (Blakey, *Roots and Herbs*): 12
"Callaway Went That a-Way" (Shorter, *Wayning Moments*): 16
"The Creature" (Unrecorded): 16
"Dead-End" (*Wayning Moments*): 32 (AA^1)
"Devil's Island" (Shorter, *Wayning Moments*): 32 (AA^1)
"El Toro" (Blakey, *The Freedom Rider*): 16
"Eva" (Blakey, *Ugetsu*): 40
"Harry's Last Stand" (*Introducing Wayne Shorter*): 21
"Infant Eyes" (*Speak No Evil*): 18[64]
"Juju" (Shorter, *Juju*): 12
"Marie Antoinette" (Freddie Hubbard, *Ready for Freddie*): 16
"Powder Keg" (Shorter, *Wayning Moments*): 24
"The Summit" (Blakey, *Meet You at the Jazz Corner of the World*): 30
"Suspended Sentence" (Lee Morgan, *Minor Strain*): 16
"Tenderfoot" (Shorter, *Second Genesis*): 16
"The 13th Thorn" (Unrecorded): 12
"Those Who Sit and Wait" (Blakey, *The Witch Doctor*): 32 (AA^1)
"United" (Blakey, *Pisces* and *Roots and Herbs*): 16

63 These AA' forms are distinct from ABAC forms, since the latter usually involve constituent 8-bar sections.

64 Although recorded after he joined Davis's quintet, Shorter wrote "Infant Eyes" earlier.

MOTIVIC STRUCTURE   One substantial difference between Shorter's 1959–63 compositions and those written after 1964 is that the later compositions rely on fewer harmonies and slower harmonic rhythm. Nevertheless, there are decided similarities. One aspect of all the compositions is their reliance on clear memorable motives in the melody. Shorter creates motivic connections through repetition of pitch, rhythm, or contour. Some compositions exclusively develop a single motive: "Infant Eyes" uses a 2-bar rhythmic motive throughout the melody of the entire composition. Several of Shorter's AABA compositions develop two contrasting motives within the A section. In these Shorter dramatizes the change in motive by a change in harmonization. For example, "One by One," "This is For Albert," and "Yes and No" use pedal point harmonies (and a slower moving melody) beneath the opening motive of the A section, creating a static harmonic field. The second motive then creates a release, with the more active harmonic progression (and more active melody) contrasting with the first portion.

By *Juju* (1964), Shorter seemed particularly interested in moving to compositions based entirely on two distinct motives. In "Deluge" (AABA), "House of Jade" (ABA), and "Mahjong" (AA^1BA), this motivic design activates the form of the piece, with one motive used in the A section and the other in the B section.

This reliance on two primary motivic ideas features in several of the Shorter compositions written for the Davis quintet, such as "Pinocchio," "Limbo," and "Prince of Darkness." In these three compositions, a contrasting motivic idea occurs during the final six measures of the form, operating as a release. Other Shorter compositions recorded by the Davis quintet—"Footprints," "Fall," "Dolores"—rely solely on a single motivic idea. "Nefertiti" similarly relies on a single motive, but Shorter treats the motive elastically, with each of the three phrases occupying different lengths of time.

Arguably, Shorter's most adventurous compositions of the 1960s are those that appear on his own 1965 *Blue Note* recording *The All Seeing Eye*, which responded in many ways to the jazz avant-garde. All of Shorter's lead sheets for these compositions abandon standard jazz harmonic labels with bass pitch and chord type; instead, Shorter writes out the horn voicings and melody. Similarly, three of Shorter's lead sheets for his compositions recorded with Davis ("Pinocchio," "Nefertiti," and "Paraphernalia") include written-out voicings: there they alternate with more typical chord symbols.

Finally, while it is difficult to itemize specific compositional influences on Shorter, it is possible to speak of shared compositional priorities with other jazz composers. Certainly a motivic focus and nonstandard harmonic progressions also apply generally to the compositions of

Thelonious Monk. The use of blues-based or minor pentatonic melodic motives recalls the compositions of Charles Mingus and John Coltrane. In addition, Booker Little's compositions, written between 1958 and 1961, show a similar interest in forms outside AABA and ABAC frameworks, unusual section lengths, and a harmonic language that makes use of hard bop progressions alongside more unusual and ambiguous progressions.[65]

TONY WILLIAMS

Tony Williams began playing drums at an early age, and he began performing publicly and freelancing while a young teenager. Although born in Chicago, he grew up in Boston, where he studied drums with Alan Dawson. "What I got basically from Alan," Williams stated, "was clarity."[66] Williams cited numerous influences, especially Art Blakey, Max Roach, Philly Joe Jones, Jimmy Cobb, Louis Hayes, and Roy Haynes. "Max Roach was perhaps the biggest influence. He brought a tremendous musicality to the drums.... From the late '40s to the early '60s, Max, Art and Philly Joe made a perfect package. I studied them all intensely, incorporating as much as I could into my own work."[67]

Williams exhibited an encyclopedic ability to study, absorb, and react to his influences. His own comments show that he closely examined not only standard drumming techniques of those who influenced him, but also the methods these players used to articulate musical form. They suggest that Williams derived from them a range of possible options to employ at important formal junctures. His comments also indicate that he consciously worked to emulate them or—instead—to provide alternate ones:

I just kept storing things and made a catalog of what drummers did and what tendencies they had, both as a whole and individually. I would listen to one drummer on many records and watch what he did at certain points in the music, during different songs and with different bands. I did that with every drummer that I admired. You find out

65 Little seemed particularly intrigued by ABA forms; see Keith Waters and David Diamond, "Out Front: The Art of Booker Little," *Annual Review of Jazz Studies* 11 (2000–2001): 1–38.

66 Paul de Barros, "Tony Williams: Two Decades of Drum Innovation," *Down Beat* 50/11 (November 1983): 15.

67 Lee Underwood, "Tony Williams: Aspiring to a Lifetime of Leadership," *Down Beat* 46 (June 21, 1979): 54.

what the guy plays and what he *doesn't* play.... At the end of a chorus maybe three drummers do one thing, while another group will do [something similar] at the beginning of a chorus or during four-bar breaks. You get this overview of what everybody does. That's how I did it.... I realized that nobody was doing certain things in certain situations, so I would.[68]

Among the quintet sidemen, Williams had the least recording experience prior to joining Davis's group in 1963, having made only three recordings. He joined alto saxophonist Jackie McLean's group in late 1962, performed on McLean's recording *Vertigo*, Hancock's *My Point of View*, and Kenny Dorham's *Una Mas* (also with Hancock). Generally more subdued than his recordings with Davis, his playing on these early three albums displays a ride cymbal technique that is sparkling, light, and airy. "My time," he claimed in 1964, "is on the cymbal and in my head...."[69]

But it was with Davis's quintet that Williams's playing helped redefine postbop drumming. Not only had Williams synthesized elements from the premier bop and hard bop players, he also imported techniques from the jazz avant-garde. His playing sometimes superimposed meters and created methods to heighten formal ambiguity. He typically maintained the timekeeping on the ride cymbal, and even at rapid tempos his cymbal patterns remained buoyant. He cultivated both regular and reverse ride patterns, developed unpredictable fills, exhibited an astonishing degree of coordinated independence, and used a wide dynamic range. On the quintet's live recordings, in particular, Williams often switched feels and tempos within compositions, and helped make the drums the center of attention along with the soloist. Herbie Hancock later recalled: "Tony Williams was a phenomenon. Nobody was playing like him. He was creating a whole new approach to drumming and we actually 'clicked.' We actually worked together very well. You know, Tony was one of the strongest elements in that band. I think a lot of what Miles told us... kind of put a lot of responsibility on the drums to give the band a certain fiery, dynamic personality."[70]

In addition to Williams's technical achievements, he developed ways to maintain the pulse while often suppressing larger metrical cues. This heightened the quintet's ability to create formal ambiguity in the context of chorus structure improvisation. By *Miles Smiles*, Williams began

68 Gene Ferriter, "The Learned Man," *Rhythm* (January 1990): 35.
69 "Drum Talk, Coast to Coast," *Down Beat* 31/8 (March 26, 1964): 15.
70 Coolman, "The Miles Davis Quintet," 27.

using different accompanimental strategies on some compositions. On "Freedom Jazz Dance," for instance, Williams frequently articulates the beat with the high-hat on all four beats of the measure, a technique he would turn to increasingly as the quintet began incorporating rock-based and R & B–based rhythms. But even while fusing rock and R & B with jazz on the later quintet recordings, Williams also developed methods for articulating pulse but avoiding overt commitment to meter. Williams's accompaniment during the improvisations during the released track of "Tout de Suite" (*Filles de Kilimanjaro*), for example, is notable for its use of rock-based rhythms without expected metrical implications.

Unaccompanied drum solos are rarer on the quintet studio recordings than on the live recordings. "Agitation" (*E.S.P.*) begins with an unaccompanied drum solo spliced in to precede the opening head statement. Like most of Williams's unaccompanied solos with the second quintet, the "Agitation" solo is metrically free and does not preserve an underlying form or consistent meter.[71]

Williams contributed three compositions to the Davis quintet studio recordings: "Pee Wee," "Hand Jive," and "Black Comedy." The first two are notable for their irregular phrase lengths that create an irregular overall form. "Pee Wee" is 21 bars, consisting of six phrases (6 + 3 + 2 + 3 + 2 + 5). "Hand Jive" is 18 bars long, consisting of an 11-bar and a 7-bar section. Similarities between Williams's two compositions and the quintet compositions written by other members are striking. "Pee Wee" and "Hand Jive" are both single section forms, and—particularly with "Pee Wee"—the use of pedal point harmonies is consistent with other quintet compositions.

During his tenure with Davis, Williams recorded two albums as a leader for the Blue Note label, *Lifetime* (1964) and *Spring* (1965). Their use of collective improvisation and departure from predetermined harmonic and formal structures show Williams's interests in avant-garde jazz. Williams contributed the compositions to these two albums. "Love Song" (*Spring*) alternates 4/4, 5/4, and 6/4, and this resembles the mixed meters heard on "Black Comedy," Williams's composition recorded with the Davis quintet on *Miles in the Sky*.

Williams did not record as prodigiously as Hancock and Carter while a member of Davis's quintet. Excluding those recordings done

---

71 In contrast, Williams's solo on the Davis quintet 1963 studio version of "Seven Steps to Heaven" does preserve underlying form and meter. For further discussion of Williams's improvisations, see Craig DeVere Woodson, "Solo Jazz Drumming: An Analytic Study of the Improvisation Techniques of Anthony Williams" (Ph.D. diss, UCLA, 1973).

with Davis, he made sixteen recordings between 1963 and 1968. They include studio recordings with Eric Dolphy (*Out to Lunch*), Andrew Hill (*Point of Departure*), Herbie Hancock (*Empyrean Isles* and *Maiden Voyage*), Grachan Moncur III (*Evolution* and *Some Other Stuff*), and Charles Lloyd (*Of Course, of Course* and *Nirvana*).[72]

RON CARTER

Bassist Ron Carter was classically trained, receiving a B.M. degree from the Eastman School of Music in 1959 and a master's degree from the Manhattan School of Music in 1961. In a 1964 interview, he identified Percy Heath, Paul Chambers, Charles Mingus, George Duvivier, and Israel Crosby as bassists that he admired.[73] Of these, undoubtedly Chambers had the strongest influence, both in terms of accompaniment and improvisation. Undoubtedly his acknowledged influences provided Carter with models for versatility and for deferring to varied ensemble situations.[74]

Carter spoke of his range of experiences prior to working with Miles, which included performances and/or recordings with Eric Dolphy, Don Ellis, Jackie Byard, Coleman Hawkins, Wes Montgomery, Thelonious Monk, Bobby Timmons, Mal Waldron, Cannonball Adderley, and Art Farmer. By 1960, Carter was recording prodigiously. Many of these early recordings, such as those made with Eric Dolphy (*Out There* and *Far Cry*, both from 1960) and with Don Ellis (*New Ideas*, 1961) show Carter working in both traditional and more modernist formats. The recordings with Ellis, for example, experiment with unusual formal designs, mixed meter, and improvisation and accompaniment based upon tone clusters rather than more traditional harmonic progressions. With Dolphy, we hear the rhythm section breaking up the 4/4 time for each soloist's first chorus in "Mrs. Parker of K.C.," and Dolphy's "Miss Ann" uses an unusual 14-bar chorus structure. These early Carter recordings display a liquid legato bass sound, and his propulsive style of walking bass is due, in part, to articulating the pulse slightly on top of the beat.

It is tempting to hear Carter on the Ellis and Dolphy recordings as playing the straight man, fulfilling a standard timekeeping role beneath the more experimental excursions of the soloists. This perception of

---

72 With the exception of the Lloyd recordings, all the other recordings are absent from the Tom Lord online discography, http://www.lorddisco.com.

73 Don Heckman, "Ron Carter," *Down Beat* 31/9 (April 9, 1964): 18.

74 This point was made to me in a communication with bassist Tommy Cecil.

Carter persists in discussions of his role with the Davis quintet, and commentators often describe Carter's playing as providing a rock-steady anchor for the other rhythm section players. Carter himself later indicated displeasure with being described as the "anchor."[75] And on the Davis quintet's earliest live recordings it is Carter who frequently initiates departures from the underlying meter and harmonic progressions, creating metric conflicts and making the form ambiguous. During Carter's accompaniment on the first-chorus B section of "Autumn Leaves" (from *Live at the 1963 Monterey Jazz Festival*, :23), he superimposes a three-beat pedal point of D over the 4/4 meter for the entire eight measures of the section. Furthermore, example 1.4 includes a transcription to the beginning of the next chorus, mm. 1–8 of Davis's first solo chorus (: 44). There Carter initiates an accompanimental pattern beneath Davis that suggests an unusual path through the harmonic structure of the composition. Carter moves chromatically: each successive downbeat moves up a half step. The first, fourth, and eighth measure (C, E♭, G) articulate the roots of the underlying harmony, and m. 3 articulates the third (D) of the underlying B♭ harmony. However, the downbeats of the second, fifth, and seventh measure (C♯, E natural, F♯) support the underlying harmonies more weakly, if at all. Rather than fulfilling a more traditional anchor role, the earliest quintet recordings often show Carter taking the lead in superimposing metric and harmonic ideas over the composition's formal structure.[76]

EXAMPLE 1.4   Carter's Accompaniment to "Autumn Leaves," mm. 1–8, First Chorus Trumpet Solo

75 See the Carter interview contained in the video *The Miles Davis Story* (CVD 54040, 2002).
76 For further discussions of reharmonization techniques in the quintet's performances of "Autumn Leaves," see Keith Waters, "Outside Forces: Autumn Leaves in the 1960s," *Current Musicology* 71–73 (2001): 276–302.

While Carter very rarely performed bass solos on the quintet record-ings, his bass accompaniment contributed significantly to the group, particularly through techniques of harmonic substitution and metrical conflict described above with "Autumn Leaves." In walking bass accom-paniments, Carter frequently provided cross rhythms and ostinatos in counterpoint to the soloists and other rhythm section players.

As composer, Carter contributed three compositions to the Davis quin-tet, "R.J.," "Eighty-One," and "Mood," all from *E.S.P.* "R.J." displays an irreg-ular formal design, with an AA¹BA form of 5/5/4/5 bars. The harmonic structure of the B section is built on a singe bass pedal point beneath shift-ing harmonies, and thus dovetails with quintet compositions written by other members of the group. "Mood" consists of a 13-bar form that relies on a bass ostinato throughout. "Eighty-One" is a 12-bar blues that the group performed in a straight eighth-note fashion, a nod to funky jazz composi-tions such as Hancock's "Watermelon Man" and Lee Morgan's "Sidewinder." Yet Hancock's frequent use of suspended fourth chords in "Eighty-One" situates the work within the quintet's more modernist harmonic sphere. The recordings attribute Davis as coauthor for both "Mood" and "Eighty-One," probably the result of alterations made to those compositions dur-ing the studio recording. (The section on studio processes above contains Hancock's description of Davis's alterations to "Eighty-One.")

THE QUINTET AND LIVE RECORDINGS

Prior to the addition of Wayne Shorter to Davis's second quintet, the group recorded a series of albums that included tenor saxophon-ist George Coleman along with Davis, Carter, Hancock, and Williams. *Seven Steps to Heaven* (May 1963) included three compositions with the new quintet in the studio, and the rhythm section in particular negoti-ates skillfully and effortlessly the meter changes in "Joshua." Despite its poor fidelity, *Live in Europe* (recorded at the Antibes Jazz Festival) won *Jazz Magazine*'s jazz album of the year. *Live in Europe* and *Live at the 1963 Monterey Jazz Festival* (both recorded during the summer of 1963, the latter released only in 2007) show remarkably innovative approaches applied to standard tunes.[77] Davis had been playing many of these stan-dards, such as "My Funny Valentine," "Stella by Starlight," and "Autumn Leaves," for a number of years. Harmonically, the group showed a supple ability to reharmonize the compositions in different ways. Metrically,

---

77 A quintet club appearance from June 1963 in St. Louis is also available as a *verité* recording. See Chambers, *Milestones*, 2, 61.

the rhythm section easily superimposed different meters, created metrical conflicts with cross rhythms, and moved in and out of double time. Along with these sophisticated harmonic and metric superimpositions, though, the group also seemed to be able to recall and channel the conventional hard bop moves of Davis's earlier rhythm sections, particularly that with Wynton Kelly, Paul Chambers, and Jimmy Cobb.

The live recordings *My Funny Valentine* and *Four and More* (both recorded on the same February 1964 concert) show a further development of improvisational prowess, group interaction, and flexibility in the context of performing standard-tune repertory. The shifts of tempos and moods within individual compositions such as "My Funny Valentine" and "Stella by Starlight" give those works the quality of multimovement suites, enhanced when Williams switches the underlying feel or ceases to play during sections of the compositions. These were the last recordings on which George Coleman appeared with the quintet. There was a disparity between the innovations of the rhythm section and Coleman's more conservative (if expressive) playing, a disparity not lost on some listeners. In a review that awarded the *My Funny Valentine* album four and one half stars, *Down Beat* critic Harvey Siders wrote of Coleman: "his ideas are too straightforward to match the harmonic and rhythmic daring of Davis, Hancock, and Carter."[78]

On the recommendation of Tony Williams, Davis replaced Coleman briefly with Boston-based tenor saxophonist Sam Rivers, whose playing was strongly allied with the jazz avant-garde. On the *Live in Tokyo* recording, Rivers's freer playing is qualitatively different from Coleman's. But while the rhythm section had by now established a continuum that ranged from the Kelly/Chambers/Cobb hard bop attitude on one side to freer positions on the other, Rivers seemed unwilling to participate in the more standard side. "It didn't really work out that well with Sam; it didn't quite mesh," Hancock acknowledged. "Sam's a great player of course. He just wasn't quite what we were looking for. We all became more certain that what we were really looking for was what Wayne had."[79]

The addition of Wayne Shorter in mid-1964 was crucial, as Hancock observed:

The differences between what Miles had been playing before the quintet crystallized [in 1964] and what we played was incredible. Like, Tony

---

78 Harvey Siders, "Review: Miles Davis, *My Funny Valentine*," *Down Beat* 32/12 (June 3, 1965): 27.
79 Mercer, *Footprints*, 96.

was introducing rhythms I had never even heard. I think what made the band unique was the interplay of the rhythm section, the way the ball passed around…and at the same time Miles and Wayne floated on top of this ever-evolving rhythm section sound. And just the way Tony mixed up the roles of different parts of the drums—the focus might be on the snare drum, or another time on the bass drum, or it might be totally the cymbals without any other parts of the drum.[80]

The live recordings made with Shorter between 1964 and 1965, *Miles in Berlin* and *Live at the Plugged Nickel*, show the group moving even further towards free jazz and abstraction in the context of standard tune improvisation. Ever exploratory, these recordings made even the innovations of the previous work seem confining. In particular, the *Plugged Nickel* recordings, made during the band's appearance at the Chicago club during the end of 1965, appeared to the members as a significant moment in the group's evolution. "I'd been in the band for a little over a year," Shorter related, "and the next thing I know we were way out there. It was like…this is what freedom means."[81]

The quintet members and critics cite the *Plugged Nickel* recordings as marking a definitive step toward free playing.[82] Hancock stated that their intent was to work against expectations to create "antimusic": "the idea was that the last thing that you would play would be what the other musicians expected you to play and just go in completely opposite directions."[83]

But while these recordings did reflect a change for the Davis quintet, they did not necessarily reflect a drastic shift in direction for the individual sidemen. Certainly other recordings made by Shorter, Hancock, Carter, and Williams during 1965—prior to the *Plugged Nickel* recordings—had already moved toward avant-garde playing. Shorter's *The All Seeing Eye*, Tony Williams's *Spring*, and Hancock's composition "Survival of the Fittest" (*Maiden Voyage*) (as well as "The Egg," from Hancock's 1964 *Empyrean Isles*) were all marked by the use of nonmetric improvisation, sound-based approaches to improvisation, and freedom from preset harmonic progressions. Thus, while the *Plugged Nickel* recordings

80 Conrad Silvert, "Herbie Hancock: Revamping the Past, Creating the Future," *Down Beat* 44/15 (September 8, 1977): 16.
81 Mercer, *Footprints*, 110.
82 Chambers, *Milestones* 2, 92–93; Coolman, "The Miles Davis Quintet," 18–20; Szwed, *So What*, 254–56.
83 Coolman, "The Miles Davis Quintet," 20.

were undoubtedly pivotal, their gravitation toward freer playing continued the sidemen's ongoing activities throughout 1965.

Video recordings of the quintet's live performances include versions
of compositions initially recorded on the studio albums. Two videos
capture the group's European tour during fall 1967 (with performances
in Karlsruhe and Stockholm), which include performance of "Agitation"
(from *E.S.P.*), "Footprints," and "Ginger Bread Boy" (from *Miles Smiles*).[84]
In contrast to the studio versions, the live performances link more decisively with the jazz avant-garde by using more frequent metrical shifts,
more extended improvisations, further departures from the underlying
harmonic progression, and a higher degree of sound-based improvisation. Shorter's and Hancock's improvisations, in particular, are at times
indebted to a "sheets of sound" aesthetic rarely heard on the studio
recordings. Particularly with the rhythm section, the video also reveals
the degree of ensemble communication and give-and-take among the
players. Carter, when initiating metrical shifts, watches carefully the
other rhythm section players. Hancock's comping occasionally drops out
as Williams's drumming becomes more active, and he observes Williams
closely, letting the piano accompaniment recede as the drum accompaniment becomes focal. In contrast to an earlier video from the quintet's
1964 Milan performance, the 1967 video performances also show the
quintet moving from one composition to another without pause, creating a large-scale medley of their sequence.

It is not entirely clear why the quintet performed so few of the studio compositions live. Coolman suggests the driving force was general
audience expectations for jazz standards.[85] It may be also that the harmonic or melodic intricacies of the studio compositions prohibited easy
memorization: at no time on the videos does the quintet use lead sheets
in performance. The composition "Footprints," one studio composition
that the group did play live, was a 12-bar minor blues and perhaps easier
to memorize than other studio compositions. In fact, Shorter claimed
that he wrote "Footprints" in response to Davis's request for a composition to play live.[86] Whatever the reason, the result is a typically a single
studio version for most of the quintet original compositions rather than

---

84 These two performances combine on the video release *Miles Davis European Tour 1967*
(Impro-Jazz, DVDIJ518). A Paris performance from the same tour was released as an audio
recording entitled *No Blues* (Jazz Music Yesterday JMY 1003). On it, the group performs live
versions of the studio compositions "Masqualero" (from *Sorcerer*) and "Riot" (from *Nefertiti*).
85 Coolman, "The Miles Davis Quintet," 21.
86 Mercer, *Footprints*, 118.

the myriad recorded live versions of standards such as "Autumn Leaves," "Walkin,'" or "My Funny Valentine."

For both the live performances and the studio recordings, the legacy of the quintet remains immense—not only through the future direction of all the quintet members, but through the original repertory as well as the implications for postbop melody, form, harmony, improvisation, and ensemble interaction.

CHAPTER 2

ANALYTICAL STRATEGIES

THIS CHAPTER PROVIDES SOME GENERAL analytical frameworks relevant to the Davis studio recordings. It disentangles knotty terms such as "modal jazz" and provides overviews of strategies in the domain of pitch, rhythm/meter, and form. Regarding pitch, these tacks include motivic cells, motivic improvisation, and phrase overlap. In the area of meter, they include accentual shift, metrical conflict, and metric modulation. Further, I examine the interaction of larger metrical groupings (hypermeter) and form, and suggest how the quintet worked to enhance formal ambiguity in improvisation by masking sectional and formal divisions.

Finally, I consider the idea of "controlled freedom" (discussed in chapter 1), describing the group's self-aware interest in uniting traditional jazz approaches with avant-garde ones. I describe how that affected the group's approaches to form in improvisation by indicating a series of intermediate levels between strict adherence to chorus structure on the one hand

and its complete abandonment on the other. The chapter concludes by showing on which levels most of the studio compositions operate. The analytical ideas throughout the chapter not only corroborate general observations made about the quintet by band members, other jazz musicians, and writers, but they also help pinpoint and highlight some of the substantial accomplishments of the quintet.

MILES DAVIS AND MODAL JAZZ

Modal jazz is a complex term, but is one central to postbop jazz. Both Miles Davis and John Coltrane are crucial figures in the development of modal jazz, particularly with their recordings of the late 1950s and 1960s. A number of writers have singled out Davis's 1958 "Milestones" as a signal point of departure, and Davis's 1959 recording *Kind of Blue* as the primary representative of modal jazz. One recent study cites Davis's 1957 soundtrack to the French film *Ascenseur pour l'échafaud* (*Lift to the Scaffold*) as an important precedent for Davis's modal jazz.[1] Representative modal jazz works by the John Coltrane Quartet include those recorded between 1960 and 1964, such as "Acknowledgement" (from *A Love Supreme*), "Impressions," "India," and "My Favorite Things."

The term itself stems from the principle that modes (or scales) provide the available pitches for improvisers. The idea of equating scales with chords was not lost on Davis. In a 1958 interview, he enthusiastically discussed how scalar organization provided a prompt for his creativity. "All chords, after all, are relative to scales and certain chords make certain scales," he stated. "When you go on this way, you can go on forever. You don't have to worry about changes and you can do more with the line. It becomes a challenge to see how melodically inventive you are."[2]

1   Jack Chambers, *Milestones: The Music and Times of Miles Davis* (New York: Da Capo, 1998), originally publ. University of Toronto Press 1983 and 1985; James Lincoln Collier, *The Making of Jazz: A Comprehensive History* (Boston: Houghton Mifflin, 1978); Ekkehard Jost, *Free Jazz* (New York: Da Capo Press, 1981), originally publ. Universal Editions, 1975; Ashley Kahn, *Kind of Blue: The Making of the Miles Davis Masterpiece* (New York: Da Capo, 2001); Andrea Pejrolo, "The Origins of Modal Jazz in the Music of Miles Davis: A Complete Transcription and a Linear/Harmonic Analysis of *Ascenseur pour l'échafaud* (*Lift to the Scaffold*)-1957" (Ph.D. diss., New York University, 2001); Frank Tirro, *Jazz: A History*, 2nd ed. (New York: W. W. Norton, 1993).
2   Hentoff, "An Afternoon with Miles Davis," in *Miles on Miles*, ed. by Paul Maher Jr. and Michael Dorr (Chicago: Lawrence Hill, 2009), 18. Originally publ. *Jazz Review* 1/2 (December 1958): 11–12.

Davis's comments during the same interview also link scales inextricably with the notion of slow harmonic rhythm:

> I think a movement in jazz is beginning away from the conventional string of chords, and a return to emphasis on melodic rather than harmonic variation. There will be fewer chords but infinite possibilities as to what to do with them.... The music has gotten thick. Guys give me tunes and they're full of chords. I can't play them. You know, we play "My Funny Valentine" like with a scale all the way through.[3]

Sources for Davis's interest in scalar/modal organization were varied. By 1958 Davis had enjoyed a decade-long friendship and association with composer and theorist George Russell, whose treatise *The Lydian Chromatic Concept of Tonal Organization* likely formed the earliest impetus for equating scales with individual chords, and for using these scales as a repository of pitches for improvisation. First published in 1953, its second 1959 edition added musical examples and was more widely distributed.[4] As the first substantial theoretical treatise on jazz, its chord/scale focus became prophetic for the development of jazz pedagogy. Davis also cited as influential his collaborations with arranger Gil Evans, pianist Bill Evans, as well as the music of Aram Khachaturian, a Russian orchestral composer.[5] (Davis's reference to Khachaturian provides an interesting contrast with John Coltrane's comments regarding his own influences for modal/scalar music, which he located within folk and world music rather than within classical music.)[6]

Pianist Bill Evans wrote the liner notes for *Kind of Blue*, and its reputation as the touchstone for modal jazz arises largely from two of its compositions, "So What" and "Flamenco Sketches." His comments emphasize the modal/scalar aspects of the two compositions. "So What," he wrote, is "based on 16 measures of one scale, 8 of another and 8 more of the first." Evans wrote about "Flamenco Sketches" that it "is a series of five scales, each to be played as long as the soloist wishes until he has completed the

---

3   Hentoff, "An Afternoon," 18.
4   George Russell, *The Lydian Chromatic Concept of Tonal Organization for Improvisation*, 2nd ed. (New York: Concept, 1959).
5   Hentoff, "An Afternoon," 18.
6   Lewis Porter, *John Coltrane: His Life and Music* (Ann Arbor: University of Michigan, 1998), 211. It is important not to use these Davis and Coltrane quotations to overstate this high/low (classical/folk) distinction. Certainly Khatchaturian, like many Russian composers after Mussorgsky, made use of folk music sources within his notated compositions.

series."[7] Cannonball Adderley's part to "Flamenco Sketches" appears in a photograph taken at the recording session to *Kind of Blue*. Published in 2000, the photograph shows five notated scales with the instructions to "play in (the) sound of these scales." Not all the five scales are visible in the photograph (Adderley's mouthpiece cap obscures the first and fifth scales). The second scale provides the pitches of E♭ dorian (modes indicated here are transposed from the E♭ key of the alto saxophone), and the third scale the pitches of B♭ major. The notes of the fourth scale are the mode of G harmonic minor that begins on D (D, E♭, F♯, G, A, B♭, C, D).[8]

Evans' descriptions for both "So What" and "Flamenco Sketches" are captivating since they provide general but distinctly technical discussion. But while they highlight the principles of scalar organization, they nevertheless suppress some of the more conventional aspects of the music. Evans's emphasis on the horizontal dimension (scales/modes) is understandable since it calls attention to novel ways in which the players conceived of aspects of musical organization. Yet his comments leave unacknowledged the degree to which the rhythm section provides an underlying harmonic framework for the improvisers, and they neglect to describe the manner in which the soloists reflect that underlying framework.

Modal/scalar organization has become a primary tenet of jazz pedagogy since the 1970s, to the extent that improvisational pedagogy suggests a fundamental equivalence between any chord and one or more associated scales. The result is an implicit treatment of *all* jazz harmonies as having a modal/scalar foundation, even with compositions not considered modal. Another result is the dominance of mode/scale considerations in the analysis of jazz improvisation.[9]

Musicians, theorists, and historians apply the term modal jazz to refer to any number of different musical features. Not all these features

7   Bill Evans, liner notes to *Kind of Blue* (Columbia/Sony 64935).
8   Kahn, *Kind of Blue*, 70. In the caption, Kahn mislabels two of the three scales visible in the photograph.
9   In this discussion, I will use the terms *modes* and *scales* interchangeably. I will not examine the relationship of jazz modality to Renaissance modality—those studies that do (and their resultant exchanges) do not meaningfully enhance the understanding of the issues surrounding modal jazz. See William Thomson, "On Miles and the Modes," *College Music Symposium* 38 (1998): 17–32; as well as Frederick Bashour, "A Different View 'On Miles and the Modes,'" and William Thomson, "Response to Frederick Bashour," both in *College Music Symposium* 39 (1999): 124–35. Nor do I here differentiate between modes of the diatonic scale and other modes, as does Barry Kernfeld in "Adderley, Coltrane, and Davis at the Twilight of Bebop: The Search for Melodic Coherence" (Ph.D. diss., Cornell University, 1981), esp. Ch. 5.

describe improvisers' use of modes; some apply more fundamentally to musical composition and accompaniment.[10] We can isolate a number of different views of the term, particularly in regard to the representative modal works by Davis and Coltrane as well as the recordings of Davis's second quintet. The following discussion identifies four general strands: modes/scales for improvisation, slow harmonic rhythm, absence of functional harmony, and "modal harmony."

1. One strand relies on a strict view of the term modal jazz—writers such as Jack Chambers, James Lincoln Collier, and Ekkekard Jost hold to the idea of scalar/modal organization as its fundamental principle.[11] It can be argued that in some cases these writers and historians have overemphasized the scalar/modal features, treating the music as if it is *purely* horizontal, or somehow devoid of an underlying harmonic framework. Writing about "Milestones," James Lincoln Collier suggests that "it is built not on chord changes but on modes."[12] "It is Davis's first completely successful composition based on scales rather than a repeated chord structure," echoes Jack Chambers about "Milestones."[13] Similarly, Chambers writes about *Kind of Blue* that "Davis's major contribution to jazz form, of which *Kind of Blue* stands as the most influential example, involves a principled shift from the

---

10 This is also one of the central points of ch. 5 from Kernfeld, "Adderley, Coltrane, and Davis."

11 Collier, *The Making of Jazz*, 431; Chambers, *Milestones*, 279 and 309; Jost, *Free Jazz*. See also Pejrolo, "The Origins of Modal Jazz," 63.

12 Collier, *The Making of Jazz*, 431.

13 Chambers, *Milestones* I, 279. Even more substantive discussions of Davis's 1958 recording of "Milestones" overemphasize its modal orientation. Ekkekard Jost (*Free Jazz*, 19) is one of many authors that describe its 8-bar A section as G dorian. But this description neglects to account for the way that Paul Chambers's bass notes during the initial chorus and throughout much of the performance reflect a resolution to F major during mm. 7–8 of each A section, as well as the C pedal point played by pianist Red Garland during mm. 1–4. So it may be accurate to describe the A section during the head to "Milestones" as a one-flat environment (considering the pitches of the melody and the piano accompaniment), but inaccurate to refer to it as G dorian, given the bass arrival points on F at mm. 7–8. But even this one-flat description fails to describe the music of the A section as it unfolds during the solos. During the second A section of Davis's first chorus on *both* the released and the alternate takes from the 1958 session, Davis's phrases resolve to B natural, the raised eleventh of F major, at the m. 7 point of harmonic resolution to F. Davis thus already departs from a one-flat environment within the first 15 measures of both his solos, negating the idea of a single mode controlling the A sections to "Milestones."

constraints of chordal organization to the different constraints of scalar organization."[14] Like Bill Evans's liner notes for "So What" and "Flamenco Sketches," these views downplay the role of harmonic organization in favor of a distinctly scalar view of the music. They also do not address the manner in which soloists use pitches from outside any underlying scales/modes.

2. A second view suggests instead that slow harmonic rhythm is more crucial to the representative modal works, particularly since improvisers frequently are not systematic in adhering to underlying modes/scales. Further, improvised musical lines may express or outline harmonies in generally conventional fashion and progress in ways that seem unmotivated by linear scalar organization. Writer Barry Kernfeld even proposes replacing the term modal jazz with "vamp style," since it describes more accurately the use of slow harmonic rhythm or bass pedal points.[15] This shifts the emphasis away from improvisation and toward composition and accompaniment. His term also places the representative Davis and Coltrane modal jazz pieces within a broader jazz compositional tradition that includes more vamp-based organization and slow harmonic rhythm, such as Afro-Cuban grooves or "cubop" works (such as Dizzy Gillespie's "Manteca"), montunos, or funky jazz.[16] And it describes a technical feature shared by these modal jazz works and some later jazz-rock fusion of the 1970s, much of which similarly relied on slow harmonic rhythm and vamps.[17]

3. Other views of modal jazz emerge in writings on Davis's second quintet. A third view of modality hinges on suppressed or absent harmonic function. In his dissertation on that quintet, Coolman defines modality as "scalar 'colors' that do not have a harmonic goal or tendency toward resolution."[18] Coolman uses the notion of absent harmonic goals and resolutions in order to describe both the linear use of modes during improvisation as well as aspects of Hancock's harmonic

---

14 Chambers, *Milestones* I, 309.

15 Kernfeld, "Adderley, Coltrane, and Davis," esp. 160–62. See also Barry Kernfeld, *What to Listen for in Jazz* (New Haven: Yale University Press, 1995), 67–69.

16 See Rebeca Mauleón, *101 Montunos* (Petaluma, Calif.: Sher, 1999).

17 Further connections between the canonic modal jazz pieces and fusion remain underexplored, such as the use of straight-eighth note improvisation, a hallmark of Coltrane's and McCoy Tyner's improvisations, as well as in much jazz-rock fusion. For a description of Coltrane's influence on rock and fusion players, see Stuart Nicholson, *Jazz-Rock: A History* (New York: Schirmer 1998), 85–87.

18 Coolman, "The Miles Davis Quintet," 47.

language ("modal voicings"). Modality in this sense applies both to improvisation and accompaniment.

4. Finally, a fourth thrust considers harmony, from the standpoint of both harmonic progression (chord-to-chord succession) and harmonic structure (chord quality). In his book *Modal Jazz: Composition & Harmony*, Ron Miller uses the term "modal harmony" to refer to nonfunctional harmonic progressions, shifting harmonies over pedal points, modally designated harmonies (for example, E lydian, E phrygian, or E aeolian), slash chord harmonies (for example, FMaj7/E), and nonstandard and nonsyntactic harmonies.[19] Miller examines a number of Davis second quintet studio compositions written by Wayne Shorter, Herbie Hancock, and Tony Williams, and he identifies Shorter and Hancock as pivotal in the development of contemporary jazz composition.[20] Miller also attempts to consider systematically many individual harmonies that emerged after 1959, and equates those harmonies with underlying seven-note modal/scalar collections. Like other authors, he indicates the problems that arise with variable or unsystematic labels for many of these harmonies.

The above four strands indicate the complexity of the term modal jazz (or modality) in discussions of Davis's (and Coltrane's) music and that modal jazz stands for a network of musical features that may appear in some combination. The discussion above suggests five characteristics, to which I have added a sixth:

1. Modal scales for improvisation (or as a source for accompaniment)
2. Slow harmonic rhythm (single chord for 4, 8, 16, or more bars)
3. Pedal point harmonies (focal bass pitch or shifting harmonies over a primary bass pitch)
4. Absence or limited use of functional harmonic progressions (such as V–I or ii–V–I) in accompaniment or improvisation
5. Harmonies characteristic of jazz after 1959 (Suspended fourth—"sus"—chords, slash chords, harmonies named for modes: i.e., phrygian, aeolian harmonies)
6. Prominent use of melodic and/or harmonic perfect fourths

19 Ron Miller, *Modal Jazz: Composition and Harmony*, vol. 1 (Rottenburg, Germany: Advance Music, 1996).
20 Ibid., 6.

To what extent do Davis's 1965–68 studio recordings exemplify modal jazz? Or, perhaps the more appropriate question now is, which compositions exhibit which of the six features indicated above? The above list suggests that the term "modal jazz" evades rigorous definition, but instead addresses a series of features that frequently overlap, or may appear in different combinations. The quintet improvisers at times adhered to pitch content of specific modes, but their improvisations just as frequently used pitch choices outside of those modes. Several compositions feature the use of slow harmonic rhythm (no. 2 above), such as "Agitation," "Masqualero," and "Freedom Jazz Dance." Yet by far the majority of the studio compositions do not consistently share that feature; many change harmonies each measure. As a result, Kernfeld's term "vamp style" is inapt. Other compositions include the use of pedal points beneath shifting harmonies (no. 3 above): Hancock's "Little One," in particular, is built on three underlying pedal points with harmonies that change above them, usually at every measure.

But nos. 4 and 5—the absence or limited use of functional harmonic progressions, and the use of nontraditional harmonies (more characteristic of jazz after 1959)—are crucial to the Davis second quintet studio recordings. Of those two, the first refers to harmonic progression: that is, chord sequences that may involve standard or syntactic harmonies (minor seventh/ninth chords, for example) but—because harmonic function is absent or suppressed—they often progress in ways that do not clearly articulate larger harmonic areas. The second applies to harmonic structure: that is, chord qualities that are not standard or syntactic. Both these characteristics describe composition and accompaniment more fundamentally than improvisation. They also reflect some of the principal compositional achievements of these recordings, which helped bring about the expansion of harmonic resources that are now incorporated into contemporary jazz composition.

Miller's term "modal harmony" is useful because it suggests some degree of continuity between Davis's 1958–59 representative modal jazz compositions and those recorded by the second quintet. Yet it is important not to overstate the degree of continuity. Certainly the second quintet works frequently feature a faster harmonic rhythm and an expanded harmonic vocabulary when compared to the 1958–59 compositions.

Much of the harmonic vocabulary that emerged during the 1960s forms now an integral part of jazz pedagogy. This is particularly true with harmonies such as "sus" chord harmonies, or with chords that relate to an underlying modal/scalar collection (phrygian harmonies, for example). Yet there are a number of harmonies that appear in the Davis second quintet studio compositions that remain unaddressed in current jazz pedagogy, perhaps because not all are as easily referable to an underlying mode/scale. Some of these less-considered harmonies are provided in example 2.1. They include the chord used in mm. 7–8 of Wayne Shorter's "Iris" (*E.S.P.*), consisting of the pitches of A♭Maj7 with both a natural and raised fifth, E♭ and E natural (for convenience, example 2.1 indicates E natural as F♭.) The lead sheet to "Iris" contained in *The Real Book* realizes this harmony merely as A♭Maj7♯5.[21] The harmony at mm. 5 of "Circle" (*Miles Smiles*) is a Dmaj triad (or DMaj7) stated above an E♭ triad.[22] Wayne Shorter's copyright deposit lead sheet to "Vonetta" labels the harmony at m. 2 as Ab+9♯; Hancock's accompanying chord on the recording (*Sorcerer*) typically states this as a "doubly-augmented" harmony, with the pitches arranged from lowest to highest as A♭–C–E–G–B–E♭ (G+/A♭+). The combination of these six pitches creates the augmented (or hexatonic) scale.[23] Herbie Hancock's "Madness" uses an eight-note chord, difficult to label in a recognizable fashion. It is possible to acknowledge this as a dense polychord, perhaps labeling it as

EXAMPLE 2.1   Nonstandard Harmonies in the Davis Quintet Compositions

21 *The Real Book*, 6th ed. (Milwaukee, Wisc.: Hal Leonard, n.d.), 218.
22 Interestingly enough, versions of this particular harmony appear as early as in the 1949–50 Davis recordings later released as *Birth of the Cool*. Davis's "Deception" uses a D triad over an E♭ triad in the horn voicings at m. 40 (:46); the final harmony of Gerry Mulligan's arrangement of "Venus de Milo" is indicated as E♭Maj7(♯9).
23 Walt Weiskopf and Ramon Ricker, *The Augmented Scale in Jazz* (New Albany, Ind.: Jamey Aebersold Jazz, 1993).

EMaj7(♭7)/A° above the B♭ bass. (For convenience, example 2.1 indicates the upper pitch as F♭ rather than E natural.)[24]

The second quintet studio compositions raise a number of fundamental analytical questions that transcend merely a catalog of novel post-1959 harmonies. How do we address harmonic progression in the absence of functional harmonic progressions? Is harmonic function sometimes present even in the absence of conventional harmonic functional progressions? Do these compositions support an overall global tonal (or modal) center—that is, do they operate within a single key? If they do operate within a single key, how do they do that? Should we understand harmonic progressions as shifts between implied or present modal/scalar collections? Should we consider bass motion independent from upper-structure harmonies? These questions, addressing compositional analysis, are pertinent not only for the Davis quintet compositions but also for any number of jazz compositions written after 1960—particularly those that feature nonfunctional harmonic progressions, nonstandard harmonies, and an overall tonal center that is ambiguous or absent.

THE SECOND QUINTET AND MODE/SCALE IMPROVISATION

While the questions above and the term "modal harmony" are weighted in favor of analysis of composition rather than improvisation, modal/scalar analyses of the improvisations can shed some light on facets of the second quintet improvisations. This is particularly true for those compositions that feature slow harmonic rhythm. One such work is "Agitation" (*E.S.P.*), which consists of two sections that alternate a loose C minor environment with an oscillation of A♭/D♭ in the bass.

If modal, "Agitation" highlights the shortcomings that arise from a view of modality that rests upon absent or suppressed harmonic goals.[25] That view sets up a crisp distinction between modality (absence of harmonic goals and resolution tendencies) and tonality (presence of harmonic

---

24 It is possible to relate most of those harmonies to scale collections, although the accompaniment and improvisations over them do not seem to have been motivated by those considerations. The "harmonic major" (A♭–B♭–C–D♭–E♭–F♭–G–A♭) corresponds to the "Iris" harmony; the "Circle" harmony corresponds to a rotation of what is sometimes called the "Gypsy" or "Hungarian Gypsy" scale, consisting of two augmented seconds (E♭–F♯–G–A–B♭–C♯–D–E♭). The "Madness" harmony loosely corresponds to the diminished (octatonic) collection (A–B–C–D–E♭–F–G♭–A♭), although this collection excludes both the bass pitch (B♭) and an upper chordal member (E) from the "Madness" chord.

25 See Coolman, "The Miles Davis Quintet," 47.

goals and resolution tendencies), a distinction with which improvisers and accompanists often appear unconcerned. Indeed, the following
examples will show how the players frequently rely on routines deeply
rooted in functional harmonic practice. Since goal-oriented harmonic
or melodic moves were a fundamental part of these improvisers' vocabulary, these players at times extended those moves into works with slow
harmonic rhythm, works frequently regarded as modal.

Example 2.2 includes two phrases of Davis's "Agitation" solo that begin
at 3:02, along with bass accompaniment.[26] Davis's two phrases appear
at the juncture of the C minor section and the A♭/D♭ bass oscillation. At
this point in the performance, the A♭/D♭ bass oscillation takes place as
Carter creates a metrical conflict through dotted quarter notes. Davis's
two phrases present melodic paths that begin by traversing C minor,
before moving to pitches that express the dominant of C minor (G7; the
bass oscillation suggests its tritone substitute, D♭7). The former occurs in
the opening measure of the first phrase in the transcription. The latter
pitches occur with the remainder of the first phrase, which express the
dominant G7 with the pitches of an ascending A♭ melodic minor scale.[27]
(Dotted slurs indicate the motion from C minor to its dominant.)

The second phrase likewise expresses the pitches of an ascending A♭
melodic minor scale, expressing the dominant.[28] Both phrases include
a chromatic passing tone A that connects B♭ to A♭. More complicated is
the passing tone A that connects G to B♭ in the second phrase, and this
motion forms one of Davis's improvisational formulas that occur in any
number of his solos.[29] Rather than implying a new or different mode, in
all three cases A natural (indicated with asterisks) embellishes but does

26 The transcription here corrects some of the rhythmic and pitch errors of Coolman's transcription that appear in Coolman, "The Miles Davis Quintet," pp. 170–71.

27 Jazz pedagogy typically regards this as a "G altered dominant" scale. See Mark Levine, *The
Jazz Theory Book* (Petaluma, Calif.: Sher Music, 1995), 70–72.

28 About these phrases, Coolman writes, "Davis' ninth phrase in mm. 72–74 is polymodal, jux-
taposing C dorian, locrian, natural and harmonic modes within a very short span. This
polymodal idea is reinforced and extended in the tenth phrase, mm. 75–78." Setting aside
questions of intention—whether negotiating four modes in the space of two and a half measures was something Davis was attempting, or that jazz musicians routinely attempt—these
analytical claims obscure the functional orientation of the two phrases. See Coolman, "The
Miles Davis Quintet," 59.

29 Further, this phrase is part of a recurring melodic formula for Davis, one that appears in
numerous solos and includes the pitches G–A–B♭–A–A♭ within a longer line. For example,
"E.S.P." (1.29), "Orbits" (1:06), "Dolores" (1:21), "Hand Jive" (1:11, 2:55, 2:59), and "Madness" (:27
and :57).

EXAMPLE 2.2 "Agitation"

not belong to the underlying mode, a mode that implies the underlying dominant harmony.

Example 2.2 also contains a phrase from Shorter's solo in "Agitation" (4:40).[30] It, like Davis's material discussed above, expresses functional harmonic moves between C minor and its dominant. The dotted slurs

30 About it, Coolman writes, "Shorter's ninth phrase in mm. 176–182, mostly in continuous eighth notes, is more chromatic than previous phrases, creating melodic tension." Coolman, "The Miles Davis Quintet," 65.

show the path, moving from C minor in the first measure, to its dominant for the following three measures, before returning to C minor. The chromaticism (indicated by asterisks), occurring in the third bar of the excerpt, can be heard as elaborating the underlying dominant. Further, the transcription brackets standard bop harmonic gestures, such as the B–D–F–A♭–G–F, outlining the dominant with flatted ninth, as well as the characteristic bebop cliché (E♭–C) that closes the phrase.[31] Moreover, even the bass is involved in establishing the harmony through clearly functional means, and the brackets indicate Carter's insertion of a standard harmonic turnaround (C–D–G–D–C) to express a functional harmonic progression.

These functional moves also occur in the piano accompaniment. About the extended C minor environment during the statement of the head of "Agitation" (*E.S.P.*), Coolman writes that Hancock's voicings "are heard primarily as C minor derivatives, with its dominant G7 (further establishing C minor) and occasional suggestions of D♭ lydian acting as a variant of the G7 dominant function commonly called a substitute dominant."[32] His description points to a harmonic environment with heightened goals and resolution tendencies.

All of this is to show how the players extended functional harmonic moves into works with slow harmonic rhythm, works that may be regarded as modal in one sense or another. It also shows potential limitations when requiring absolute distinctions between modality and tonality, since the players rarely relied on such sharp distinctions in practice.

To summarize: the term modal jazz remains elusive because it often refers to a range of musical features, and these features sometimes differ when applied to the representative Davis and Coltrane modal works or to the second quintet studio recordings. Modal scales, slow harmonic rhythm, pedal point construction, absent/suppressed harmonic goals, nontraditional or nonsyntactic harmonies, and fourth-based harmonic and melodic structures may appear to varying degrees in this repertory. These features describe aspects of improvisation as well as composition and accompaniment. All interact in distinct ways and apply to a range of music described as modal.

31 This rhythmic and contour gesture, similar to the opening gesture of Dizzy Gillespie's "Groovin' High," may be likely the onomatopoeic origin of the term "bebop."
32 Coolman, "The Miles Davis Quintet," 57. This description, applied to what Coolman describes as Hancock's "modal voicings," contradicts his notion of modality with absent or suppressed harmonic goals.

MOTIVIC ANALYSIS

We were actually tampering with something called DNA in music
in a song. Each song has its DNA. So you just do the DNA and
not the whole song. You do the characteristics. You say, "Okay,
I will do the ear of the face, I will do the left side of the face. You
do the right side of the face." ... Everyone ... took a portion of a
certain characteristic of the song and—you can stay there. And
then you do eight measures of it, and then you make your own
harmonic road or avenue within a certain eight measures.

(SHORTER ON THE DAVIS QUINTET AND
"DOLORES")[33]

Mode/scale labeling provides a means to address improvisation. Yet
pitch considerations independent of interval, rhythm, contour, as well
as meter, form, and voice-leading provide a decidedly one-dimensional
view of musical improvisation. Motivic analysis provides one method
of addressing pitch in tandem with interval, rhythm, and contour. One
early motivic analysis appears in Gunther Schuller's 1958 article "Sonny
Rollins and the Challenge of Thematic Improvisation," in which he identified melodic motives used by Rollins within his improvisation on "Blue
Seven."[34] Schuller's analysis focuses on how Rollins later restates and
transforms motives used earlier both in the head and at the beginning of
his improvisation.
    Later writers have criticized Schuller's appeals to structural unity
and cohesion since that approach seeks to validate jazz through its
adherence to Western European values for musical coherence.[35] Their
critique suggests that such Western European analytical methods are
inappropriate for jazz, an African-American music. More recent scholarship has shown that the motives that Schuller highlighted appeared
in any number of Rollins's improvisations from the same time period.

---

33 Eric Nemeyer, "The Magical Journey: An Interview with Wayne Shorter," *Jazz Improv* 2/3
    (1999): 75.
34 Contained in Gunther Schuller, *Musings: The Musical Worlds of Gunther Schuller* (New York:
    Oxford University Press, 1986), 86–97. Originally publ. *Jazz Review* 1 (November 1958).
35 Ingrid Monson, *Saying Something: Jazz Improvisation and Interaction* (Chicago: University
    of Chicago, 1996), 135–36; Robert Walser, "Deep Jazz: Notes on Interiority, Race, and Criti-
    cism," essay in *Inventing the Psychological: Toward a Cultural History of Emotional Life in
    America*, ed. Joel Pfistner and Nancy Schnog (New Haven: Yale University, 1997).

Thus, Rollins derived the motives in his "Blue Seven" solo from his vocabulary of melodic formulas.[36]

Despite the criticisms of Schuller, it seems reasonable to assume that jazz musicians sometimes create musical relationships based on repetition and elaboration during improvisation. To indicate these motivic correspondences merely suggests that jazz players may create such musical relations while improvising, that subsequent improvised phrases may relate to a greater or lesser degree to earlier phrases, and that it is profitable to point out these relations in order to hear them. Those critical of Schuller's approach rightly point out that it highlights principles of organic unity, and downplays the ways in which jazz arises from larger social constructions. Yet to abandon completely any consideration of musical motives erases the opportunity to consider how or when those musical relationships take place during improvisation. Further, it leaves unaddressed those players whose improvisations cultivate techniques for motivic improvisation—improvisers dedicated to, in Lester Young's apt phrase, "telling stories."[37]

Certainly many improvisers appear committed to exploring motivic relationships, and to developing musical ideas that emerge out of previous ones by continuing some aspects of pitch, rhythm, contour, or interval. Barry Kernfeld has discussed the issue of motivic improvisation, identifying as a key feature a liberal use of space between each motivic statement, which then allows time to prepare the next. He lists Count Basie, Thelonious Monk, John Lewis, Benny Carter, Paul Desmond, and John Gilmore as representative motivic improvisers.[38]

Motivic improvisation took on greater urgency in the context of modal jazz and avant-garde jazz in the late 1950s and 1960s. This is particularly evident with compositions that abandoned chorus structure frameworks. Since the players no longer negotiated a predetermined harmonic progression, many relied on principles of motivic organization. Motivic organization has provided the focus of a number of published analyses

---

36 Benjamin Givan, "Gunther Schuller and the Challenge of Sonny Rollins: Musical Context, Intentionality, and Jazz Analysis," paper delivered at national meeting of the Society for Music Theory, 2006. Givan suggests that, rather than deriving his improvised motives from the melody, Rollins derived the melody from one of his frequently used improvised formulas.

37 Nat Hentoff, "Prez," *Down Beat* (March 7, 1956): 9.

38 Kernfeld, *What to Listen For*, 143–46. Kernfeld also examines the motivic orientation to the opening bars of Sonny Rollins's solo on "St. Thomas" (*Saxophone Colossus*), indicating the saxophonist's use of inversions, transpositions, intervallic extensions, and ornamentations of the opening notes of the melody.

of such improvisations, particularly those by Ornette Coleman, John Coltrane, and John Gilmore.[39]

The discussion in chapter 1 of the primary soloists of the quintet—Davis, Shorter, and Hancock—argued that each had cultivated techniques for motivic improvisation prior to the formation of Davis's quintet in 1963–64. All applied these techniques within standard-tune and hard bop contexts, and they would continue to pursue those implications with further rigor after Davis formed the quintet, both with compositions that maintained chorus structure as well as those that abandoned it. Certainly for the Davis second quintet the absence of a fixed underlying harmonic progression in the "time, no changes" compositions invited such techniques for motivic improvisation.

MOTIVIC CELL

The term "motivic cell" describes a technique in which a soloist states and develops an underlying identifiable short motive. What constitutes a motivic cell is flexible, but these motives may be identified through repetition of interval, rhythm, contour, pitch, or some combination of those elements. In this context I will consider motivic cell improvisation as one that relies on transpositions, and these transpositions may be independent of the underlying tonal or modal center. Improvisers may derive motivic cells from features of the composition on which they are improvising, or a motivic cell may instead emerge spontaneously during improvisation. The following two examples illustrate how improvisers use motivic cells that are derived from, in one instance, the bass ostinato and, in another, a portion of the composition's melody.

Perhaps the most famous use of a motivic cell comes from John Coltrane's solo from "Acknowledgement," the first movement of his 1964 recording *A Love Supreme*. Following an introduction, "Acknowledgement" then uses a four-note bass ostinato based on the pitches F–A♭–F–B♭. During one portion of Coltrane's solo (at 4:56), he uses solely that four-note motive and subsequently transposes that motive freely,

39 Michael B. Cogswell, "Melodic Organization in Two Solos by Ornette Coleman," *Annual Review of Jazz Studies* 7 (1994–95), 101–44; Jost, *Free Jazz*, 44–65; Kernfeld, *What to Listen For*, 146; Lewis Porter, "John Coltrane's *A Love Supreme*: Jazz Improvisation as Composition," *Journal of the American Musicological Society* 38/3 (Fall 1985), 593–621; Lewis Porter, *John Coltrane: His Life and Music* (Ann Arbor: University of Michigan, 1998); Gunther Schuller, *A Collection of the Compositions of Ornette Coleman* (New York: MJQ Music, 1961).

ultimately transposing it so it begins at least once on each of the twelve pitch classes.[40]

There Coltrane uses the underlying foundation of the movement—the bass ostinato—as the resource for improvisation. Coltrane's motivic cells maintain the rhythm, the intervallic structure, and the contour from the bass ostinato, but Coltrane transforms those cells through transposition. We may also note that "Acknowledgement" is considered a salient example of modal jazz, but this is due to the rhythm section's use of a single primary tonal center that is articulated through pedal point in the bass. Since Coltrane freely transposes the motivic cell, there is absolutely no adherence in this portion of the solo to a single mode as a resource for improvisation.

Toward the end of his solo from "Pinocchio," saxophonist Wayne Shorter uses a motivic cell in a similar fashion (*Nefertiti*, 3:08). Like Coltrane's, Shorter's is a four-note motive, freely transposed.[41] The rhythm section's accompaniment to Shorter's solo from "Pinocchio" provides an example of "time, no changes": that is, the group maintains an underlying 4/4 meter, but abandons "Pinocchio's" underlying harmonic progression and 18-bar form stated during the head. Given the freer harmonic and formal context, Shorter relies here on developing the motivic cell heard initially during the head. Example 2.3 contains this ending portion of Shorter's solo.

EXAMPLE 2.3   Motivic Cell Improvisation at the End of Wayne Shorter's Solo on "Pinocchio" (3:08)

40 Porter, "Coltrane's *A Love Supreme*," and Porter, *John Coltrane*, 242–43.
41 This is not to suggest that the motivic cells of Coltrane's "Acknowledgement" solo formed a direct influence on Shorter's use in "Pinocchio." Despite the chronology (the recording of "Pinocchio" occurred 2½ years after "Acknowledgement"), motivic consistency was already a general principle of Shorter's compositions and improvisations.

The transcription indicates that Shorter refers to the opening motive of "Pinocchio," and he states the motivic cell seven times. Unlike Coltrane's solo from "Acknowledgement," Shorter does not preserve the rhythm and intervals consistently. Instead, he preserves the contour from the head's opening motive, and transposes the motivic cell freely during those measures. Yet, even while Shorter abandons the precise rhythmic and intervallic relationships, the relationship with the motive from the head is unmistakable. The final statement of the cell uses precisely the pitches from the opening phrase of the head, before the horns return to the head statement. The lower part of Example 2.3 also shows the opening melody as written on the copyright deposit to Shorter's lead sheet, showing the relationship between it and the rhythm of the motivic cell from the improvisation, as well as the melody as played by the quintet on the recording.[42]

This portion of the solo indicates a profitable way to interpret Wayne Shorter's comments above regarding DNA within a composition. If we consider Shorter's comments in light of the "time, no changes" improvisations, this can suggest that—in the absence of chorus structure—Shorter relies here on a motivic cell derived from the composition's melody. This provides a profoundly different view of the improvisational strategies than that offered by Jack Chambers, who suggests instead a modal/scalar basis for these compositions. Shorter's compositions, Chambers writes, "consist of brief, melodic catch-phrases...that get repeated arbitrarily in the opening and closing ensembles. The point of the catch-phrase is to encode the scale that is available to the improviser."[43] In the instance of "Pinocchio," this misses the mark since the melodies and improvisations do not articulate scales in systematic fashion. Instead, in "Pinocchio's" melody, what is encoded—Shorter's idea of DNA—is the motive and its potential for motivic cell improvisation.

MOTIVIC INTERACTION

For a number of the Davis quintet studio recordings, motivic improvisation takes on heightened importance. It occurs not only within individual improvisations, but also between two solos, as one solo ends and another begins. The idea of beginning a solo by echoing material that concludes

---

42 Lead sheet to "Pinocchio," Library of Congress Copyright Deposit Eu 42286 (March 13, 1968).

43 Chambers, *Milestones 2*, 99.

old
respectable

the previous solo was already a venerable jazz practice by the 1960s.[44] Yet with the Davis studio recordings this practice appears prominently, in some instances with the use of short motivic cells. Example 2.4 shows how, at the conclusion to Shorter's solo and the opening of Hancock's solo from "Hand Jive" (*Nefertiti*, 5:21), both players develop a two-note motive based on the interval of a perfect fourth.

Shorter states the motive eight times, each as an ascending perfect fourth, and with the first pitch played as a dotted quarter note or as a quarter note. (Shorter plays the first statement as two consecutive perfect fourths, G#–C#–F#.) Note too the extensive use of space between motivic

EXAMPLE 2.4   Motives at the End of Shorter's and Beginning of Hancock's Solo on "Hand Jive" (5:21)

44 See Paul Berliner, *Thinking in Jazz: The Infinite Art of Improvisation* (Chicago: University of Chicago, 1994), 669–71.

statements, particularly between motives 1 and 2, and between motives 5 and 6. Hancock then begins the piano solo with the two-note motive stated each measure for the first four measures. Motives 1–3 involve the same overall rhythmic profile, although the third statement inverts the two-note motive, now a descending perfect fourth. And Motive 4 consists of two consecutive perfect fourths. By mm. 5–6, Hancock departs from the perfect fourth motivic cell, and at mm. 7–11 Hancock commits to a new idea, based upon a three-note stepwise motive. The motivic profile between the pair of three-note motives at mm. 7–9 at first is based primarily on the similar rhythm, since that heard at m. 7 is played as three descending pitches (F5–E♭–D♭), while at m. 8–9 as a lower-neighbor gesture (B4–A–B). The following two statements of the motive (mm. 10–11) continue the lower-neighbor motion. Measures 12–13 then move to another brief two-note motive, now a pair of ascending eighth notes.

Here, consecutive solos perpetuate a single motive as one concludes and the following begins. The continued two-note idea is treated as a motivic cell, transposing a perfect fourth. And Hancock's solo follows this with two different motives, a three-note idea (mm. 7–11), and an ascending two-note idea (mm. 12–13). All this suggests that motivic improvisation operates for the quintet as a significant premise. The soloists reiterate brief memorable ideas punctuated by a liberal use of space. The brevity of these motives, here consisting of only two or three pitches, suggests a highly concentrated view of motivic improvisation, one that provides an alternative to longer lines and characteristic eighth-note hard bop improvisation.

Yet it is important to acknowledge that even the most motivically oriented improvisations on the studio recordings do not completely abandon their hard bop orientation and a more consistent eighth-note organization. We may hear some of the improvisations as alternations between the two, shifting between compact motivic organization and more characteristic eighth-note hard bop lines. Even the "time, no changes" improvisations also include improvisational paths characteristic of hard bop. Despite a "no changes" environment, the soloists do at times suggest implied harmonies, ones that they express or outline within an eighth-note language. In many ways, the détente between motivic improvisation and longer eighth-note hard bop phrasing explains part of the ongoing appeal of these recordings.

MOTIVIC EXPANSION

In addition to overt motivic processes described above, other connections apply. Shorter, in particular, uses techniques of motivic expansion. Here, with each subsequent motivic statement the improviser gradually lengthens and extends in range an original idea. Example 2.5 contains a transcription of Shorter's solo that begins at m. 12 of his solo in "Orbits" (*Miles Smiles*, 1:47). Shorter states a four-note ascending motive consisting of the pitches G, A♭, B♭, and C, which is then answered with the same four pitches, now descending (C, B♭, A♭, and G, m. 13). The subsequent two motives then each refer to those pitches at their outset. At m. 14, the motive begins by joining the upward and downward motion heard in mm. 12–13, beginning with an ascent that eliminates the opening pitch G (A♭, B♭, C), and followed by a descent consisting again of C, B♭, A♭, and G (mm. 14–15). Note that here the motive continues downward to E♭. Thus the motive increases in duration (now occupying five beats) and range. The following motive (mm. 16–18) begins with the C–B♭–A♭–G descent and this time continues downward even further, to B. Thus in this final statement the motive again extends in duration and range. (For range considerations, I disregard the overblown pitch at m. 15, the probable result of a squeaky reed.)

In this instance, motivic identity depends on the opening pitches, and the pitch relationship between each motive is evidently audible. But motivic expansion comes about through the consistent extension of duration and intervallic distance. This suggests a different type of continuity than the motivic cell organization described earlier with "Pinocchio" and "Hand Jive." Those cells feature free transposition. More significantly, they rely on a fixed and discrete number of pitches and a largely consistent time span for each motivic restatement.

The distinction between motivic cells and motivic expansion is important. Motivic expansion provided Shorter with a consistent technique for improvisation.[45] But motivic expansion not only sheds light on

EXAMPLE 2.5   Motivic Expansion in Shorter's Solo on "Orbits" (1:47)

45 See Coolman, "The Miles Davis Quintet," for a description of this phenomenon in Shorter's solos to "Agitation" (p. 63) and "Masqualero" (pp. 106–7).

Shorter's improvisations, it also reveals a profound *compositional* discovery for Shorter, one heard during the final studio recordings made with the Davis quintet, particularly *Nefertiti*. This involved the application of motivic expansion to his compositional melodies. While the melodies to Shorter's earlier compositions rely on motives based on pitch, rhythm, and contour, these typically recur with a generally fixed and discrete number of pitches, occupy a generally consistent time span, and are metrically consistent (i.e., appear in the same location with the measure). By *Nefertiti*, however, Shorter was applying principles of motivic expansion to "Nefertiti" and "Pinocchio." Chapter 6 will show how recurrent motives in the melody of those two compositions expand and contract. This created a significant compositional breakthrough for Shorter. It allowed a high degree of elasticity with those compositions' melodies, used instead of motives with a consistent rhythmic/metric identity.

CONTINUITY AND PHRASE OVERLAP

"He's got that sort of inevitable one-thing-follows-the-next, follows-the-next, follows-the-next thing that is so rare in modern improvisers."
(PAT METHENY ON HERBIE HANCOCK)[46]

"Herbie has a great linear harmonic sense, in that his phrases are elongated in a very beautiful way—they not only come out of something, they automatically lead back into something else."
(OSCAR PETERSON ON HERBIE HANCOCK)[47]

Motivic analysis presents the ways in which improvisers spontaneously create overt musical relationships. Subsequent motives use repetition on some level, either through exact repetition or through repetition that preserves elements of pitch, rhythm, interval, or contour. But motivic repetition is not the sole means for creating ongoing musical relationships in improvisation. Metheny's and Peterson's comments above describe compelling features of Hancock's improvisations. Both call general attention

---

46 Interview, *Jazz Profiles*, "Herbie Hancock," National Public Radio (April 2000). Quoted in Jeremy Yudkin, *Miles Davis, Miles Smiles, and the Invention of Post Bop* (Bloomington: University of Indiana, 2008), 80.
47 Conrad Silvert, "Herbie Hancock: Revamping the Past, Creating the Future," *Down Beat* 44/15 (September 8, 1977): 16.

to musical continuity, inevitability, and connection. These features may arise from overt motivic connections. But they may also transcend them, as Peterson's comments imply ("they not only come out of something, they automatically lead back into something else"). So how do we address this?

One section of Hancock's solo from "Circle" (*Miles Smiles*) shows in a compelling manner these features that Metheny and Peterson describe. This portion from the solo appears as a long extended melodic phrase. But it is not the length by itself that creates the notion of ongoing continuity, nor solely the continuation of a single motive or motivic cell. The passage overlaps melodic ideas, so that the conclusion of one extended idea forms the beginning of a new one, which is itself then treated to motivic continuation. Example 2.6 models the principle, showing how this creates an ongoing continuity. We can understand the improvisational principle generally as a *phrase overlap*. The conclusion of one idea then forms the beginning of a new series of motives.

EXAMPLE 2.6   Phrase Overlap

In the Hancock example, the relationship of overlap to musical form is crucial. Here the overlap straddles the end of Hancock's second chorus and beginning of the third, masking the formal division. Example 2.7 contains a transcription of the section (3:25). Toward the end of the second chorus, Hancock initiates a passage based on ongoing eighth-note triplets. The excerpt begins here with the harmony of C-9 at m. 41 (Hancock's extended triplet line begins two measures earlier, at m. 39). At the harmonic change to F13(♭9), Hancock now initiates D major broken triads over F13♭9 (mm. 43–44). (The groupings of these triads frequently create a metrical conflict, a principle discussed later in this chapter.) Note that Hancock continues that D major harmony while moving to the successive B♭Maj7 harmony at mm. 45 as well as the Emin7(♭5) harmony at m. 46. The use of the same D major triad as an upper structure for all three harmonies (F13♭9, B♭Maj7, Emin7(♭5)) heightens the seamlessness in this portion of the phrase. Hancock then raises the D triadic structure up a half-step to E♭ over the A7 chord (mm. 47–48), before ending the triplet patterning at the top of the

EXAMPLE 2.7   Phrase Overlap in Hancock's Solo on "Circle" (3:25)

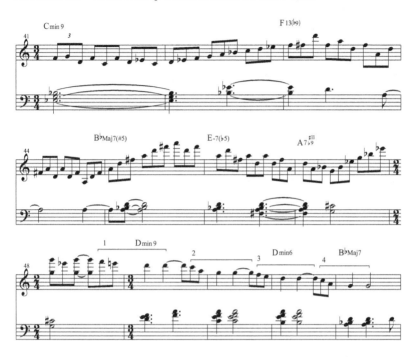

form. There is a dropped beat at m. 48 that in no way detracts from the magic of the passage. The rhythm section adjusts immediately to that 2/4 bar, showing the group's uncanny rapport and adaptation in support of the soloist.

The phrase overlap comes about at the end of this triplet section and the beginning of the next chorus. Out of the triplet figure Hancock launches a new motive during the last bar of this second chorus (m. 48), the bar of 2/4 meter. Note how this motive emerges with the stepwise descent in that measure (F–E), which then connects to D on the first measure of the new chorus. Each successive measure then perpetuates that motive, keeping the same contour and rhythmic shape each bar for four bars (mm. 49–52). Thus the end of the triplet arpeggio at m. 48 initiates the motive that, repeated, dominates the first four bars of the next section.

As Oscar Peterson stated about Hancock's phrases, that "they not only come out of something, they automatically lead back into something else." The principle of phrase overlap provides a means for improvisational continuity that transcends repetition of a single motive. Instead it links two successive ideas. The technique depicts the inevitability and continuity described by Pat Metheny and Oscar Peterson above, and the overlap effect is one that can convey a sense of endless melody. With "Circle," the overlap occurs at the top of the form, blurring the formal division. Subsequent chapters will show that overlap operates not only in Hancock's improvisations, but also among other soloists of Davis's quintet, and these techniques of phrase overlap often interact with underlying form in similar ways.

METER, HYPERMETER, AND METRICAL CONFLICT IN IMPROVISATION

Pitch relationships provide the primary focus for published analyses of jazz improvisation. Analyses discussed above call attention to pitch-based ideas related to modes/scales, motives, and phrase overlap. Yet it is easy to overlook the complex role of rhythm and meter in improvisation. These considerations extend from expressive microtimings—playing ahead or behind the beat, or varying subdivisions of the beat (such as swing vs. straight eighth notes)[48] through techniques for elasticizing the harmonic rhythm, accentual shift, metrical conflict (or superimposition), metric modulation, and hypermeter.

ELASTICIZING THE HARMONIC RHYTHM

One significant method for creating metric flexibility comes about through elasticizing the harmonic rhythm. In the context of improvisations with compositions that maintain an ongoing meter and harmonic progression, this can take place in a number of ways. A soloist can continue to play or imply a harmony beyond its given harmonic rhythm, continuing it for several beats beyond the expected point of harmonic change. Typically the result is that, as the harmonic rhythm of the continued harmony lengthens, the following harmony becomes

---

48 See, for example, Fernando Benadon, "Time Warps in Early Jazz," *Music Theory Spectrum* 31/1 (2009): 1–25; Jeffrey Collier and James Lincoln Collier, "Microrhythms in Jazz: A Review of Papers," *Annual Review of Jazz Studies* 8 (1996): 117–139; Vijay Iyer, "Embodied Mind, Situated Cognition, and Expressive Microtiming in African-American Music," *Music Perception* 19/3 (2002): 387–414.

foreshortened.[49] Conversely, a soloist may anticipate the upcoming harmony by several beats. Here the relationship of foreshortened and extended harmonic rhythm is reversed from the situation described above since the harmonic rhythm for the earlier chord is compressed, while that of the following chord is expanded.

Other factors can manipulate harmony to elasticize the harmonic rhythm. With harmonic insertion a soloist may imply additional harmonies, thus changing the perception of the harmonic rhythm. With harmonic deletion, a soloist may imply fewer harmonies, again potentially changing the perception of the harmonic rhythm.[50]

All these techniques for elasticizing harmonic rhythm form part of the improvised jazz tradition, since they allow soloists flexibility in the context of compositions with a consistent underlying meter and harmonic rhythm. Certainly particular improvisers cultivated these techniques to become a prominent feature of their improvisations.

METER, ACCENT, AND ACCENTUAL SHIFT

There are additional ways to play with meter flexibly, even when the underlying meter is regular. Some techniques are quite subtle, but they still can work to make the underlying meter more ambiguous. One particular technique is through accentual shift. This can occur in relation to eighth-note bebop-oriented phrasing displaced from its typical metrical placement. Example 2.8 shows an eighth-note line that adheres to the underlying meter. This takes place particularly with the first four eighth notes in both complete measures (shown with brackets). Following the lead-in of three eighth notes, the groupings on the downbeat form a four-note ascending arpeggio. During the second measure the groupings likewise form a four-note descending arpeggio. These four-note groupings here appear in a conventional metrical position, and conform to the underlying meter.

As a point of comparison, we can examine Example 2.9, the end of Hancock's first 32-bar chorus on "E.S.P." (*E.S.P.*, 4:22; the entire solo is

---

49 For a discussion of elasticized harmonic rhythm in the Bill Evans Trio performance of "Autumn Leaves," see Henry Martin and Keith Waters, *Jazz: The First Hundred Years*, 2nd ed. (Belmont, Calif.: Thomson Schirmer, 2006), 307–8.

50 Examples of harmonic insertion and deletion appear in Scott DeVeaux, *The Birth of Bebop: A Social and Musical History* (Berkeley: University of California Press, 1997). DeVeaux discusses Lester Young's use of harmonic deletion (112–14), and Charlie Parker's frequent insertion of iii7–♭iii7 harmonies during the eighth measure of 12-bar blues choruses to "Tiny's Tempo" (377–80).

EXAMPLE 2.8   Bebop Line Aligned with Meter

transcribed in chapter 3.) In contrast to the above example, the phrasing is shifted over by one beat, shown by the brackets above the upper clef. This creates a subtle accentual shift, and the phrasing appears a beat away from a more conventional metric placement. This is especially clear with the first and third brackets, indicating the four-note arpeggios that began on the downbeats in the example above. The brackets show how the grouping of pitches in Hancock's line subtly create an accentual shift, appearing a beat away from the more conventional and expected version. Note, too, how at the end of Hancock's phrase the groupings come back into phase with the meter. This is made especially vivid by comparing the three-note (Bb-G-G#) displaced lead-in at mm. 27–28 that returns in m. 31, now aligned more clearly with the meter. Chapter 3 discusses the solo in more detail and also considers the ways in which Hancock elasticizes the harmonic rhythm.

These considerations of accentual shifts make a number of assumptions about grouping structures and meter in improvisation. One assumption is that certain groupings (or improvisational shapes) have

EXAMPLE 2.9   Accentual Shift in Hancock's Solo on "E.S.P." (4:22, m. 27ff.)

a characteristic and expected metric placement. Thus, if in Hancock's excerpt the characteristic and expected metric placement of the four-note ascending and descending arpeggios is on the downbeat (or third beat of the measure), Hancock's displacement creates a subtle dislocation away from the underlying meter. This accentual shift may be considered a type of syncopation: here the initiation of groupings creates accents that do not align with the metrical beats that appear on the downbeat and third beats of the measure.

In certain improvisational situations these accentual shifts can create metrical ambiguity by obscuring the listener's location of the metric downbeat. This is not to say that all such accentual shifts work in the same way. For example, drums that emphasize backbeats (on beats 2 and 4) in a 4/4 meter create syncopations by accenting the second and fourth beats of the measure, but these syncopations are part of the fabric of many jazz idioms, and normally do not disorient listeners familiar with those idioms. Whether or not different listeners metrically reorient themselves in the face of accentual shift such as in Hancock's passage above may be due to any number of perceptual factors, such as musical experience or familiarity with the recording.

In addition, accompanimental strategies on the part of the rhythm section can play a role in metrical ambiguity in these situations. In the face of accentual shift, clear unambiguous accompaniment can encourage listeners to maintain the underlying meter on the one hand, while ambiguous accompaniment might encourage listeners to shift the perceptual location of the downbeat on the other. With the Davis quintet, the rhythm section accompaniment is a significant consideration given the players' accompanimental strategies that ranged between metrical clarity and metrical ambiguity.

METRICAL CONFLICT

I use the term metrical conflict to refer to grouping patterns that suggest one or more meters distinct from an underlying meter. This term will be used generally in place of other terms such as metrical superimposition, poly-rhythm, polymeter, and cross rhythm. We may distinguish metrical conflict from accentual shift in the following manner. Accentual shift is a type of metric displacement that *maintains* an underlying meter, but uses groupings that may shift the perception of the metrical downbeat. Metrical conflict instead implies metrical groupings *distinct from* the underlying meter.

Metrical conflict formed an important strategy for members of the Davis quintet, one that had important implications during improvisation.

Its use by soloists and/or the accompanying rhythm section provided techniques for tension and release. Further, metrical conflict can create formal ambiguity since it has the potential to obscure important formal divisions in a composition. In both improvisational and accompanimental situations, metrical conflict relies on the players' ability to maintain the underlying meter even while creating musical events that conflict with it.

Example 2.10 provides a transcription of one of the more complex examples of metrical conflict from the second quintet studio recordings. This occurs during the B section of Wayne Shorter's solo on "Dolores" (*Miles Smiles*, 2:38). Carter creates a metrical conflict through dotted quarter notes during the first three bars of the excerpt, stating a single pitch of D. This creates a level of 3/8 that conflicts with the underlying 4/4 meter. But this is not the only metrical conflict taking place. Against Carter's accompaniment Shorter paraphrases the melody, but his use of quarter-note triplets subtly implies a different meter than either the underlying 4/4 meter or Carter's implied 3/8. The quarter-note triplet groupings suggest a level of 6/4 meter.

Shorter obscures the meter further. Note that by the third bar of the excerpt, Shorter's groupings become shifted one beat later. The pitch material stated on the downbeat of m. 52 now returns with that one beat shift. (Carter abandons the consistent 3/8 conflict by m. 54.) Thus, Shorter's ideas create two levels of conflict. They imply a meter of 6/4 through

EXAMPLE 2.10   Metrical Conflict in "Dolores": Shorter, Carter, and Williams (2:38)

the use of quarter-note triplets, and they subsequently create an accentual shift of that meter once the melodic material returns. Both Carter and Shorter create a complex network of rhythmic conflicts heightened by Williams's accompaniment, which sets up yet further conflicts. The excerpt includes the high-hat accents played by Williams in mm. 54–56.

Despite the dizzying array of simultaneous metrical conflicts, all the players come back into metrical focus following this 6-bar section. Thus each of the players subliminally preserves the underlying 4/4 meter even while creating metrical conflicts with it. As Shorter paraphrases the melody to the next section, all the players return to a regular 4/4 meter with the bass and drums returning to more typical timekeeping roles.

This excerpt from Shorter's solo on "Dolores" indicates how metrical conflict creates a rich source for tension and release, especially intensified since each player implies meters that conflict both with the underlying 4/4 meter and with each other. Here these conflicts last for the duration of the 6-bar section of "Dolores" before the players resolve the metrical conflicts and return to the underlying 4/4 meter at the onset of the following 8-bar section of the form. (The form and improvisations to "Dolores" are discussed more thoroughly in chapter 4). Since the metrical conflicts here operate within a single formal section, they heighten the metrical ambiguity within the section, rather than across the larger formal sections.[51]

FORMAL AMBIGUITY, HYPERMETER, AND METRIC MODULATION

Nevertheless, metrical conflicts, accentual shifts, and elasticized harmonic rhythm *can* cut across formal divisions of a composition. Formal divisions can become blurred when those conflicts continue across them. The result is not only metric ambiguity, but also formal ambiguity.

One way to model formal ambiguity is through the idea of *hypermeter*. Hypermeter is a term used by musical analysts to refer to metrical groupings that are larger than a single measure (such as 4, 8, 16, or 32 measures). Hypermeter suggests that these larger metrical groups often operate in more or less the same way that measures do. That is, in music with meter, musical cues typically allow listeners to group beats cyclically: listeners

---

51 For further discussion of accentual shift and metrical conflict, see Keith Waters, "Blurring the Barline: Metric Displacement in the Piano Solos of Herbie Hancock," *Annual Review of Jazz Studies* 8 (1996): 19–37; and Waters, "Outside Forces: 'Autumn Leaves' in the 1960s," *Current Musicology* 71–73 (2001–2): 276–302.

perceive the first metric pulse of each measure as structurally equivalent (beat 1), perceive the second metric pulse of each measure as structurally equivalent (beat 2), and so forth. In these cases, we typically understand the first beat of a measure as metrically accented. Metric accent does not require that the downbeat be played more loudly or forcefully, merely that the musical cues allow the listener to hear it as having "beat 1" status. Thus, the examples of accentual shift and metrical conflict described above may create situations that suspend those metrical cues.

The idea of hypermeter suggests that larger metrical groupings operate analogously. In these cases, musical events allow listeners to hear larger metrical groupings of, for example, 4, 8, 16, or 32 bars in the same way. As listeners may hear downbeats of measures as metrically accented, so too may listeners hear the beginning of a hypermetric group as metrically accented. We may refer to these beginnings as hypermetric downbeats. Just as the notion of metrical accent does not require downbeats to be played more loudly or forcefully, neither are hypermetric downbeats required to be played more loudly: rather, musical cues allow the listener to hear this hypermetrical downbeat as having "bar 1" status. Rhythm section conventions often involve the drummer setting off 8-, 16-, or 32-bar divisions, frequently an eighth note in advance or after the hypermetric downbeat.[52]

Example 2.11 models hypermeter at the 16-bar and 32-bar level by providing durational reductions. Each notated beat corresponds to four bars (16-bar reduction) or eight bars (32-bar reduction). Both reductions suggest that the hypermetric downbeat receives a stronger metrical accent than the other measures. The second (32-bar) reduction represents the larger formal divisions within a 32-bar AABA standard-tune form. For the analysis of jazz, hypermeter is an attractive construct. It is a principle intuited by improvisers who articulate longer musical spans by providing a release point that gives stronger metrical weight to the larger divisions of the formal structure. It is important to make clear that, as with meter, hypermeter need not require groupings of 4 bars (and their multiples) and may occur with other metrical groupings. However, the jazz standard repertory often privileges those groupings of 4, 8, 16, and 32 bars.

Hypermeter thus helps illustrate formal ambiguity since it may show how metric conflict can camouflage 4-, 8-, 16-, or even 32-bar divisions. Formal ambiguity, as a general principle, seems to have been an important

---

52 Paul Berliner describes the role of drums and piano in establishing what he calls "structural markers." See Berliner, *Thinking in Jazz*, 622–629.

EXAMPLE 2.11   Model of 16-Bar and 32-Bar Hypermeter

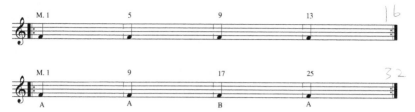

goal for the Davis quintet. A number of commentators have called attention to formal ambiguity in the context of the quintet's live recordings, which often feature improvisations over 32-bar jazz standards.[53] The players themselves addressed this. Bassist Buster Williams, who substituted for Ron Carter in live performances with the quintet, described his experiences with the group in compelling fashion:

> Playing with Miles, I learned how to keep a structure in mind and play changes so loosely that you can play for some time without people knowing whether the structure is played or not, but then hit on certain points to indicate that you have been playing the structure all the time. When you hear these points being played, you just say, "Wow! It's like the Invisible Man. You see him here and then you don't. Then all of a sudden you see him over there and then you see him over here." And it indicates that it's been happening all the time.[54]

Williams describes the role of formal ambiguity through harmony. His comments suggest how the players maintain an underlying form, but—by elasticizing (or suppressing) the harmonic progression—they withhold the crucial musical cues that make apparent the hypermeter and larger formal divisions.

Comparison of the group's earlier live recordings with later versions of the same compositions make clear how the group continued to develop methods to heighten formal ambiguity while playing jazz standards. Chapter 1 discussed Ron Carter's accompaniment to "Autumn Leaves" (*Live at the 1963 Monterey Jazz Festival*) in which dotted quarter notes

53 Henry Martin, "The Nature of Recomposition: Miles Davis and 'Stella by Starlight,'" *Annual Review of Jazz Studies* 9 (1997–98): 77–92. Todd Coolman also discusses Davis's "Stella by Starlight" in "The Miles Davis Quintet," 121–53.
54 Berliner, *Thinking in Jazz*, 340.

implied a meter that conflicted with and challenged the underlying 4/4 meter. Carter's conflicting meter here begins with the beginning of the B section of the form (m. 17), and lasts for eight bars, thus upholding the larger 8-bar divisions of the 32-bar composition. In contrast, the 1964 version of "Autumn Leaves" (from *Miles in Berlin*, recorded scarcely a year later) reveals a metrical conflict that takes place during the final chorus of Wayne Shorter's solo. But here the conflict creates formal ambiguity since it continues throughout mm. 9–32 of Shorter's final chorus (7:29) and cuts across the internal formal and hypermetric divisions of "Autumn Leaves."

Not only does formal ambiguity arise through the metrical conflict, but it also stems from a suppressed harmonic progression. Hancock's long-short comping pattern appears every three beats, suggesting a metrical conflict of 3/4 at odds with the underlying 4/4 meter of "Autumn Leaves." At the same time, the piano accompaniment remains frozen on the opening C- harmony (with an added Maj7) for the remaining bars of the form. By m. 17, Carter remains on a 1-bar ostinato for the remainder of the chorus, deleting the underlying harmonic progression. Thus the players subliminally retain the underlying form and meter, even while erasing many of the musical cues that make apparent the internal divisions of "Autumn Leaves."[55] Only at the end of the chorus does the group resolve those conflicts and return to playing the underlying harmonic and metric cues.

Thus the 1963 and 1964 versions of "Autumn Leaves" both show metrical conflict. But while the earlier version creates metrical ambiguity (through Carter's accompaniment), the later version raises the stakes: the extended continuation of the metrical conflict as well as the suppressed harmonic rhythm create and enhance the formal ambiguity.

When all the members of the group participate in the same metrical conflict, the ensuing result is commonly described as *metric modulation*. The quintet's performance of "Footprints" (*Miles Smiles*) uses metric modulation: it begins in 6/4 and shifts to 4/4 meter during the trumpet solo. Example 2.12 includes the bass riff to "Footprints" for both meters. The group preserves the measure but alters the pulse (measure-preserving), so that the original six beats then occupy four beats. Example 2.13 also indicates that a different example of metric modulation occurs in "Limbo" (*Sorcerer*), which shifts from 3/4 to 4/4 as the group moves from the head into the solos. In contrast to "Footprints," the group preserves

<hr/>

55 However, Hancock does change the register of the harmony to coincide with the 8-bar divisions.

EXAMPLE 2.12   Metric Modulation in "Footprints" and "Limbo"

the pulse but alters the measure (pulse-preserving). Now the pulses remain consistent, but the measure lasts a beat longer.

GROUP INTERACTIONS

Playing with Miles, importance was placed on everything you did, even when you weren't soloing. There was that tendency to think that the whole evening was the composition. As far as everybody in the group thinking that way, it was up to each individual to be on his own to help create images and illusions, to sort of spread the peripheral of sight as seen by the audience.

(WAYNE SHORTER ON THE DAVIS QUINTET)[56]

Recent analytical jazz literature has stressed the role of improvisation as a collaborative group activity.[57] These writers stress the role of ensemble communication during improvisation, and downplay the analysis of individual solos. The discussion of metric modulation in the previous section shows one way in which group interaction took place among members of Davis's quintet. Since the quintet was renowned for an almost telepathic level of communication among members, considerations of group interaction seem urgent in the context of analysis, and solo improvisation examined independently of the ensemble ignores collaborative and participatory aspects of group improvisation.

56 Tim Logan, "Wayne Shorter: Doubletake," *Down Beat* 41/12 (June 20, 1974): 17.
57 Berliner, *Thinking in Jazz*; John Brownell, "Analytical Models of Jazz Improvisation," *Jazzforschung* 26 (1994): 9–29; Tor Dybo, "Analyzing Interaction during Jazz Improvisation," *Jazzforschung* 31 (1999): 51–64; Robert Hodson, *Interaction, Improvisation, and Interplay* (New York: Routledge, 2007); Monson, *Saying Something*.

In these analyses, consideration of group interaction normally takes one of two forms. The first regards how the group circulated pitch motives, rhythmic motives, or other ideas between two or more players. Implied metric layers begun by one player and echoed by another become a significant means of group interaction among members of the quintet. Another way that such circulation takes place is through consecutive solos: one improvisation ends with a specific melodic or rhythmic motive, and the next soloist begins by responding to that motive. The discussion of motives above pointed out this technique during "Hand Jive" (*Nefertiti*). In it, the beginning of Hancock's solo echoed and continued the perfect fourth motive that concluded Shorter's previous solo.[58]

The second way the analyses consider group interaction is by examining the means by which quintet members aided one another in helping resolve formal, metric, or harmonic ambiguity. Many of the studio compositions posed significant improvisational challenges and required heightened reliance among group members during improvisation. The above discussion of Hancock's solo on "Circle" pointed out how the accompanying players accommodated Hancock's inadvertent 2/4 bar at the end of his second chorus. Many of the analyses will highlight ways in which group members provided cues in those situations.

Some appeals to promote analysis of group interaction—and to demote analysis of individual solos—suggest that the former examines "process" while the latter examines "product."[59] But this dichotomy is overstated. It prohibits the view of individual jazz improvisation as processive, that jazz improvisers work out and develop improvisational ideas in real time, and that they may respond to their own ideas or motives stated during the flow of improvisation. Moreover, it can be argued that group analysis sometimes offers limited analytical observations, ones that stress overt repetition occurring among different ensemble members. Yet certainly for the quintet the role of group interaction, response, and communication is crucial.

MILES DAVIS AND CIRCULAR COMPOSITIONS

"Circular compositions" took on enhanced importance during the 1960s, and Davis's quintet recorded several circular works. Circular compositions are works composed in such a manner that, following the initial

---

58 For another example, see Todd Coolman's discussion of a "three-way signaling" at the end of Shorter's solo and beginning of Hancock's solo during "Agitation" (*E.S.P.*), Coolman, "The Miles Davis Quintet," 73 and 75.

59 Brownell, "Analytical Models," 13–22.

statement of the head, the top of the repeating chorus structure no longer sounds like the beginning of the form.[60] Circular compositions thus contain a formal overlap that disguises the top of the form. This overlap typically arises through one of three conditions: (1) melody: the opening phrase of the composition sounds as a continuation of the previous phrase(s); (2) harmony: the opening harmonic progression continues a sequence begun at the end of the form; and (3) hypermeter: irregular metric groupings suggest a continuation into the top of the form.

Circularity is by no means limited to jazz composition, and certainly folk music and European classical music provide antecedents.[61] Probably the *locus classicus* for jazz circular compositions is "Blue in Green" (from Davis's *Kind of Blue*, 1959). In the liner notes, Bill Evans merely acknowledges "Blue in Green" as a 10-bar circular composition, without further comment.[62] Given that its 10-bar form cuts across the typical 4-bar divisions of standard tunes, its circularity arises from the third condition noted above, that of hypermeter. The harmonic structure of "Blue in Green" also contributes to its circularity, as its opening G minor harmony continues a sequence begun in the final two measures (Amin7, Dmin7).

Davis's quintet recorded a number of circular tunes. For "Nefertiti" (*Nefertiti*), the melody supports its circularity. It contains three phrases, and its first phrase continues a sequence begun by Phrases 2 and 3. It is possible that this melodic circularity provided one motivation for the group to record "Nefertiti" as a series of repeated statements of the melody, without improvisation by horns and piano. Chapter 6 examines the melodic structure of "Nefertiti" more thoroughly.

The circularity of "Vonetta" (*Sorcerer*) arises from hypermeter. It contains 15 implied bars, thus the return to the top of the form sounds as if completing a 16-bar hypermetric cycle. It is important to acknowledge, however, that irregular hypermetric groupings do not necessarily create circular tunes. For example, "R.J." (*E.S.P.*) is a 19-bar noncircular composition.

60 Steve Larson, Henry Martin, Steven Strunk, and Keith Waters, "Circular Thinking: A Round-table on 'Blue in Green' and 'Nefertiti,'" paper given at the national meeting of the Society for Music Theory, Montreal Canada (October 2009). Many of the ideas discussed in this section on circular tunes have profited by correspondence with Alexander Stewart.

61 Phillips Barry in 1909 writes of circular folk tunes in "Folk-Music in America," *Journal of American Folklore* 22/83 (1909), 77; circularity is at work in the genre of the round, as well as in works such as Bach's perpetual canon from *Ein Musikalisches Opfer*, and Chopin's Mazurka in F minor, op. 68, no. 3 (posthumous), in which the performer is instructed to repeat *senza fine*.

62 Evans, Liner notes to *Kind of Blue*.

Writers on jazz have not devoted substantial attention to circular compositions.[63] Some jazz musicians have regarded them from standpoints that differ from the three criteria outlined above. Herbie Hancock seemed to consider the absence of cadences as a condition for circularity. Describing his own composition "Maiden Voyage," he stated that it "doesn't have any cadences; it just keeps moving around in a circle."[64] (Certainly the absence of a cadence at the end of the 10-bar form plays a role in magnifying the circularity of "Blue in Green." The presence of the m. 3 cadence likely motivated the players on the recording to end the performance there.)

Others have pointed to formal designs such as AAB (for example, Horace Silver's "Song for My Father") as circular, particularly in light of more-standard formal AABA forms. Thus the return to the first A section in an AAB form may be heard as completing a "missing" final A section, creating circularity. And certainly harmonic turnarounds serve a more general type of circularity since they consist of harmonic insertions that create links across formal boundaries. Possibly the most celebrated circular tune is Steve Swallow's "Falling Grace" (originally recorded on the 1966 Gary Burton album *The Time Machine*), which is circular from the standpoint both of harmony and hypermeter: its opening harmony continues a sequence begun in the final two measures, and its two sections consist of 14 + 10 bars.

DAVIS, THE AVANT-GARDE, AND FORM IN IMPROVISATION

The relationship of Davis and the jazz avant-garde has proved problematic for Davis biographers, given Davis's denunciations of a number of avant-garde players, such as Ornette Coleman, Archie Shepp, and Eric Dolphy.[65] Yet his quintet sidemen were inspired by the avant-garde, and the *Live at the Plugged Nickel* recordings in particular moved decisively toward freer approaches by abandoning, at times, meter, form, and harmonic structure. And the use of "time, no changes" on some of the Davis quintet studio recordings resulted in the elimination of chorus structure by departing from the harmonic and hypermetric structure heard during the initial

63 Jeffrey Magee proposes a view of Davis's composition "Solar" as circular in "Kinds of Blue: Miles Davis, Afro-Modernism, and the Blues," *Jazz Perspectives* 1/1 (May 2007): 19.

64 David Baker, Lida Belt, and Herman Hudson, eds., *The Black Composer Speaks* (Bloomington, Ind.: Afro-American Arts Institute, 1978), 122.

65 Waldo Martin, "Miles Davis and the 1960s Avant-Garde," essay in *Miles Davis and American Culture*, ed. Gerald Early (St. Louis: Missouri Historical Society Press, 2001), 107–16.

statements of the head. Further, the absence of piano comping on the "time, no changes" compositions suggested to many listeners a response to Ornette Coleman's pianoless quartet recordings of the late 1950s.

Coleman's 1959 quartet recordings, *The Shape of Jazz to Come* and *Change of the Century*, and his notorious New York debut at the Five Spot the same year, provided for many musicians the entry point for a type of jazz shorn of many of its syntactic conventions. Coleman's 1960 recording *Free Jazz* provided a label for the music, which was also identified at the time as avant-garde jazz, or the "New Thing." While many writers and critics heard Coleman's 1959 recordings as departing completely from the principles of chorus structure, more recent scholarship points out ways in which the quartet preserved an underlying form during some of the improvisations.[66]

Earlier examples of free collective improvisation extended at least a decade prior to Coleman's recordings, including pianist Lennie Tristano's 1949 recordings of "Intuition" and "Digression." Billy Taylor has pointed out earlier recordings that made use of free improvisation that were done in the early 1940s by Erroll Garner as well as by Stuff Smith and Robert Crum. And writer Barry Ulanov included an interview with trumpeter Roy Eldridge, in which he discussed recording a free improvisation with drummer Clyde Hart that would have been made prior to 1945, the date of Hart's death.[67] But it was the emergence of Coleman's quartet, the work of pianist Cecil Taylor, saxophonist Albert Ayler, and the later recordings of John Coltrane that had a broader impact upon the jazz community in general, and Davis's second quintet in particular.[68]

There are myriad ways to underscore differences between standard and avant-garde approaches to jazz. Jost's study of free jazz describes changes in instrumental technique, use of nontempered intonation, and collective improvisation.[69] An additional method revolves around the

66 Eric Charry, "Freedom and Form in Ornette Coleman's Early Atlantic Recordings," *Annual Review of Jazz Studies* 9 (1997–98), 261–94. Kurtis Adams critiques some of Charry's conclusions in "Ornette Coleman and *The Shape of Jazz to Come*" (D.M.A thesis, University of Colorado–Boulder, 2008).

67 Billy Taylor, *Jazz Piano: A Jazz History* (Dubuque, Iowa: Wm. C. Brown, 1983), 189; and Barry Ulanov, *A History of Jazz in America* (New York: Viking, 1952), 239. I would like to acknowledge Carl Woideck for calling the Garner, Smith, and Eldridge recordings to my attention.

68 Hancock discussed Tony Williams's interest in Paul Bley, Gary Peacock, and Ornette Coleman. Regarding Ornette Coleman, Hancock described how Williams "got me interested in Ornette and got me to the point where I could get into it." Ray Townley, "Hancock Plugs In," *Down Beat* 41/17 (October 24, 1974): 15.

69 Jost, *Free Jazz*.

notion of form during improvisation. For example, standard small group improvisation typically relies on chorus structure. This assumes a set of principles for the improviser and rhythm section, identified in the left-hand side of figure 2.1. The upper left-hand box indicates that chorus structure preserves from the head three levels from the metric hierarchy: hypermeter, meter, and pulse. In the jazz tradition, 32-bar AABA and ABAC forms provide common formal paradigms. Thus repeated choruses establish hypermetric regularity at the 32-bar level. Figure 2.1's left-hand lower box also indicates that the rhythm section and soloist preserve the harmonic progression and harmonic rhythm from the head.

Jazz historians frequently use negative values to describe how form operates in improvisation during free jazz: the music abandons consistent meter, tonality, and cyclic form altogether.[70] The right-hand boxes of figure 2.1 suggest that in the context of free improvisation musicians frequently abandon all three metric levels maintained in chorus structure, and abandon harmonic progression and harmonic rhythm. (Ornette Coleman's *Free Jazz*, recorded in 1960, and John Coltrane's *Ascension*, recorded in 1965, provide two examples.) The two sides of figure 2.1 indicate a common and useful binary model to accentuate differences in the relationship of underlying form to improvisation. The left side indicates

Traditional   **Free Jazz**

Chorus Structure	Rhythm section/soloist abandon consistent:
Rhythm section/soloist preserve (from head): • Hypermeter (often 32 bars) • Meter • Pulse	• Hypermeter • Meter • Pulse

| Rhythm section/soloist preserve (from head):
 • Harmonic Progression
 • Harmonic rhythm | And abandon:
 • Harmonic progression
 • Harmonic rhythm |

FIGURE 2.1   Form in Improvisation

70 J. Branford Robinson, "Free Jazz," entry in *The New Grove Dictionary of Jazz*, ed. Barry Kernfeld (New York: St. Martin's Press, 1988 and 1994), 404–5.

allegiance to chorus structure and its three attendant metric levels; the right side suggests the rejection of chorus structure and those three metric levels. Naturally, this dichotomy is oversimplified, but it provides a useful model to dramatize significant differences.

However, it is possible to provide a more nuanced view of formal solutions and attitudes in the 1960s, one that more richly describes formal practice and that more closely acknowledges Hancock's notion of "controlled freedom," described in chapter 1. There exists the possibility for intermediate stages between chorus structure (which preserves harmonic structure and three metric levels of hypermeter, meter, and pulse) on the one hand, and the abandonment of harmonic and metric structure on the other. This allows further methods to consider form in improvisation, relative to the number of metric levels preserved from the head and relative to harmonic progression. Figure 2.2 provides a model that does this. The example provides six different possibilities, indicated from left to right as Level 3, Levels 2a and 2b, Levels 1a and 1b, and Level 0. The level number (3, 2, 1, 0) corresponds to the number of metric levels preserved from the head. Thus the leftmost Level 3, corresponding to chorus structure, indicates the consistent preservation of three levels from the metric hierarchy: hypermeter, meter, and pulse.

Levels 2a and 2b indicate the consistent preservation of two levels from the metric hierarchy: meter and pulse. At this level, the hypermeter created by repeated choruses is absent. The lower boxes of 2a and 2b differ according to whether the rhythm section and soloist maintain the harmonic progression (2a preserves the harmonic progression, 2b abandons harmonic progression). Thus Level 2b indicates the practice referred to as "time, no changes." With this, the rhythm section and soloists maintain two metric levels of pulse and meter but abandon hypermeter. Further, the group does not preserve the underlying harmonic progression from the head.

Levels 1a and 1b indicate the consistent preservation of only one level from the metric hierarchy, that of pulse (with this level, both consistent hypermeter and meter may be absent). The lower boxes of 1a and 1b differ according to whether the rhythm section and soloist maintain the harmonic progression (1a preserves the harmonic progression, 1b abandons the harmonic progression). And the rightmost Level 0, corresponding to typical notions of free jazz, preserves no levels from the metric hierarchy.

Beneath the boxes are listed most of the Davis's quintet compositions recorded on their first five studio recordings. This displays the group's fluid and flexible relations to form during improvisation. These formal

Level 3	Level 2a	Level 2b ("Time, no changes")	Level 1a	Level 1b	Level 0
Chorus Structure Rhythm section/soloist preserve (from head): • Hypermeter (often 32 bars) • Meter • Pulse	Rhythm section/soloist abandon (from head): • Hypermeter. But preserve consistent: • Meter • Pulse	Rhythm section/soloist abandon (from head): • Hypermeter. But preserve consistent: • Meter • Pulse	Rhythm section/soloist abandon consistent: • Hypermeter • Meter. But preserve consistent: • Pulse	Rhythm section/soloist abandon consistent: • Hypermeter • Meter. But preserve consistent: • Pulse	Rhythm section/soloist abandon consistent: • Hypermeter • Meter • Pulse
Rhythm section/soloist preserve (from head): • Harmonic progression • Harmonic rhythm	Rhythm section/soloist preserve (from head): • Harmonic progression (*but not harmonic rhythm*)	Rhythm section/soloist abandon (from head): • Harmonic progression • Harmonic rhythm	Rhythm section/soloist preserve (from head): • Harmonic progression (*but not harmonic rhythm*)	And abandon: • Harmonic progression • Harmonic rhythm	And abandon: • Harmonic progression • Harmonic rhythm
"Iris" (25-bar chorus) "E.S.P." "Eighty-One" "Little One" "Mood" "RJ" "Gingerbread Boy" "Footprints" "*Pinocchio*" (Hancock solo) "Limbo" (alternate take) "Vonetta" "Prince of Darkness" "Pee Wee" "Fall" "*The Sorcerer*" (Davis/ Shorter solos) "*Dolores*" (Shorter solo)	"*Madness*" (Hancock solo; second half) "Freedom Jazz Dance" "Agitation" "Paraphernalia" "Country Son"	"Orbits" "*Pinocchio*" (Davis and Shorter solos) "*The Sorcerer*" (Hancock Solo) "*Madness*" (Davis and Shorter solos) "*Dolores*" (Hancock solo) Hand Jive	"*Madness*" (first half of Hancock's solo) *N.B. Compositions in italics reside at more than one level.		

FIGURE 2.2   Form in Improvisation: Miles Davis Quintet Studio Recordings

strategies offered the group a number of intermediate stages between traditional and avant-garde approaches, allowing a continuum along which the group ranged freely.

Further, the list of compositions includes in italics those compositions that appear in more than one location, revealing the group's use of different strategies within the same composition. "Pinocchio," for example, appears under both Level 3 and 2b. On the recording Hancock's piano solo preserves chorus structure (Level 3) while Davis's trumpet solo and Shorter's saxophone solo do not (Level 2b: "time, no changes"). Thus, "Pinocchio" suggests different formal strategies within the same composition, and might suggest that the group did not determine the formal strategy beforehand. Note, too, that Hancock's solo on "Madness" itself resides on two levels: it begins on Level 1a before moving to 2a.

It is important to acknowledge that Davis made use of some of these intermediate levels in earlier works. For example, Level 2a also describes "Flamenco Sketches" (*Kind of Blue*, 1959). Since the players determined the lengths of each of its five harmonic sections spontaneously during performance, "Flamenco Sketches" thus preserves harmonic progression but abandons consistent hypermeter. Davis revisited that technique with "Teo" (*Someday My Prince Will Come*, 1961).

These levels suggest a nuanced way to understand Hancock's notion of "controlled freedom," which he described as the negotiation of traditional and avant-garde approaches. They also reveal a highly flexible set of strategies by which the quintet offered challenges to accepted notions of chorus structure on the studio recordings. The levels provided do not faithfully apply to all the studio recordings, and those omitted from the example are discussed in further detail in the subsequent chapters. "Circle," for example, consists of an additive form that allowed for inserted 4-bar sections during the improvisations. "Riot" uses an underlying 16-bar form during the improvisations that is not derived from the head, and the tonality migrates down a half-step with each subsequent solo. "Dolores," "Masqualero," and "Stuff" also stray from this model, and are examined more thoroughly. The Davis quintet's final studio recording, *Filles de Kilimanjaro*, departed even further; chapter 7 discusses those compositions in detail.

CHAPTER 3

E.S.P.

SHORTLY AFTER WAYNE SHORTER JOINED Davis's quintet September 1964, the group made their television debut on the Steve Allen show (it aired September 22 and 25), which included a striking performance of "So What."[1] A European tour began shortly after; the recording *Miles in Berlin* chronicles further one of their earliest performances.

By the time the group entered the Los Angeles studios January 20–22, 1965, to record *E.S.P.*, many of the quintet members had already moved well past their hard bop roots. Hancock's recordings *Inventions and Dimensions* (August 1963) and *Empyrean Isles* (June 1964) departed from the elaborate quintet/sextet arrangements of his earlier two Blue Note recordings. *Inventions and Dimensions* was largely improvised in the studio according to some generally sketched frameworks, with bassist Paul Chambers, drummer Willie Bobo, and percussionist Oswaldo Martinez.

---

1   See http://matthewasprey.wordpress.com/tag/miles-davis/.

Empyrean Isles featured a series of thematically related titles, a precursor to the "concept albums" that would emerge with rock artists during the decade. With the Davis rhythm section, the quartet performances (with trumpeter Freddie Hubbard) of *Empyrean Isles* also included a foray into free collective improvisation, "The Egg." Wayne Shorter's *Speak No Evil* (December 1964, with Hancock and Carter) included compositions that merged sections of slower harmonic rhythm with faster, frequently non-functional, progressions ("Speak No Evil" and "Witch Hunt").

Trumpeter Kenny Dorham provided the *Down Beat* review for *E.S.P.* December 1965. His ambivalent review awarded the recording 4½ (out of 5) stars, at the same time denouncing it as cerebral and unemotional: "Emotionally, as a whole, this one is lacking. It's mostly brain music.... This type of music has that drone thing that I don't like, but because of the almost flawless presentation, I give five stars—but only four stars for the writing and effort—and no stars for the over-all sound. E.S.P. music in general is monotonous—one long drone."[2]

Overall, not an auspicious review for the quintet's first studio recording made with Shorter. In hindsight, Dorham seems to have missed either much of what was innovative about the playing and compositions, or—at least—to have not appreciated the aesthetic. Certainly the more introspective works, such as "Mood," maintain a static hypnotic quality due, in part, to the unyielding bass ostinato throughout, often done in tandem with Shorter's saxophone obbligato.

While it may be easy to critique Dorham for missing the newer aspects of *E.S.P.*, this omission may indicate their subtlety. Too, many of the celebrated facets of the later studio recordings are not yet in evidence on *E.S.P.* There are no examples of "time, no changes" compositions, which began to appear only on the quintet's second studio recording, *Miles Smiles*. And in contrast to the quintet's live performances, *E.S.P.* offered original compositions that generally challenged standard 32-bar formal frameworks, ones stitched together through a consistent harmonic vocabulary, frequent pedal point construction, and that largely avoided standard harmonic turnarounds.

Dorham also seemed uninterested in remarking on the unusual formal construction of many of the compositions. "R.J.," for example, is a 19-bar composition, written in an AA'BA form consisting of 5 + 5 + 4 + 5 bars. Its irregular 5-bar phrases created some significant challenges for the soloists, and within the first chorus of the piano solo, the group added an

2   Kenny Dorham, Review of Miles Davis, *E.S.P.*, *Down Beat* 32/27 (December 30, 1965): 34.

Dorham avoided tunes with irregular bar numbers

additional beat and one half while negotiating the 5-bar phrases. "Mood" is a circular composition, whose 13-bar form brought about its circularity. Dorham was more forthcoming in describing other technical aspects. Writing about "Eighty-One," a 12-bar blues with a straight-eighth rhythmic feel, he described it as a "deviation from the blues, a modal type of blues."[3] Here his use of the term modal likely reflected the harmonic language, which relies significantly on suspended fourth chords in place of more traditional dominant chords.

Of the compositions on *E.S.P.*, "E.S.P.," "Iris," and "Eighty-One" received a degree of visibility due in part to their inclusion in jazz fake book compilations. "Agitation" became one of the few studio compositions that the quintet played live, often using it as an opening composition.

"IRIS"

TRANSFORMATIONS

Wayne Shorter's "Iris" underwent a series of transformations en route to its recording. In many ways these transformations show Davis's and the quintet's interest in eliminating more standard harmonic progressions and challenging some precepts of chorus structure. We can trace these transformations through three stages. The first stage derives from Shorter's lead sheet, reproduced as example 3.1. It reveals "Iris" as a 10-bar composition in 4/4 meter, consisting of two 5-bar phrases.[4] The second stage applies to the statements of the head by the group on the recording. Example 3.2a provides a lead sheet from the opening head statement. On the head statements, the quintet recorded "Iris" as a 16-bar waltz, with each measure of Shorter's 4/4 lead sheet played as 2 bars in 3/4. The result is that the irregular 5-bar phrases of the lead sheet now become regularized to more standard 8-bar phrases. (It may be useful to consider the lead sheet's notated 10 4/4 bars as 20 2/4 bars—this shows more clearly how the group contracted the lead sheet's structure on the recording.)

The third and final stage applies to the form of "Iris" during improvisations. Example 3.2b shows that, rather than basing the improvised choruses strictly upon a repeating 16-bar cycle taken from the head (typical of chorus structure treatment), the group uses a 25-bar cycle. They do

3 For more on "Eighty-One," see Jeffrey Magee, "Kinds of Blue: Miles Davis, Afro-Modernism, and the Blues," *Jazz Perspectives* 1/1 (May 2007): 21–24.
4 Library of Congress deposit, Eu 863488 (January 26, 1965). Shorter's mm. 2–3 are peculiar since m. 2 consists of 3½ beats, while m. 3 consists of 4½ beats.

EXAMPLE 3.1   Recreation of Shorter's Lead Sheet to "Iris"

EXAMPLE 3.2a   "Iris" Head on Recording

this by playing first a single 16-bar chorus (derived from the harmonic structure and form of the head). Added to this each time is a chorus with doubled harmonic rhythm (8 bars), followed by an additional ninth measure. The result is a 25-bar chorus structure. Note that during mm. 18–19 and mm. 22–24 the harmonic rhythm includes two chords per measure, and there the group frequently implies 6/8 meter, playing the harmonies as dotted quarter notes.

EXAMPLE 3.2b   Form in Improvisation (= 25 bars), mm. 1-16 from Head; 17–25 Doubled Harmonic Rhythm + 1 Bar

These three stages show a path that begins with overall irregular metric groupings (lead sheet, 10 bars). The group then regularizes these metric groupings (head on recording, 16 bars). Finally, the group alters this structure into irregular metric groupings during the solos (form during improvisations on recording, 25 bars). They also suggest that—contrary to claims made by members of Davis's quintet—the group did make alterations to Shorter's compositions, and in the case of "Iris" these changes were substantial.[5]

On the recording appears alterations of some of the harmonies from Shorter's lead sheet. (Remember that one notated measure of

5   It is possible that Shorter's lead sheet was not the one used in the studio. Nevertheless, the Library of Congress deposit date is January 26, 1965, a mere four days after he recorded it with Davis. Whether or not the group used the lead sheet for the studio recording, Shorter's submission of the 4/4 10-bar composition suggests that this version was for him somehow definitive.

the 4/4 lead sheet is generally equivalent to two measures of the 3/4 performance.) In the lead sheet (example 3.1) the EMaj7 harmony that begins m. 2 returns again at m. 3. In contrast, on the recording (example 3.2a) the group replaces that m. 3 harmony with B♭7alt in the analogous place at m. 5. This avoids duplicating the same EMaj7 chord heard prior to the G♭Maj7 chord. Additionally, the harmony at the end of the first half of the composition is different. At mm. 4–5 of the lead sheet, the chord that harmonizes the melody pitch E is CMaj9. In comparison, the studio recording uses the significantly more unstable harmony A♭Maj7(♮5, ♯5) at mm. 7–8.

What is especially revealing is how the group eliminates the more conventional harmonic progressions contained in Shorter's lead sheet. Example 3.1 shows a resolution from D♭7 (end of m. 3) to CMaj9 (mm. 4–5). Yet example 3.2a shows that the progression from the recording moves from D♭7(♯11) to A♭Maj7(nat5/♯5) at mm. 6–8, and therefore avoids the more standard harmonic resolution. Similarly, the studio recording eliminates the harmonic turnaround included in the notated lead sheet at the end of the form. Example 3.1 includes a motion G+9 to C9♭5 (mm. 9–10), setting up a conventional harmonic turnaround that links back to F minor at the top of the form, In contrast, on the recording the group plays merely D♭7(♯11) during the head at mm. 15–16, deliberately omitting the functional dominant.

These changes show a calculated effort to suppress the functional harmonic progressions from Shorter's lead sheet at mm. 3–5 and 9–10. There the D♭7 CMaj9 and G+9 C9♭5 progressions fulfilled a role in clarifying the form. These functional progressions ended each half of the composition, with the latter creating an explicit harmonic turnaround to the return to the top of the form.

On the recording, the group replaces these progressions with generally nonfunctional progressions. And these replacement harmonies also help clarify the form. But rather than through functional means, they articulate each half of the form by means of less standard harmonies, ones strikingly more dissonant than those used during the rest of the composition. This is particularly evident at mm. 7–8, where the final harmony of the first half of "Iris" is A♭Maj7(♮5/♯5), which uses both E♭ and E♮ in the piano voicing.[6]

6   Hancock used versions of this A♭Maj7♮5/♯5 harmony earlier, in the 1964 Davis live recording of "My Funny Valentine," mm. 5–6 of the piano solo. The Real Book indicates this harmony in "Iris" merely as A♭Maj7♯5: see The Real Book, 6th ed. (Milwaukee, Wisc.: Hal Leonard), 218.

In comparison, the harmony at the end of the form during the head is a more conventional harmony, with the D♭7(♯11) at mm. 15–16 recalling the harmony at mm. 11 and 13. But during the improvisations the group makes a significant change there. Both m. 16 and mm. 24–25 insert an additional harmony (see example 3.2b), in which Hancock plays Dmaj(♭9) (and occasionally adds pitches from the D/E♭ octatonic collection), while Carter maintains D♭ in the bass. Like the A♭Maj7(nat5/♯5) at mm. 7–8 and 20, this Dmaj(♭9)/D♭ is a nonstandard jazz harmony, one significantly more unstable than the other harmonies. In both instances, a nonstandard harmony with heightened dissonance serves a formal role: A♭Maj7(nat5/♯5) appears at mm. 7–8, at the midpoint of the 16-bar and 9-bar cycles, Dmaj(♭9)/D♭ appears at mm. 16 and 24–25, at the end of the 16-bar and 9-bar cycles. These dissonant harmonies precede the minor harmonies at the top (mm. 1 and 17) and midpoint (mm. 9 and 21) of those cycles during the improvisations.

In contrast to the A♭Maj7(nat5/♯5) and D(♭9)/D♭ harmonies, most of the other individual harmonies are generally standard and syntactic ones. However, their sequence—the harmonic progression—is not completely standard or syntactic. This is especially true of mm. 1–8, which is significantly more harmonically fluid and active than mm. 9–16. A pair of chromatic neighbor chords decorates the opening F–11 harmony (EMaj7♯11, G♭Maj7♯11). While the progression seems to largely avoid the patterns of functional harmony, we may regard the m. 3 harmony (G♭Maj7♯11) as a third-related substitution for E♭–6/9. In this case, it derives from the more standard progression Fmin11 EMaj7♯11 (or F♭Maj7♯11) E♭min6/9.[7] Minor third related dominant chords (B♭7alt, D♭7(♯11)) then proceed to the mm. 7–8 A♭Maj7(♮5/♯5) discussed above. Since this mm. 7–8 harmony includes both E♭ and E♮, it telescopes within a single harmony the E♮–E♭ motion of the melody, the half-step melodic gesture that links across the two halves of the form, at mm. 8–9.

The move to C minor (at mm. 9–10) provides a harmonic and melodic release to mm. 7–8, and the subsequent harmonies for the remainder of the composition pivot around C minor, elaborated with D♭ in the bass that supports several different harmonies: D♭7(♯11) (mm. 11, 13, and 15–16), and AMaj7/D♭ (m. 14). The harmony at m. 14 appeared in Shorter's lead sheet merely as an AMaj9 harmony, but here Carter maintains the D♭/C♯ pedal in the bass.

---

7 This same interpretation involving G♭Maj7 as substituting for E♭ appears in Lex Giel, *The Music of Miles Davis* (Milwaukee, Wisc.: Hal Leonard, 2004), 291–92.

The extent to which "Iris" is in a single key is an interesting one to contemplate. In his analysis, Steven Strunk suggests an interpretation in the key of F minor, the opening harmony to "Iris." He states that the second half of the composition (mm. 9–16) elaborates the minor dominant (C minor) through the upper neighbor D♭ harmonies. Here the D♭7(♯11) harmonies act as tritone-related dominant chords to the C minor harmonies with which they alternate.[8] *The Music of Miles Davis* indicates the key of "Iris" as E♭ major. Although the harmony of E♭ major is nowhere in evidence in "Iris," that analysis indicates the opening progression composition as an altered ii–V–I cadence: F–11 operates as a ii chord, EMaj7♯11 as a tritone-related substitute for V, and G♭Maj7♯11 as a "minor third substitute for the implied E♭Maj7 (I)."[9] The difference between the two analyses—with two different proposed keys of F minor or E♭ major—highlights the tonal ambiguity of the composition. Although progressions of individual harmonies may suggest isolated individual key areas, the idea of a global tonic harmony for the entire composition remains elusive. Shorter's copyright lead sheet deposit would favor Strunk's interpretation of F minor since the final two harmonies (G+9 C9♭5) create a turnaround back to F minor at the top of the form. That the group elected to delete those two harmonies—the ones that evidently mark F minor as the key of the composition—reveals much about the players' commitment to harmonic ambiguity.

Like many of Shorter's compositions recorded by the quintet, the form to "Iris's" head is a 16-bar single section form. However—unlike many of Shorter's compositions—its melody does not consistently rely on continuing motives that retain rhythmic, contour, or pitch relationships. But this is not to say that these types of motivic correspondences are completely absent. The second half of the composition loosely mirrors the first half in several ways. Most obvious is the overall rhythmic similarity: both halves begin and end with pitches held longer than a measure (compare mm. 1–2 with mm. 9–10, and mm. 7–8 to 15–16). In addition, the melody's acceleration occurs analogously in both halves, at mm. 5 and 13, and the latter transposes precisely the pitches of m. 5. The harmonic rhythm of both halves is identical: the chord progression to each half of the head statements moves at 2/1/1/1/1/2 bars.

---

8   Strunk further claims that the AMaj7/D♭ (or B♭♭Maj7/D♭) operates as a neighboring chord to the D♭7 harmony, maintaining the same bass pitch, but relying on stepwise elaboration of the upper voices. Strunk's analysis does not take into account the additional Dtriad(♭9)/D♭ that appears during the improvisations. See Steven Strunk, "Notes on Harmony in Wayne Shorter's Compositions, 1964–67," *Journal of Music Theory* 49/2 (Fall 2005): 304–6.

9   Giel, *The Music of Miles Davis*, 291–92.

Poetic and lyrical, Shorter's solo also displays an intricate rhythmic sense that creates subtle conflicts with the meter, revealing some ways in which Shorter's phrases sometimes seem to transcend the beat or float above it. A transcription of the solo appears as example 3.3. Shorter's solo consists of a complete 25-bar cycle (16 bars from head and 9 bars with doubled harmonic rhythm: see above) as well as an incomplete cycle of 16 bars. Since Shorter does not complete a second 25-bar cycle, the unfinished cycle creates some confusion and formal ambiguity at the beginning of Hancock's solo, a point to which I return after discussing Shorter's improvisation.

EXAMPLE 3.3   Shorter Solo on "Iris" (3:34)

Shorter begins his solo in the second measure of the opening 25-bar cycle, since Davis paces his prior solo to conclude at the top of the form. Much of Shorter's improvisation loosely paraphrases the melody. This is particularly evident at the beginning of the solo in which Shorter begins with G, then elaborates it before moving to B♭ at the downbeat of the third measure (3:37). During the melody to the head of "Iris" this G–B♭ pitch pair is also heard on the downbeats of mm. 2–3. Thus the opening move of Shorter's solo echoes it. But while deriving it from the melody, Shorter elaborates this pitch pair further, continuing with a chromatic slide to D♭ at m. 4. While B♭ is the upper pitch during the first four measures of the head to "Iris," Shorter extends the melodic direction higher at the beginning of the solo.

A subtle detail, this motion from B♭ to D♭ at mm. 3–4 nevertheless provides a lyrical and consistent path for Shorter at the beginning of each 16- and 9-bar section, recurring at mm. 17–18 (4:04), and at mm. 27–28 (4:21). At all three places Shorter consistently arches the melody to D♭ as the uppermost pitch. Yet in each of the three instances, the B♭–D♭ pitch pair emerges through remarkably different circumstances. Both mm. 4 and 28 attain D♭ plaintively through a delicate slide, but note that the move to D♭ appears at the G♭Maj7(♯11) harmony m. 4, but with the earlier EMaj7(♯11) harmony at m. 28. And at mm. 17–18 the upward path to D♭ emerges through much increased rhythmic activity above the doubled harmonic rhythm.

These eighth-note triplets heard throughout mm. 17–22 bear scrutiny since they play such an important role in the solo. Their use begins much earlier, at mm. 5. But it is not merely the use of this rhythm, but their groupings that warrant attention. For example, at m. 5 Shorter paraphrases the m. 5 melody to "Iris" (3:41). This occurs through the pitches G♭–A♭–B♭–A♭–C♭–B♭, and at m. 6 Shorter departs from the melodic paraphrase by moving the line sequentially. Here the two-note sequences B♭–A♭ and C♭–B♭ ending m. 5 thus continue to D♭–C♭ and E♭–D♭ at m. 6. But these two-note groupings, cast within eighth-note triplets, form a subtle metrical conflict, as indicated by the brackets.

And it is exactly this same grouping that obtains at mm. 18–19, while Shorter makes his second B♭–D♭ pitch pair connection (4:05). Again, like at mm. 4–5, these pitches group similarly into descending pairs. And by m. 19, drummer Williams responds to these groupings by articulating quarter-note triplets that correspond to the first of every pair of Shorter's two-note groupings before returning to a ride pattern by the last beat of the measure. (Example 3.3 includes Williams's cymbal pattern at mm. 19–20 above the saxophone part.) The resultant interplay, with both Shorter and Williams maintaining the same 2/8 grouping of triplets, creates a subtle disruption of the underlying 3/4 metrical fabric. Shorter and Williams maintain that metrical conflict only briefly, with Shorter's two-note groupings taking place in mm. 18–19, and Williams's quarter-note triplets merely appearing at m. 19.

A different degree of metrical interplay between Shorter and Williams takes place at mm. 21–23 (4:10). Shorter maintains the earlier metrical conflict by grouping pairs of eighth-note triplets, initiating that grouping at the end of m. 21 and continuing through m. 23 (note the single acceleration of two-note groupings into sixteenth notes the final beat of m. 22). At m. 23 Williams responds in a different manner. Here he states the third triplet of each eighth-note triplet. (See example 3.3 for Williams's cymbal part in these measures.) Thus Williams's groupings avoid the beat but hew to the meter more overtly, while Shorter's 2/8 triplet groupings conflict with the underlying 3/4 meter. One further point about Shorter's two-note groupings at mm. 21–23 is their sawtooth contour (alternation of ascending/descending contours), a feature that occurs in a number of Shorter's solos. All these metrical conflicts create the sense of acceleration in relation to the underlying pulse and triple meter, allowing the improvisation to move inside and outside of metrical focus.

There are other details of Shorter's solo that show how his phrasing works to delicately obscure the beat. This occurs with his use of eighth-note triplets, and the following discussion focuses on how Shorter states and restates a chromatic pitch motive of B♭–A–A♭ in ways that align or do not align with the underlying pulse. For example, the second beat of m. 13 (3:56) Shorter states these three chromatic pitches, with B♭ appearing on the second beat of the measure (indicated by the broken slurs). Thus here the pitches align with the meter. But earlier, during the final beat of m. 7 and first beat of m. 8, an eighth-note triplet displaces the same chromatic pitches. Here they begin on the second triplet of the third beat and continue through to G the following measure (3:46). Since unaligned with the pulse, this displacement obscures the sense of downbeat at m. 8. As that phrase continues, the effect of dislocation from the meter creates a dazzling tightrope effect. The metric ambiguity clarifies as Shorter realigns with the meter at m. 9, the beginning of the second half of the 16-bar section. (Note too a similar metric dislocation with the same chromatic B♭–A–A♭ at the very end of Shorter's solo. At m. 41 Shorter's B♭ now anticipates the third beat by a triplet, again obscuring the pulse.) This metric flexibility corroborates one commentator's description of Shorter's phrases that "intentionally floated over and past the beat instead of getting down inside it."[10]

Much of Shorter's lyricism arises from his connections with and responses to the extended C minor sections at mm. 9–12 (3:48) and 34–37 (4:34). These sections provide a point of stable lyrical repose that clearly expresses the underlying harmonic progression. In contrast, Shorter consistently reharmonizes the AMaj7/D♭ harmony mm. 14 and 39, replacing that harmony with one that implies A♭min9 (or D♭13sus). With this reharmonization, Shorter provides a more typical harmony to alternate with the surrounding D♭7(♯11) harmonies.

In sum, Shorter's use of consistent elaborated pitch pairs (B♭–D♭) at the top of the form, subtle metrical conflicts (often stated in dialogue with drummer Tony Williams), and the use of chromatic paths (B♭–A–A♭) in varying relationships to the underlying pulse operate in delicate balance, creating a solo that is lyrical, subtly dramatic, and metrically flexible. At the end of Shorter's solo, he does not complete two 25-bar cycles, however. After completing the first 25-bar cycle, he ends his solo after another 16 bars, without continuing into the following 9 bars with the doubled harmonic rhythm. This undoubtedly caused the rhythm section some confusion at the beginning of Hancock's solo. It was likely unclear for the pianist and bassist whether to complete the missing 9 bars with the doubled harmonic rhythm, or merely return to the top of the 25-bar cycle.

10 Mark Gridley, *Jazz Styles*, 10th ed. (Upper Saddle River, N.J.: Prentice Hall, 2009), 277.

EXAMPLE 3.4 Opening Measures to Hancock's Solo on "Iris": Bass and Piano Out of Phase, mm. 1–8 (4:49)

Example 3.4 shows how they negotiate that question during the first 8 bars of Hancock's solo (4:49).

Initially it appears that Hancock chooses to return to the top of the 25-bar form, as he continues the Fmin9 voicing across the first measure into the second measure of his solo. However, Carter continues the form (into m. 17) with the doubled harmonic rhythm, since his m. 1 F yields to E at m. 2. Here Hancock adapts to Carter, playing mid-measure of m. 2 a voicing to accord with Carter's E, and the next measure playing the

B♭7(alt.) voicing that aligns with m. 19. However, at mm. 3–4, it is unclear which interpretation Carter has opted for, since the bass pitches suggest neither possibility, and Hancock omits any left-hand voicings between mm. 4–8. But by the fifth measure, Carter reconsiders and plays the harmonies from the top of the form, moving to B♭ in m. 5, D♭ m. 6, and A♭ (decorated with G) mm. 7–8. By m. 9, both players are in phase with one another.

These events at the beginning of Hancock's piano solo show how the players in real time solve and transcend the discrepancies of form that arise in performance. This occurs later in Hancock's solo as well, as piano and bass move out of alignment at the end of Hancock's first chorus into the beginning of his second. Here the bassist has added an extra bar at the end of the first chorus, and is out of phase for the first seven measures, before coming back into phase with Hancock. The bassist adds an additional bar again at the end of Hancock's second chorus, and here it is Hancock who adapts, allowing the extra bar and coming into phase with Carter. Thus Hancock's second chorus lasts 26, rather than 25, bars.

Following Shorter's solo, all these adaptations during Hancock's solo indicate the degree of unruffled flexibility and adaptability on the part of the performers. Shorter's early departure creates a formal wrinkle to which the players adapt through careful listening and response, one of many such situations that arise during the studio recordings. Certainly Davis's "first take" aesthetic is in evidence here, and clearly the spirit of the overall performance took precedence over minor and subtle discrepancies that arose during the performance. Such discrepancies create momentary—and spontaneous—formal ambiguities, working in counterpoint with the decided—and predetermined—harmonic ambiguities of "Iris."

"LITTLE ONE"

HARMONIC STRUCTURES

"Little One" remains one of Hancock's most ambitious compositions. The Davis Quintet recorded it on *E.S.P.*, and Hancock recorded it again some two months later, with the same rhythm section, on *Maiden Voyage*. It is a remarkable composition, but less acknowledged than some of Hancock's other 1960s compositions. Possibly it did not circulate as widely in fake books as other Hancock compositions since its out-of-tempo melody is likely less easy to be recreated by other players: the 3/4 waltz tempo of "Little One" begins only with the improvisations. The rubato opening recalls some of the Ornette Coleman/Don Cherry out-of-tempo head statements, heard on recordings such as the Coleman Quartet performance of "Lonely Woman" (*The Shape of Jazz to Come*, 1959).[11]

The harmonic progression heard during the melody is loosely related to that used during the improvisations, and it remains Hancock's most adventurous excursion into shifting harmonies over fixed bass pedal points. The technique of shifting pedal point harmonies was one Hancock had already used in a number of compositions. Chapter 1 included examples from "Three Wishes" (1961) and "King Cobra" (1963), and their use in those compositions—both of which share with "Little One" the same tonal center of F—provide significant precedents for "Little One." These focal pedal point harmonies allowed Hancock to explore what he described as his fascination with "chord color in music."[12]

Several writers have supplied brief analyses of "Little One." Barry Kernfeld describes the large-scale bass pedal point organization, but does not examine the individual harmonies. Ron Miller indicates individual harmonies (or modal labels for them), and his score annotations make many of the same points as Kernfeld in relation to pedal points and the half-step approaches to them. In a 2005 article, I examine the individual harmonies from the standpoint of underlying modal/scalar collections, showing how some of the harmonic progressions reflect modal changes that shift by a single pitch.[13]

The analysis here examines those ideas. The following discussion concentrates on the harmonic progression used to support the improvisations in "Little One," before turning to Davis's improvisation. During the improvisations, the formal design is a 24-bar repeated chorus structure. Despite the complexity of the individual harmonies, the overarching bass motion of "Little One" relies on three focal pitches. Example 3.5a contains a bass reduction, showing those pitches as F, E♭, and B♭. In his discussion of "Little One," Barry Kernfeld describes this F–E♭–B♭ structure as

---

11 Barry Kernfeld pointed out the relationship between "Little One" and "Lonely Woman" in a private communication.

12 Liner notes to *Takin' Off*. Reprinted in liner notes to *Herbie Hancock: The Complete Blue Note Sixties Sessions* (B2BN 7243 4 95569 2 8), 10.

13 Barry Kernfeld, "Adderley, Coltrane, and Davis at the Twilight of Bebop: The Search for Melodic Coherence (1958–59)" (Ph.D. diss., Cornell University, 1981), 168; Ron Miller, *Modal Jazz: Composition & Harmony*, vol. 1 (Rottenburg, Germany: Advance Music, 1996), 88; Keith Waters, "Modes, Scales, Functional Harmony, and Nonfunctional Harmony in the Compositions of Herbie Hancock," *Journal of Music Theory* 49/2 (Fall 2005): 333–57.

"subdominant-oriented."[14] This interpretation arises by considering the bass motion from the standpoint of tonal functions, with B♭ operating as subdominant of F, and E♭ as "subdominant of the subdominant." Such subdominant progressions (with major triads, in progressions such as F–E♭–B♭–F) were to become a standard feature of rock music during the mid-1960s and 1970s.[15] But Hancock's coloristic harmonies over these three pedal points are significantly more intricate than the triadic structures of subdominant-oriented rock progressions.[16]

EXAMPLE 3.5a   F–E♭–F–B♭ Large Scale Bass Motion in "Little One;" F–B♭–C Opening Sonority

Note, too, that this large-scale bass organization with F, E♭, B♭ creates an inversion of a perfect-fourth chord (in pitch-class set nomenclature, this harmony is [027]). The right-hand side of 3.5a also includes the opening and primary sonority of "Little One," which uses an inversion of a perfect fourth chord, an Fsus4 harmony that Hancock typically realizes as F, B♭, C above the bass pitch F. Thus both the large-scale bass organization as well as the opening primary sonority use an inversion of a perfect fourth chord, revealing the allure of that particular sonority on different architectural levels.

CHROMATIC PROGRESSIONS.   Example 3.5b contains the overall harmonic progression to "Little One." The arrivals on E♭ (m. 6), F (m. 13) and

14 Kernfeld, "Adderley, Coltrane, and Davis," 168.
15 For example, "Baby I Need Your Loving" and "Without the One You Love" (Four Tops), "Gloria" (Them), "I Can't Explain" (The Who), and "Hey Jude" (The Beatles) use this I–♭VII–IV progression. These examples were generously provided to me by Walt Everett.
16 Hancock used a related subdominant organization in "Theme to Blow Up," recorded in 1967 with Bobby Hutcherson. There the bass pitches progress through E, A, and D. *Herbie Hancock: The Complete Blue Note Sixties Sessions.*

B♭ (m. 21) come about through upper chromatic bass motion (indicated in 3.5a by stemless noteheads). These half-step descents clarify each of the E♭, F, and B♭ arrival points. They do so because the upper chromatic harmonies (based on F♭/E, G♭, and C♭/B) are akin to more functional harmonies. They rely on general principles of tritone substitution, yet their relationship to tritone substitution chords is veiled.

EXAMPLE 3.5b   Harmonic Progression for Improvisation

The general principle of tritone substitution proposes the equivalence of tritone-related dominant harmonies, since the active and directed chordal thirds and sevenths are maintained (and merely swap positions between the tritone-related harmonies): typically V7 harmonies become replaced by ♭II7 harmonies. In order to show how Hancock transforms those harmonies, we examine first the chromatic bass motions at mm. 5–6 and at 20–21. Note that the upper chromatic chord at m. 5 is Dmin/E, leading to E♭min11 at m. 6. The upper chromatic chord at m. 20 is Amin/B, leading to B♭min7♭5 at m. 21. The Dmin/E and Amin/B upper chromatic chords are transpositions of one another. Example 3.6a shows how both correspond to more conventional tritone-related dominants. Dmin/E is similar to E7♭9, yet it differs from E7♭9 since it replaces the chordal third (G♯) with a suspended fourth (A). Amin/B does the same with B7♭9, replacing the chordal third (D♯) with E. Thus both these upper chromatic harmonies at mm. 5 and 20 operate as suspended fourth chords, rather than more traditional dominant harmonies.

Similarly, the harmony at mm. 11–12 (G♭13sus) leads chromatically down to the Fmin9 harmony at m. 13. Again, this upper chromatic harmony operates as a suspended fourth chord, rather than a more standard dominant harmony (such as G♭13). Again, the substitution of the suspended fourth for the chordal third alters somewhat the general principles of tritone substitution. And there are further transformations that appear here as well: the harmony at mm. 9–10 (EMaj7♯11/E♭) also contributes to this progression.

Example 3.6b is meant to illustrate Hancock's transformation of a more functional three-chord progression at mm. 9–13. The left side of the example indicates tritone substitution from the standpoint of ii–V pairs. It shows how a resolution to F is effected through D♭min9 to G♭13, a tritone substitution for the ii–V pair Gmin9 to C7♯9/♭13. For the purposes of the subsequent discussion of "Little One," we label the D♭min9 as "x" (a subdominant/pre-dominant harmony), the G♭13 as "y" (a dominant harmony), and the resolution to F as "z" (a tonic harmony).

EXAMPLE 3.6b   Tritone-Related ii–V Pair and Its Transformation at mm. 11–13 of "Little One"

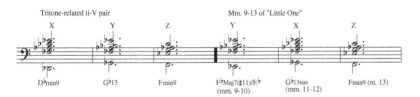

The right side of example 3.6b includes the three-chord progression to "Little One" at mm. 9–13. Note that the upper structure to "Little One's" G♭13sus harmony is identical to the upper structure of the x chord. The x and y chords also help show how the harmony *prior* to the G♭13sus harmony plays a role in the ultimate motion back to Fmin9 at m. 13. The F♭/EMaj7♯11/E♭ at mm. 9–10 is the last of a series of colorful harmonies that occur above the E♭ pedal point. But not only does it conclude the E♭ pedal point section, it participates in the return to F. While the upper structure of F♭/EMaj7♯11/E♭ is similar to that of the G♭13sus at mm. 11–12, there is a crucial difference. At mm. 9–10 the chord contains B♭, while at mm. 11–12 the chord contains instead C♭.[17] And the upper structure of the harmony at m. 9–10 is precisely that of the y chord, the dominant harmony. Thus here Hancock has reversed the typical position of upper structure harmonies. Instead of the more conventional x to y (pre-dominant to dominant) motion, he suggests instead a move from y to x (dominant to pre-dominant). Further, the bass pitch E♭ of the EMaj7♯11/E♭ harmony corresponds to neither the original x nor y bass. Rather, it continues the already existing pedal point. As a result, the G♭–F bass motion at mm. 12–13 adheres to the typical half-step bass motion that occurs with tritone-substituted dominants and their resolutions, but the use of E♭ beneath the mm. 9–10 y chord provides an unusual bass pitch, one that completes the E♭ pedal point section.

In sum, the three-chord sequence alludes to a conventional harmonic progression, while reinterpreting it in musically significant ways. The two chords at mm. 9–12 ingeniously transform a functional progression, and help clarify the return to F at m. 13. The sequence of harmonies shows a reliance on standard harmonic practice while at the same time expanding its possibilities.

All these upper chromatic harmonies discussed above (Dmin/E, Amin/B, G♭13sus) operate as sus chord harmonies. Such suspended fourth harmonies figure in several of Hancock's mid-1960s compositions, particularly "Maiden Voyage." In "Little One," the meaning of all three harmonies relies on their resolution—rather than stand-alone harmonies, they operate functionally as substitute dominant harmonies that then resolve downward by half-step.

All this so far examines the way in which the harmonies bring about arrivals to the three pedal points of E♭ (m. 6), F (m. 13), and B♭ (m. 21), without regard to the progression of pedal point harmonies themselves. And it is the harmonic activity over the pedal points that creates much of the composition's harmonic magic.

17 Ron Miller's analysis does not take into account the difference between those two harmonies, and indicates the upper structure harmonies at mm. 11 and 12 as the same. See Miller, *Modal Jazz*, 88.

MODES/SCALES. It is tempting to consider the harmonic progression to "Little One" in terms of progressions of underlying modes/scales. And by doing so it is possible to understand some of these progressions in surprisingly systematic ways. The first two harmonies oscillate between the Fsus4 harmony and a cluster chord, perhaps best represented as D♭Maj7♯11/F (or E♭13/F). (See example 3.5b.) By regarding the opening Fsus4 harmony as representing the F dorian mode (F G A♭ B♭ C D E♭ F), the mode/scale collections for the harmonies at mm. 1–4, 6, 7, 9, and 10 increase systematically by a single flat over the F and E♭ pedal points. Thus through mm. 1–10 each successive modal/scalar collection changes consistently by a single pitch. This is shown in table 3.1 (the single changed pitch appears in bold for each collection).

The example in table 3.1 does not include the chromatic passing chord (Dmin/E) of m. 5, nor does it include the harmony at m. 8 (BMaj7♯5/E♭).[18] And while this example seems to provide a systematic way of understanding the mm. 1–10 progression, it is worth acknowledging the general problems that arise here by simply equating chords with seven-note modal/scalar collections.

The first problem stems from the harmonic accompaniment, since Hancock's comping often does not articulate all seven pitches from the suggested mode/scale, either simultaneously or successively. For example,

TABLE 3.1   E5–E♭5 Modes/Scales in the Harmonic Progression of "Little One"

m. 1 F sus4	(F G A♭ B♭ C D E♭ F)	F dorian (3 flats)
m. 2 D♭Maj7♯11/F	(F G A♭ B♭ C **D♭** E♭ F)	F aeolian (4 flats)
mm. 3–4 (repeats mm. 1–2)		
m. 6 E♭–11	(E♭ F **G♭** A♭ B♭ C D♭ E♭)	E♭ dorian (5 flats)
m. 7 EMaj7♯5/E♭	(E♭ **F♭** G♭ A♭ B♭ C D♭ E♭)	Mode of D♭ melodic minor ascending (6 flats)
m. 9–10 EMaj7♯11/E♭	(E♭ F♭ G♭ A♭ B♭ **C♭** D♭ E♭)	E♭ phrygian (7 flats)
mm. 11–12 G♭13sus	(G♭ A♭ B♭ C♭ D♭ E♭ F♭ G♭)	G♭ mixolydian (7 flats)

18 Miller omits this m. 8 harmony. Miller also provides an incorrect bass pitch for m. 19. See Miller, *Modal Jazz*, 88. The mm. 8–9 progression (EMaj7♯5/E♭ BMaj7♯5/E♭) must have appealed to Hancock, who used the identical harmonies at mm. 34–35 of "Dolphin Dance," also on Hancock's *Maiden Voyage* recording.

Hancock frequently realizes the first Fsus4 harmony as merely a three-note chord, without additional pitches.[19] A second problem stems from the improvisations, since the improvisers seem not to be guided by relying on 7-note mode/scale considerations (Hancock and Shorter both avoid the use of A♭ over the Fsus4 harmony). A third problem arises from the remainder of the composition since the harmonies do not progress in a similar fashion via underlying chord/scales that shift by changing one element. Instead, the harmonic progressions over the return to the pedal point F (mm. 13–18) as well as B♭ (mm. 21–24) emerge largely from voice-leading considerations, with many of the upper structure harmonies moving by whole step or half step. This is particularly clear at mm. 12–14 (Fmin9 Gmin9/F G♭Maj7♯11/F), as well as mm. 22–24 (G/B♭ G♭Maj7/B♭).[20] Thus mode/scale considerations can play at most a provisional role in explaining the harmonic progressions of "Little One."

The harmonic richness of "Little One" moves the group and 1960s jazz composition into new terrain. The composition explores changing harmonies over bass pedal points to an unprecedented degree. Additionally, those pedal points arrive through descending chromatic bass motion. These chromatic chords facilitate motion to the major points of arrival on E♭, F, and B♭. While they help clarify those points of arrival, they do so through harmonic function that is weakened, since all three (Dmin/E m. 5, G♭sus9 m. 11, Amin/B m. 20) function as tritone substitution chords, altered through the addition of a suspended fourth.

DAVIS'S SOLO

DAVIS AND THE FSUS4 CHORD.   The discussion above pointed out the problems that arise with Hancock's m. 1 and m. 3 harmony of Fsus4 (F, B♭, C) from the standpoint of chord/scale identification. This is particularly true when equating that harmony with an underlying 7-note mode/scale, since that would require identifying a chordal third, which in this case

---

19 Additionally, Hancock occasionally substitutes the natural 7th for the flatted seventh at the m. 6 E♭ minor harmony, as during Davis's first chorus.

20 The role of the F♯min7/F at m. 19 is unusual, and perhaps there is a better label for it since Hancock occasionally adds the pitches C (and E♭) to the chord. It is possible to consider it as the first of a tritone-related ii–V pair (F♯min7 B7♭9), with the following Amin/B harmony as the second element of that pair. Ron Miller (p. 88) identifies this harmony as F♯min7(♭5), although Carter plays F natural here, and Hancock consistently includes C♯ in the chord.

might either be A♭ or A natural.[21] Thus, the question arises: is the context of the Fsus4 harmony major, minor, or neither? The m. 2 harmony of D♭maj♯11 (or F aeolian) that follows could suggest a minor context for the Fsus4 chord. Yet the opening melody to "Little One" includes A natural in its first phrase. During their solos both Hancock and Shorter studiously avoid playing either pitch on this chord during their solos, so in these cases neither supplies a major or a minor context. (On the later version of "Little One" recorded on Hancock's *Maiden Voyage*, tenor saxophonist George Coleman and trumpeter Freddie Hubbard rely on A♭ while playing over this initial harmony in the form, suggesting a minor context.)

In contrast, Davis's solo offers a study in how he negotiates and reevaluates that harmony in real time over the course of his three choruses. It suggests a remarkably rapid learning curve in adapting to that harmony, and altering the harmonic implications of the opening 4 bars in each chorus. A transcription to the entire solo appears in example 3.7. Simply put, Davis undertakes a path that moves from a two-flat environment during mm. 1–4 of Chorus 1, to a three-flat environment the same place at Chorus 2, and to a four-flat environment at the same place in Chorus 3. With it, we can hear how Davis works out and rethinks the implications of the Fsus4 harmony during the performance.

EXAMPLE 3.7   Davis Solo on "Little One" (1:19)

21 Kernfeld discusses the same issue relative to Freddie Hubbard's solo on the Dsus harmony of "Maiden Voyage," in *What to Listen for in Jazz* (New Haven: Yale University, 1995), 147–51.

EXAMPLE 3.7 Continued

We can describe mm. 1–4 of Davis's first chorus (1:19) as a two-flat environment (with B♭ and E♭). This environment, with Davis's use of A natural, thus implies a major context for the Fsus4 harmony. A simple description of the pitch content however misses the richness of Davis's motivic organization, particularly from a rhythmic standpoint. It is possible to hear Davis elaborating the upbeat-to-metric downbeat ideas in ingenious ways. Example 3.7 brackets each of these motivic two-note descents. The initial statement of D–F into m. 1 becomes transformed in the following measure. Here Davis preserves the two-note descent across the barline (E♭5–C5), but two pitches (G4–A4) precede that descent. The crisply articulated pitches on the downbeats of mm. 1 and 2 shape the relationship of the two motives. Davis restates the descending motive across the barline into m. 3 (F5–F4), now extending the two-note relationship with an additional pitch. And, finally, Davis in m. 3 displaces the two-note descent (B♭–E♭) and displaces it to end not on the metric downbeat of m. 4, but one eighth note earlier. Thus the four descending two-note motives respond to the 4-bar organization here, one motive per measure. But—characteristically for Davis—he treats these four motives loosely and flexibly, rather than predictably and mechanically.

Modal analysis describes Davis's pitch content at the Fsus4 chord at mm. 1 and 3 as F mixolydian. It is likely that the opening to Davis's solo is a response to the opening motive of the melody, which similarly uses A natural (the melody opens with the pitches E♭–C–G–A–B♭–C–A). Certainly this is not the first time a soloist begins an improvisation by alluding to the melody of the composition. And, in fact, several of Davis's pitch choices in his solo relate quite closely to that opening melodic idea.

By Davis's second chorus (1:55) he has abandoned A natural in the opening measures, now replaced with A♭ (heard at m. 27). This alters the harmonic climate, a minor mode interpretation of Fsus4 replacing Davis's major mode interpretation from Chorus 1. Although Davis does not play B♭, the presence of E♭ and A♭ identify these measures as a three-flat environment. (The E natural in m. 27 is passing. Davis plays neither D natural nor D♭ here.) Similar to mm. 1–4, the measures that open Chorus 2 are highly motivic, and again the motives relate as two-note motives that preserve their rhythmic identity. Here Davis's rhythm articulates the downbeats and midpoints of each measure. The relationship between m. 25 and m. 26 is especially clear: both express an ascending contour (F4–F5, and E♭5–G5) with short staccato pitches. Measure 27 maintains its relationship to the previous two measures primarily through rhythm, since the opening two pitches of A♭5–G5 similarly suggest a level of 6/8, a rhythmic idea picked up by Hancock in his accompaniment. But in contrast to mm. 25 and 26, the contour descends, and the opening pitch of A♭ is held rather than played clipped.

Finally, Davis's third chorus moves to a four-flat environment at mm. 50–53 (2:32; the D natural held across the barline into m. 53 is a passing tone). Thus here the pitch content reflects F aeolian, which Davis applies to both Fsus4 and D♭Maj7♯11/F harmonies. The material here is not as overtly motivic, although mm. 52–53 recalls Davis's phrase played earlier (at mm. 46–47).

A comparison of the opening 4 bars to each of Davis's three choruses reveals a process of revision undertaken in real time. The ambiguity of the opening Fsus4 harmony creates an opportunity to Davis to offer solutions that change during the course of the improvisation. As suggested above, the opening to Davis's first chorus might have been encouraged by the opening melody to "Little One." Naturally it is impossible to read Davis's intentions. But it is nevertheless interesting to speculate that Davis's use of A natural, the major third above the bass F, provided for him a subtle clash. And it is perhaps this clash that motivated a change to the minor third A♭ during the second chorus, and to move to a four-flat environment by the final chorus. These alterations show a subtle but meaningful reconsideration of these opening bars, and the meaning of the Fsus4 harmony. These alterations highlight more generally the potential major/minor ambivalence of sus chords, and Davis's fluid responses to them.

MOTIVIC ORGANIZATION.   The above showed Davis's reliance on two-note rhythmic motives to open his first and second choruses. Certainly those passages at mm. 1–4 and 25–27 projected related motivic ideas each measure, and done in a way that preserved some aspects of rhythmic or contour while still making changes in other dimensions. All of this provides a crucial way of hearing Davis's improvisations here and elsewhere: his motives create relationships that are memorable, lyrical, highly creative, and—perhaps above all—flexible. Even in the case of ideas that begin as two-note motives, successive motives undergo alteration and reinterpretation and forgo rote repetition.

And these types of motivic relationships guide much of Davis's solo. They provide a way to hear how Davis spontaneously creates continuous relationships in an immediate context. By considering Davis's entire solo, it is useful to acknowledge the limitations of chord/scale analysis, since Davis seems unconcerned with careful negotiation of each individual harmony. Instead, the solo attains much of its expressive power through memorable and malleable motives.

Davis works out these immediate motivic relationships elsewhere during the course of the solo. These motivic echoes are sometimes subtle, but present nevertheless. The transcription uses brackets to indicate five of them. At mm. 13–14 (1:37) Davis creates a sequence of ascending step-wise fourths (M1), F4–B♭4 followed by G4–C5 (the melodic line continues beyond m. 14: the motivic designation is meant merely to highlight the recurrence of the ascending perfect fourth). Here the two ascending fourths appear in different rhythmic guises. The first begins on the downbeat of m. 13, while the second is displaced to the upbeat of the first beat at m. 14, and the restated perfect fourth continues to ascend. Further, the second ascending fourth at m. 14 is rhythmically compressed relative to the one at m. 13. Davis rhythmically alters the sequential relationship.

Similarly, a three-pitch descending motive (M2; 1:45) appears across the barline into m. 19 (E, E♭, D♭), and Davis rhythmically alters the descending third in its sequential reappearance at mm. 19–20 (E♭, D♭, C♭). At mm. 21–22 (1:50) Davis ends a melodic shape with a descending sixth gesture of E♭5–G4, and echoes that gesture a step lower with the same upbeat-to-metric-downbeat descending sixth, moving into m. 23 with D♭–F (M3). Note that Davis tailors the end of M3b to ascend a half step to G♭5, here carefully negotiating the half step that is a prominent feature of the harmony at that measure. Measures 29–34 contain two consecutive motives (M4 and M5). M4 (2:00; mm. 29–30) maintains the identical rhythm and ascending contour (B4–F5, E5–A♭5). M5 (2:03; mm. 31–34) preserves rhythm and descending contour, and Davis enhances the rhythmic relationship by delaying the appearance of the downbeat pitches at mm. 31–34.

Note that Davis restates all five motives (M1–M5) at the measure level. All but one appear with two motivic statements over two measures, and the final motive M5 appears with four motivic statements over four measures. All create continuity by maintaining interval, contour, or rhythm, with the motivic repetitions fluid rather than predictable.

Finally, there is one pitch motive that recurs throughout the solo. It relies on the elaboration of E5–E♭5, and this becomes the focal motive of the solo. Unlike motives M1–5, which appear strictly in consecutive measures, the E5–E♭5 motive appears frequently across the entire solo, and spans longer portions of the solo than merely at 2- and 4-bar levels. Table 3.2 lists the occurrences of this pitch motive, and the transcription indicates these appearances with dotted slurs. The two pitches are often elaborated in distinct ways. In some instances this pitch motive is preceded by F5, and in some instances D♭ follows it. Table 3.2 lists the appearances of this pitch motive in the first column. The letters in parentheses in the first column indicate when Davis uses the motive in the analogous place

TABLE 3.2   E5–E♭5 Motive in Davis's Solo on "Little One"

(A) Mm. 5–6 (1:25)	Dmin/E	E♭min9	(F E E♭)
(B) 8–10 (1:29)	BMaj7♯5/E♭	EMaj7♯11/E♭	(E E♭ E E♭)
(C) 15–16 (1:41)	G♭Maj7♯11/F		(C D♭ E E♭ C)
(D) 17–18 (1:43)	D♭Maj7♯11/F		(C D♭ E E♭)
(E) 18–19 (1:45)	D♭Maj7♯11/F	F♯min7/F	(E E♭ D♭)
(F) 35 (2:09)	G♭13sus		(G F E E♭ E)
(C) 40–41 (2:17)	G♭Maj7♯11/F		(F E E♭ D♭ E♭ E E♭)
(A) 54–55 (2:38)	Dmin/E	E♭min9	(F E F E E♭ D♭)
(B) 57–58 (2:42)	BMaj7♯5/E♭	EMaj7♯11/E♭	(E E♭ D♭ E E♭)
(F) 60–61 (2:47)	G♭13sus		(E E♭ D D♭ C♭)
(D) 67–68 (2:56)	D♭Maj7♯11/F		(E E♭ D♭)

in the form. For example, (A) indicates Davis's use of the elaborated E–E♭ motive at mm. 5–6 in both Chorus 1 and 3. The second column indicates the harmonies over which the motive appears, and the third column lists the pitches used in each instance of the motive in order to show how it is elaborated during the course of the solo.

Clearly Davis treats this idea loosely, but each recollection of the half-step E–E♭ motive echoes earlier statements of it. The motive provides Davis with a recurrent pitch path throughout the solo, one that operates as a point of reference. This points to a more general practice with a number of Davis solos that offer similar frequent returns to a focal motive that elaborates two or three pitches. Rather than taking place only within an immediate context, motives such as the E–E♭ pitch motive described above (as well as those heard in Davis's solos to "Freedom Jazz Dance" and "Petits Machins") provide a returning reference point across the entire improvisation.[22] The recurring semitone idea heard in "Little One" recalls the half-step flamenco gestures heard prominently in Davis's earlier *Sketches of Spain*, an ongoing facet of Davis's searing ballad playing tradition.[23]

The solo is also notable due to Davis's deft handling of additional bars that the rhythm section appends to the 24-bar form. Pianist Hancock and bassist Carter add an additional bar at two identical places in the form during Davis's second and third choruses. The first appears at m. 37 (2:12). The rhythm section maintains the G♭13sus chord for an extra bar,

22 Jeremy Yudkin describes a recurrent "x" motive for Davis's solo in "Freedom Jazz Dance," in *Miles Davis: Miles Smiles and the Invention of Post Bop* (Bloomington: Indiana University Press, 2008), 111–14. Chapter 7 here discusses the primary motive to "Petits Machins."

23 Acknowledgments to Barry Kernfeld for pointing out the relationship to *Sketches of Spain* in a private communication.

and Davis quotes the opening two pitches (E♭–C) from the melody to "Little One." At m. 62, the rhythm section again adds an extra bar (2:49), and here Davis merely holds the second pitch G across the barline. The effect is seamless. The continuation of his melody through to A5 at m. 64 shows Davis effortlessly responding to the Gmin9/F harmony, and negotiating the additional bar without issue. All this reveals Davis's flexibility in the face of spontaneous formal alterations.

The discussion above pointed out two types of methods to hear Davis's motives. The first involved the use of repeated motives in an immediate context, often appearing in consecutive measures. The second involved the use of the single half-step E5–E♭5 motive that reappears throughout the improvisation, operating as a consistent reference point. And although "Little One" is one of Hancock's more harmonically dense and complex compositions, Davis seems uninterested in negotiating and expressing each harmony carefully, in contrast to the way that, for example, George Coleman would on the later version of "Little One" from Hancock's *Maiden Voyage* recording. Nevertheless, the solo underscores Davis's motivic orientation, and its unerring conviction and urgency make for a compelling improvisation, one steeped in Davis's romantic ballad playing.

"E.S.P." Extra Sensory Perception

COMPOSITION

The melody to "E.S.P." is notable for its foregrounding of the perfect fourth interval. This is not the first Shorter composition to explore this interval. Shorter's "Suspended Sentence" (Lee Morgan and Thad Jones, *Two Stars at Birdland*, 1961) and "Ping Pong" (in the B section, from Art Blakey's *Ugetsu*, 1963) project the interval. Earlier uses of the perfect fourth interval include John Carisi's "Israel," recorded by Davis (1949) and released as part of the *Birth of the Cool* sessions, which arpeggiates a pair of three ascending fourths at mm. 9–10, and Warne Marsh's "Marshmallow." But with "E.S.P." the perfect fourth interval becomes the central focus of the composition's melody, as it was with Shorter's "Witch Hunt" (*Speak No Evil*, 1964), which similarly arpeggiates perfect fourths. This brings to the melodic dimension what was becoming a distinct feature of harmonic accompaniment in the 1960s, most notably pianist McCoy Tyner's fourth-based comping with the John Coltrane Quartet. Later Shorter compositions recorded by Davis's second quintet, such as "Orbits," and "Nefertiti," project the interval in more subtle ways. Its bald use in "E.S.P." functions, it would seem, as a token of mid-1960s modernism.

Example 3.8 provides a lead sheet of the head to "E.S.P." The form of the composition is a repeated 16-bar structure with a first and second ending (AA'). The opening E7 harmony (indicated as E7 alt; Shorter's lead sheet notates it as E+9 (♭5)) initially plays a dual role. At the outset of the composition, it provides an embellishing chord for the overall FMaj7 tonic that appears first at mm. 3–4. At mm. 5–6, E7 also provides a link to the ensuing E♭Maj7 harmony. Thus it begins as a lower chromatic neighboring chord (resolving to F) before it is reconfigured as an upper neighbor chord (resolving to E♭).[24] Further, much of the composition seems to investigate the notion of dominant chords that move chromatically upward. For example, mm. 9–12 provide an upward resolving chromatic path (D7(♯9) E♭7(♯9) E7(♯9) FMaj7♯11), a path that reverses the more typical downward chromatic resolution of dominant seventh chords.

EXAMPLE 3.8   Head to "E.S.P."

24 Strunk, "Notes on Harmony," 307.

The discussion of "Iris" above showed how for the recording the quintet excised the lead sheet's functional harmonic progressions at the end of each half of the composition. In comparison, "E.S.P." retains its functional progressions in the last 4 bars of each half. Thus it is unlike most of the Shorter compositions written for the quintet, which avoid standard harmonic cadences and turnarounds. In fact, the AA' form of "E.S.P." resembles many of Shorter's earlier AA' compositions, which include a motion to the V harmony (half-cadence) at the end of the first ending, and a motion to the I harmony (full cadence) at the end of the second ending. Yet "E.S.P" transforms those earlier harmonic conventions of Shorter's. The first ending of "E.S.P." concludes with a G♭Maj7 harmony in place of a more standard C7 (or G♭7) at m. 16. And the progression at the second ending employs D♭min9 G♭13 at m. 31, providing a tritone-related ii–V substitution that leads to the final tonic harmony at m. 32.

During head statements, Hancock avoids playing any harmonies at mm. 9–11, and 14–16 of both 16-bar sections. Since he is consistent in not playing those measures during the head, this was likely part of a predetermined strategy worked out in the studio. Such decisions contributed to the specific and unique identity of the studio compositions.

Example 3.8 shows that the melody's opening fixes the downward arpeggiated perfect fourths of C–G–D. These fourths form a stable point against which the underlying harmonies move chromatically. This poses an opposite strategy relative to the group's performance of Eddie Harris's "Freedom Jazz Dance" (*Miles Smiles*): it involves a single static harmony beneath chromatically shifting arpeggiations of perfect fourths.

While these arpeggiated perfect fourths form the primary motive for the first 8 bars, the following melodic material develops this intervallic idea in more elaborated fashion. Between mm. 9–12 Shorter offers a pair of veiled sequences each measure. The first forms a descending whole step and descending minor third (D–C–A) at mm. 9–10, with the same intervallic relation at mm. 10–11 (G–F–D) (shown with dotted slurs). Here the sequence is intervallic, not rhythmic, but both gestures span a filled-in perfect fourth. The second begins with an ascending fourth that links to a descending minor third, initially at mm. 11 (D–G–E) and again at m. 12 (F–B♭–G) (indicated with brackets). Unlike the mm. 9–10 sequence, this mm. 11–12 sequence also extends to rhythm. And this set of intervals appears earlier as G–C–A (mm. 6–7, shown with dotted brackets), precisely at the point the melody moves away from the strict perfect fourth organization. Overall the melody explores the perfect fourth interval overtly at mm. 1–6, and in elaborated fashion mm. 6–7 and 9–12.

Also notice the return to perfect fourth organization here during the final two measures of the melody. The descending perfect fourth E♭–B♭ (m. 31) is then answered by an ascending perfect fourth A4–D5 the final measure. These two measures create a subtle melodic circularity linking to the opening phrase of the composition, with the descending fourth (E♭–B♭, m. 31) followed by an ascending fourth (A–D, m. 32), which then links to the descending fourth of the opening phrase (C–G, m. 1). But the implied circularity is suppressed by other factors, such as the cadential progression at mm. 31–32. Further, the group states the melody only once at the beginning of the performance, and once at the end. Since the group never returns directly to the m. 1 melody after mm. 31–32, the performance does not exploit the implied circularity.

HANCOCK'S SOLO

Hancock's two-chorus solo, contained in example 3.9, displays some general features heard in a number of his improvisations. Note the left-hand comping, which alternates 3–4 note voicings with individual pitches, all of which set up a buoyant rhythmic counterpoint with the right-hand lines. Note too, a characteristic feature of many of his bop lines, which begin on the second beat of the measure, initiated with three descending chromatic pitches, such as at mm. 8, 22, 25, and 41.

EXAMPLE 3.9   Hancock Solo on "E.S.P." (4:00)

EXAMPLE 3.9   Continued

It is also possible to hear the solo as moving between tightly compact motivic organization (typically at the beginnings of 16-bar and 32-bar sections) and longer bop lines (typically at the ends of 16-bar and 32-bar sections). The following discussion focuses on two primary features specific to this solo. The first feature is a flexible grouping of pitches (based on G–A♭–B♭–B) that begin each of the four 16-bar sections, often setting up the compact motives. The other feature involves Hancock's consistent reharmonizations during the final 4 bars of each 16-bar section, often supporting the longer bop lines. These reharmonizations alter the harmonies stated during the head.

PITCH GROUPING. Hancock's two-chorus solo begins after Davis's. Davis concludes his solo (4:00) by overlapping with the beginning of the 32-bar form by 3 bars. He ends his solo with a melodic idea that Hancock immediately picks up. Rather than repeating Davis's phrase exactly, though, Hancock maintains the rhythm and contour, and alters the pitches, initially beginning a minor third higher than Davis. Hancock's pitches of G, A♭, B♭, and B natural provide him with a reference point to negotiate the beginning of each 16-bar section, particularly at the E7alt harmony. This G–A♭–B♭–B pitch grouping recurs transformed at similar places in the form. Hancock realizes that pitch grouping in a number of distinctly different ways.

In mm. 4–7 of his first chorus (4:04), Hancock limits himself to the four pitches of G, A♭, B♭, and B natural. Hancock preserves the rhythm and contour of Davis's previously stated idea consistently. However, by limiting the pitch content so severely, Hancock's reliance on Davis's contour forces an intriguing harmonic substitution at m. 7. Here Hancock's A♭ in the melody, duplicated in the left-hand harmonies during that measure, substitutes E♭sus13 in place of the composition's E♭Maj7. Thus Hancock flexibly reevaluates this harmony in service of echoing Davis's motive while using his four note-pitch grouping.

Hancock's second 16-bar section (4:14) begins with a restatement of those same four pitches. This ascending gesture at m. 18 (G–A♭–B♭–B) reflects quite closely the one heard at mm. 4–5 (B♭–G–A♭–B♭–B). And the material that follows the motive at mm. 19–20 abandons the G–A♭–B♭–B environment, as Hancock reverts to a bebop gesture that instead expresses and outlines the underlying FMaj7 harmony.

The beginning to Hancock's second chorus (4:27; mm. 33–40) provides a pitch grouping related to the G–A♭–B♭–B pitch motive. Likewise four pitches, this pitch grouping now consists of D–G–A♭–B♭, stated identically in mm. 33 and 34 (labeled M1a in the transcription). And this motive becomes a malleable point of departure during the opening 8 bars of this chorus, as Hancock's phrase organization responds significantly to the harmony and to the underlying 4- and 8-bar sections. Following the opening two statements of this motive, m. 35 begins with the identical contour and rhythm heard at mm. 33–34, but Hancock alters the pitch content to express the FMaj7♯11 harmony (D–G–A–B–A, M1b). Moreover, Hancock's three ideas create a larger phrase organization, with mm. 35–36 heard as responding to mm. 33 and 34. In fact, this lyrical phrase structure, consisting generally of 1 + 1 + 2 measures and known as "sentence" structure, is one that organizes any number of jazz and popular song melodies.[25] M1b ends with a classic bebop gesture of two descending eighth notes begun on a metrically strong beat (G–C).[26] Thus not only are Motives M1a and M1b related, but also the larger phrasing based on these motives creates a lyrical 4-bar grouping.

Further, there is a larger musical rhyme taking place between mm. 33–36 and 37–40. Measure 37 opens with the same pitches and rhythmic shape of M1a, and is then absorbed into a longer line, with m. 38 expressing the octatonic (diminished scale)[27] collection, and m. 39 outlining the E♭Maj7 sonority. Further, note that Hancock ends that 4-bar gesture at m. 40 with the same bebop rhythmic gesture that ended m. 36 (shown with asterisks), setting up a broader lyrical relationship between mm. 33–36 and 37–40, with the second 4-bar section responding to the first 4-bar section. While the chorus begins with tightly compact motivic organization at mm. 33–36, the opening motive becomes absorbed into a longer line (at mm. 37–40): all provide lyrical paths through the 4- and 8-bar organization.

---

25 For example, such 1 + 1 + 2 phrasing provides the organization for the opening 4 bars of "Blue Monk," "Dat Dere," "Tenderly," "Ain't Misbehaving," "Darn That Dream," and "Memories of You." The same proportion applies in 2 + 2 + 4 organization for the opening 8 bars of compositions such as "Yesterdays," "The Very Thought of You," "Willow Weep for Me," "Over the Rainbow," "My Funny Valentine," "Cottontail," "If You Could See Me Now," and "When I Fall in Love." In discussions of European classical music, analysts use the term "sentence structure" to describe this type of phrase structure. Arnold Schoenberg uses the term in his *Fundamentals of Musical Composition*, ed. by Gerald Strang and Leonard Stein (London: Faber and Faber, 1967), chapter 5.

26 This rhythmic and contour gesture, similar to the opening gesture of Dizzy Gillespie's "Groovin' High," may likely be the onomatopoeic origin of the term "bebop."

27 The octatonic collection (or diminished scale) refers to a symmetrical collection of alternating half and whole steps. Because of its symmetry, this eight-note collection has three distinct forms, including the one that begins on C/C♯, on C♯/D, or on D/E♭.

The beginning of the final 16-bar section (4:40; mm. 49–54) again relates integrally to the G–A♭–B♭–B pitch grouping. The first two phrases each end with those four pitches, at mm. 50–51 and 53. However, in this chorus, the four-note idea becomes absorbed into a larger octatonic (diminished scale) framework. Earlier choruses distinguished the harmonic progression, with G–A♭–B♭–B expressing the E7alt harmony, but with the subsequent melodic material differing by expressing the resolutions to FMaj7 (and E♭Maj7). Yet here the consistent octatonic frame obliterates the distinction between the harmonies of E7 and FMaj7.

This section also contains a subtle example of cat-and-mouse interplay between Hancock and Carter. Carter's anticipation of the bass pitches at the downbeats to mm. 49 and 53 seem to invite Hancock to respond, and he plays marked pitches in the bass register of the piano, outside of the midrange register typically used by the left hand. Carter's bass anticipation to E at m. 49 encourages a response by Hancock in his bass register (the last eighth note of m. 49) where he plays B2, the fifth of the E7 harmony. Three bars later Hancock states C2, the fifth of the F harmony, on the downbeat of m. 52. In return Carter anticipates the downbeat of m. 53 with E. This interaction shows a moment of subtle interaction and communication between the players.

Variations of the G–A♭–B♭–B pitch grouping heard at the opening of Hancock's solo appear near the opening to each of the 16-bar sections of "E.S.P." Rather than regarding it as an overarching organizational tool for the solo, it may be more apt to consider it as a comfortable reference point used by Hancock to negotiate the opening E7 harmony. At mm. 17–18 and mm. 33–36 the pitch grouping then yields to other material that expresses the ensuing FMaj7 harmony. And at mm. 33–36 and mm. 49–52 the pitches allow for further motivic development—the former negotiates the harmonic change from E7 to FMaj7, the latter submerges the harmonic change beneath the prevailing octatonic environment.

REHARMONIZATIONS. A number of other features of the solo are noteworthy. Hancock reharmonizes the final 4 bars of each 16-bar section, bypassing or altering a number of the harmonies stated during the head and played by Hancock behind the other soloists. At m. 16 (4:13), Hancock avoids the pitches related to the G♭Maj7 harmony, instead outlining an FMaj7 harmony. This perhaps was motivated by a desire to avoid what might have been an uncomfortable direct move from the head's G♭Maj7 (m. 16) to E7alt (m. 17). The transcription at mm. 14–16 proposes in parentheses an underlying harmonic progression, showing the omission of G♭Maj7 as part of a longer range and more standard reharmonization. It suggests a move linking A7alt (or E♭7) to D7alt (m. 14), moving to Gmin11 (first half of 15), C7 (second half of m. 15, first half of 16) and FMaj7 (last half of 16). This also affords Hancock a seamless common-tone strategy into the following section and the E7 harmony (m. 17), with G ending the previous m. 16 FMaj7 arpeggiation before forming the ♯9 of the E7alt harmony.

Chapter 2 discussed the accentual shift that occurs at mm. 28–31 within Hancock's longer bop-oriented phrase. This section, which ends his first chorus (4:23), also effects a reharmonization of these final bars of the chorus. The implied harmonies are indicated in parentheses in the transcription, and they show how the reharmonization supports the accentual shift. The pitch material suggests that Hancock bypasses the D♭9(♯11) of m. 29, replacing it with FMaj7 (or Dmin9). Further, Hancock omits the m. 30 Gmin7 harmony. Instead mm. 30–31 elasticizes the 1-bar m. 31 progression (D♭min9 G♭13) from the head into 2 bars. The line comes back in phase with the harmony and the meter at m. 32, as Hancock returns to Fmaj7. The phrase indicates Hancock's ability to move outside the metric frame by using reharmonization to effect the accentual shift.

Hancock's second chorus also offers similar reharmonization techniques in the final 4 bars of each 16-bar section. The melodic line at mm. 47–48 (4:39) implies a progression from D♭min7 to G♭7, overriding the harmony from the head (Gmin7 G♭maj7). And the final bars of Hancock's solo form another reharmonization (4:50): Dmin7 in m. 61 replaces the D♭9(♯11) harmony of the head, and in mm. 62–63 D♭min7 G♭7 is elasticized to appear over 2 bars (rather than the single bar from the head). Here, the phrasing also creates a subtle accentual shift with the groupings anticipating the barlines at mm. 62 and 63 by one beat (shown by brackets).

All these reharmonizations during the final bars of each 16-bar section reveal a supple view of the underlying harmonic progression, and the elasticity is heightened with the use of subtle accentual shifts. There are other aspects to the solo that convey rhythmic elasticity, such as the series of motives (M2a–d) at mm. 57–61 (4:47). Their beginning pitches (A♭–A–B♭–B) shape a longer ascending chromatic line that leads to the C6 at m. 61. Note that the motives begin on the downbeat at mm. 57 and 58, shift to begin on the second beat of m. 59, and shift again to the third beat of m. 60. All these motives create a compelling direction to the solo, enhanced by the elasticized rhythmic shape, as M2b (m. 58) appears one measure following M2a, while M2c and M2d appear five beats after M2b and M2c respectively (mm. 59–60).

Such elasticity calls attention to the degree of rhythmic freedom already attained by Hancock. This freedom sounds unfettered in the context of up-tempo compositions such as "E.S.P.," despite the challenges of the underlying harmonic progression. Here Hancock expresses metrically flexible groupings within the 32-bar composition, with constituent sections of 4, 8, and 16 bars. Its remarkable effortlessness contrasts with Hancock's solo on "R.J." which includes 5-bar phrases. There the odd numbers of bars pose some clear impediments, as the group drops a beat and a half within Hancock's initial chorus. Thus Hancock was still working out the implications of odd-numbered measure groupings at faster tempos. But steeped in the tradition of standard tune compositions, with regular groupings of 4, 8, 16, and 32 bars, Hancock had already developed any number of remarkably elastic strategies for solos that highlighted lyrical motives and flexible reharmonizations, all operating within an eighth-note oriented bop language.

"AGITATION"

"Agitation" is organized more freely than the other compositions on *E.S.P.* Following a spliced-in drum solo that begins the track, the composition features two alternating sections. The first loosely states a tonal center of C minor, the second involves the oscillation of A♭ and D♭ in the bass. Although the head to "Agitation" supports 4-bar sections, the improvisations alternate these sections freely and their lengths vary. The compositional design of two alternating sections—of spontaneously determined length—looks ahead to later Davis compositions, such as "It's About That Time" (*In a Silent Way*, 1969).

The form of the opening head follows. A represents the C minor sections, stated with a syncopated G pedal point in the bass, and B represents the A♭/D♭ bass oscillation. Carter typically effects the change to the B section one measure early.

A1 (4 bars)   A2 (4)   B (4)
A1 (4)   A2 (4)   B (4)
A2 (4)

The composition gives the effect of a loose sketch. The sawtooth contour (alternating primarily descending and ascending motion) of the melody to the A section descends in two waves. The upper pitches of A1's contour consist of the pitches of the C natural minor scale, descending stepwise from G5 (although Davis's opening pitch of his first A1 statement begins with A natural). A2 uses D♭5 and B natural for its initial opening upper pitches (suggesting pitches from the dominant of C minor), before descending stepwise to D4 through the natural minor scale. The B section provides a 4-bar release played by the rhythm section without trumpet melody. Later recorded live versions of "Agitation" (such as the two versions on the *Live at the Plugged Nickel* recordings) abandon the B section with its A♭/D♭ oscillation. With the absence of this contrasting section in these live performances, the solitary 8-bar melody further contributes to the loose sketch quality of the composition.

The head melody to the A1 section begins with the third beat of the measure, as Shorter plays in loose imitation two beats behind. A published transcription of the head and Davis's solo on "Agitation," contained in *Miles Davis Originals Vol. 1*, incorrectly displaces the melody to begin on the downbeat of the measure.[28] As a result the head and solo are similarly displaced two beats for most of the transcription. During the third B section within Davis's solo, the quintet adds three beats (see the following diagram), and the published transcription here and within 7 bars of the following A section migrates its way to correspond with the meter played by the group. (The out head in the transcription is then given its correct metric placement.)

Here is the form for the solo sections:

DAVIS:

A (G pedal): 10 bars (2:23)
B (A♭/D♭): 8 (2:32)
A (Walking bass): 28 (2:39)
B: (A♭/D♭ in dotted quarter notes): 12 (3:04)
A: (Walking bass): 16 (3:14)
B: 14 bars + 3 beats* (3:28)
A: 12 bars + 10 bars (1/2 time) (3:40)
B: 10 (3:59)
A: (Walking bass): 4 (4:08)

SHORTER:

A: (G pedal, dotted half note): 16 (4:11)
B: (A♭/D♭): 16 (4:25)
A: (Walking bass) 40 + (G pedal): 16 (4:38)
B: 16 (5:25)
A: 16 (Walking bass) (5:38)

---

28 *Miles Davis Originals, Vol. 1* (Milwaukee, Wisc.: Hal Leonard, n.d.), 5–9.

A: 16 (Walking bass) + 14 (G pedal) (5:51)
B: (D♭/A♭): 16 + 1 beat* (6:15)
A (Walking bass) 36 + 2 beats* (6:28)
Transition to out head: (G pedal) 11 bars (6:58)

The chart indicates a number of things about the performance. The variable lengths of each A and B section indicate that the group determined them spontaneously during the performance. The number of sections played diminishes with each consecutive solo. The asterisks in the chart indicate where the group adds additional beats to the underlying 4/4 meter, a result of the loose metrical feel of the performance.[29] And also note that the final two solos rely primarily on an underlying hypermeter of 8 and 16 bars. Shorter's solo, in particular, maintains that underlying hypermeter consistently. Thus, despite the clearly spontaneous aspects of the form—and Shorter's remarkably creative improvisation—the group relies during this solo on comfortable and regular hypermetric routines of standard tune improvisation.

Yet even in those sections of regular hypermetric groupings, the results are often remarkable. One example occurs in Shorter's second A section (5:11), during the 16-bar segment with the G pedal point in the bass. Example 3.10 provides a transcription of the saxophone, piano, and bass parts. Against the syncopated bass (played on the second and fourth beats of the measure), Hancock's accompaniment sets forth a modified clave rhythm. But while the *son clave* pattern in a 4/4 meter often appears as a 2-bar cycle of 3 + 3 + 4 + 2 + 4 eighth notes,[30] Hancock's appears differently by stating cycles of 10 eighth notes. Following the initial measure of 3 + 4 + 3 grouping, mm. 2–11 consistently state groupings of 4 + 3 + 3 eighth notes. As a result, the comping pattern reappears every 5 beats, and the larger pattern recurs over five-measure cycles (mm. 1–5, 6–10). Ultimately the comping yields to a more regular grouping of three eighth notes (mm. 13–15).

By the 6th bar, Shorter's solo focuses on the development of a single gesture, one that largely involves upper eighth-note and eighth-note triplet elaborations that descend to a longer pitch, typically a dotted quarter note. The asterisks indicate those longer pitches that appear beginning at m. 6. It

29 These additional beats are not included in either the Coolman or the *Miles Davis Originals* transcriptions.
30 See Christopher Washburne, "The Clave of Jazz: A Caribbean Contribution to the Rhythmic Foundation of an African-American Music," *Black Music Research Journal* 17/1 (1997): 59–80.

EXAMPLE 3.10   Sixteen-Bar A Section during Shorter's Solo on "Agitation" (5:11)

is interesting to hear how many of those longer pitches appear 5 beats apart, and thus seem to respond to Hancock's 5-beat cycles. Most of Shorter's longer pitches in mm. 6–7 (C♯ and F♭) begin at the same time as Hancock's 5-beat cycles. The majority of Shorter's held pitches in mm. 8–12, although displaced from Hancock's groupings, nevertheless create 5-beat cycles.[31]

The passage shows the group's ease in improvising a section with a regular underlying hypermeter of 16 bars. But the groupings within the piano accompaniment and saxophone solo create a profound series of conflicts with the underlying meter. The result is anything but predictable and regular. Further, the passage shows the group's commitment to creating an improvisational space, one that allows the players time to quietly and unhurriedly explore those rhythmic and motivic ideas within the open form.[32]

IN THE DISCUSSION OF MODAL jazz, chapter 2 considered "Agitation," and suggested that its connection to modal jazz arises from its slow harmonic rhythm. Chapter 2 also suggested that—with some exceptions—slow harmonic rhythm was not a consistent feature of the quintet compositions in the same way that it was, for example, in the compositions that the John Coltrane Quartet recorded. Further, a comparison of "Agitation" with any number of recordings by Coltrane's quartet that

---

31 This passage is one of the more problematic ones in Todd Coolman's transcription of "Agitation." See Coolman, "The Miles Davis Quintet of the Mid-1960s: Synthesis of Compositional and Improvisational Elements" (Ph.D. diss., New York University, 1997), 176 (m. 213ff). Much of the passage is displaced by two beats, the piano rhythms are incorrectly realized, and several of the parts are misaligned. Despite its many impressive features, Coolman's "Agitation" transcription contains a number of such problematic passages, including mm. 73–78 (retranscribed here in chapter 2), mm. 276–90 (bass is displaced by a beat), mm. 306–14 (unaligned parts due to additional beats), and mm. 324–41 (piano part is displaced by an eighth note).

32 It is Carter who makes the shift to the B section by replacing the consistently syncopated G pedal of these 16 bars with the motion to the D♭/A♭ bass oscillation. Notice that despite the shift in bass, Hancock's harmonies maintain the C minor orientation of the previous

likewise rely on slow harmonic rhythm reveals some strong aesthetic differences. The Davis quintet is less consistently explosive and explores more regularly a softer dynamic range and a heightened use of space.

These traits are in evidence throughout most of *E.S.P.* It seems that Kenny Dorham's overall dissatisfaction with the recording (in his *Down Beat* review, discussed at the beginning of this chapter) came about in response to those features. It may also be that *E.S.P.* was too strongly detached from the hard bop tradition. Dorham's own album *Una Mas* (recorded in 1963) included both Herbie Hancock and Tony Williams in the rhythm section, and it maintains far more evident ties to hard bop than does *E.S.P.* It was the following studio recording (*Miles Smiles*) that provided the quintet enhanced critical acclaim. It offered novel solutions while at the same time accentuated the quintet's connections to both the hard bop tradition and the avant-garde.

section, creating a subtle clash. Todd Coolman describes a number of such bass/piano clashes in "Agitation," formed by the piano maintaining C minor-oriented harmonies that conflict with the Ab/Db bass during the B section. Coolman, "The Miles Davis Quintet," 61.

CHAPTER 4

MILES SMILES

MILES SMILES, RECORDED OCTOBER 24–25, 1966, followed a difficult year and a half for Davis. Health problems necessitated a hip operation in April 1965 and a follow-up procedure that August. Davis recovered sufficiently to perform live during the fall and winter, most notably the performances from Chicago's *Plugged Nickel* recorded that December. The following month Davis returned to the hospital to treat a liver ailment.

Meanwhile, the interim period was one of the most fertile for the other quintet members, who were consistently at the Rudy Van Gelder studios recording a series of Blue Note albums. Shorter recorded four sessions, ultimately released as *The Soothsayer* (with Carter and Williams, March 1965), *Etcetera* (with Hancock, June 1965), *The All Seeing Eye* (with Hancock and Carter, October 1965), and *Adam's Apple* (with Hancock, February 1966). With its series of maritime-titled compositions—supported by evocative liner notes—Hancock's *Maiden Voyage* (March 1965) was, like *Empyrean*

Isles, a concept album. Recorded with the Davis rhythm section (along with saxophonist George Coleman and trumpeter Freddie Hubbard), its harmonic language, impressionistic textures, and improvisations position *Maiden Voyage* as one of the highlights of the 1960s Blue Note catalog. Tony Williams's *Spring* (with Shorter and Hancock, August 1965) revealed Williams as a prolific composer. All these recordings reflect the intense ferment taking place mid-decade: introspective modal harmony compositions stand cheek-by-jowl with free jazz and assertive postbop.

In comparison with *E.S.P.*, the recorded sound of *Miles Smiles* was decidedly richer, with Davis placed significantly higher in the mix. While the earlier recording was made in the Columbia studio in Los Angeles, *Miles Smiles* was made in Columbia's celebrated 30th St. studio in New York. And for the entire quintet, the music on *Miles Smiles* moved significantly beyond that of *E.S.P.* The album won record of the year in the 1967 *Down Beat* Reader's Poll, a poll that also awarded the quintet first place for best combo, and Davis first place for best trumpeter. Despite his recent health problems, Davis's playing on *Miles Smiles* shows him in impressive control, technically and musically. On *Miles Smiles* the quintet further developed its celebrated sense of airy openness and space. This is the first Davis studio recording on which Hancock stops comping behind entire solos, and his own solos on those compositions ("Orbits," "Dolores," "Ginger Bread Boy") avoid left-hand accompanimental chords.[1] The album offers further challenges to chorus structure, particularly through the use of "time, no changes" on compositions such as "Orbits." "Circle" makes seamless use of an additive form by inserting additional 4-bar sections during the solos. Many of the solos concentrate on motivic improvisation arising from melodic paraphrase. On "Ginger Bread Boy" and "Footprints," the group rethinks conventional attitudes toward the 12-bar blues. With "Ginger Bread Boy," the group transforms Jimmy Heath's 12-bar blues into a 16-bar form. "Footprints" refits a 12-bar minor blues with an unconventional harmonic turnaround, subjecting it to metric modulation that shifts the 6/4 meter into 4/4. For many musicians and critics *Miles Smiles* remains the group's quintessential studio recording, one that best represents the effortless negotiation between the traditional and the experimental.[2]

1 However, these are not Hancock's first solos to avoid traditional left-hand comping. On "Tee" (from Tony Williams's *Spring*) and "Mellifluous Cacophony" (from Sam Rivers's *Contours*), both from 1965, Hancock largely avoids playing with his left hand during his solos.

2 See, for example, Jeremy Yudkin, *Miles Davis, Miles Smiles, and the Invention of Post Bop* (Bloomington: University of Indiana, 2008).

Dan Morgenstern's review of *Miles Smiles*, like Kenny Dorham's *E.S.P.* review, awarded the album 4½ stars.[3] Morgenstern was less stinting in his praise than Dorham. Like Dorham, he called attention to the quintet's relation to the avant-garde. While describing Davis as one of the "spiritual fathers" of the new jazz, he described some similarities between Davis's and Don Cherry's playing. Morgenstern avoided discussing some of the more ragged ensemble passages, such as the melody to the out head of "Dolores." No doubt—as in most assessments of the recording—such problems were easily trumped by the features that Morgenstern did detail: the rhythm section cohesion, the quintet's ability to move from "inside" to "outside," and the high level of improvisational prowess.

"DOLORES"

HEAD

The form to the head of "Dolores" is intriguing. There are three principal sections, consisting of 8 + 6 + 8 measures (Sections A–C). Between these three sections occur 8-bar interludes: these consist only of bass and drums keeping time (Interludes 1 and 2). Shorter's lead sheet copyright deposit contains the melody and chord symbols for the three principal melodic sections, and merely indicates the interlude sections with the instructions "8 ad lib."[4] On the recording the piano does not play during statements of the head (save for during the final head statement at the end of the performance). Overall, then, the form of the opening head statements consists of 38 bars: 8 + 8 (interlude) + 6 + 8 (interlude) + 8. Example 4.1 contains the statement of the head as played during the introductory chorus, along with the bass accompaniment.

The melody throughout all three sections is based nearly entirely on a 2-bar rhythmic motive. The motive contains a melodic overlap, so the ending pitch of one motive forms the beginning pitch of the following. The motive is stated three times during Section A, twice during Section B, and again three times at Section C. The pitch content of Sections A and C is nearly identical, save for the first 2-bar motive (at mm. 1–2 and mm. 31–32).

3   Dan Morgenstern, Review of Miles Davis, *Miles Smiles*, *Down Beat* 34/13 (June 29, 1967): 28.
4   Library of Congress Copyright Deposit Eu 982066 (March 1, 1967).

EXAMPLE 4.1   Opening Head to "Dolores"

Example 4.1 includes the harmonies stated or implied by the bass and melody. (Chords in parentheses, such as at mm. 20–21, are supplied to indicate additional harmonies taken either from Shorter's lead sheet or from the later V.S.O.P. performance of "Dolores," recorded in 1977.[5] Example 4.1 also indicates chord root without chord quality when chord quality is ambiguous.) Two published lead sheet versions of "Dolores" contain harmonic progressions that depart from the recording to greater or lesser degrees, since they do not reflect the harmonies implied by the bass on the recording.[6] Such departures in those lead sheets are due, perhaps, to the absence of piano comping during the head.

What remains unclear are a number of harmonies to the third section (mm. 31–38) since some of the bass pitches are inaudible during mm. 34–35. But it may be possible to determine them based upon Carter's accompaniment during the solos and Shorter's lead sheet (as well as the later V.S.O.P. performance), all of which provide a clue here to the harmonic identity of Section C. All suggest that the harmonies to Section C are those played by Carter during Interlude 2. It is likely that Carter performed Interlude 2 by

5   The recording *The Quintet: V.S.O.P.* included Davis quintet members Shorter, Hancock, Carter, Williams as well as trumpeter Freddie Hubbard (Columbia C2 34976).

6   Yudkin, *Miles Davis*, 105; "Dolores" Lead Sheet, *Jazz Improv* 2/3 (1999): 90.

reading ahead and playing the harmonic progression of Section C from the lead sheet. Only in the final bars of Section C does Carter return to Shorter's notated harmonies.[7] Given all this, a reconstruction of the harmonic progression of the three sections is as follows:

Section A
Dmin   Fmin7 B♭7   E♭Maj7 Amin7 D7 F–11   Amin7(♭5) D7 D♭9sus4
(8 mm.)

Section B
Gmin9 D7   Gmin9   Fmin9   Emin9 E♭
(6 mm.)

Section C
Gmin7 Fmin7 B♭7   E♭Maj7 Amin7 D7 F–11   Amin7(♭5) D7 D♭9sus4
(8 mm.)

Note that Sections A and C differ in their opening harmonies (D minor for Section A; G minor for Section C), but otherwise the two 8-bar sections are indicated similarly. Significantly, both end with the same harmony (D♭9sus4), which provides a prominent formal signpost for the soloists. In the case of Davis, the analysis will show how that D♭sus9 harmony allows him to negotiate the overall A section in his first and second choruses. In the case of Shorter, the tenor saxophone solo begins out of phase with the bass. When Carter plays the D♭ harmony (mm. 19–20), this provides Shorter a signal that allows him to reorient himself in the form and come back into phase with the bass.

IMPROVISATIONS *Ambiguity*

The issue of form during the improvisations is fascinating. It is also the cause of some debate. Yudkin states that the solos "hew to the eight-bar patterns, eschewing the six-bar phrase." Bob Belden states that the underlying metric design beneath the solos is 8 + 8 + 6 + 8. John Szwed suggests that the "soloists do not adhere to any harmonic structure," suggesting an example of "time, no changes."[8]

7   It may be also possible that Carter determined his bass pitches during the solos from Interlude 2, rather than from Section C.
8   Yudkin, *Miles Davis*, 107; Bob Belden, Liner Notes to *Miles Davis Quintet 1965–68* (Columbia 67398), 73; John Szwed, *So What: The Life and Times of Miles Davis* (New York: Simon
and Schuster, 2002), 259.

There is ample reason for the ambiguity. Davis's and Shorter's solos rely on repeated cycles of Sections A, B, C, and do not use the interludes stated in the head. However, the *length* of each of the three sections varies according to the soloist. During the trumpet solo, the bass and trumpet are out of phase. Carter maintains the 8 + 6 + 8 organization from the head, while Davis plays the three sections as 8-bar sections during the solo. proof ?

Shorter, in contrast, maintains the 8 + 6 + 8 division from the head. Although he begins his solo out of phase with the bass, the D♭ harmony supplied by Carter provides an evident harmonic signpost, allowing Shorter to return to phase within the first 20 bars. Hancock's solo, in contrast, does not rely on the three sections. Instead, his solo moves to the "time, no changes" format. Thus the lengths of the underlying formal sections and the formal strategy differ according to the three soloists. Undoubtedly any decisions regarding these improvisational strategies emerged spontaneously during improvisation. Proof ?

The following discussion will focus primarily on Carter's accompaniment and Davis's solo. It shows how both players express Sections A, B, and C of "Dolores," but each is out of phase with one another. It then concludes by regarding the opening to Shorter's solo, showing how he begins out of phase with Carter, but eventually moves in phase.

CARTER. Example 4.2 provides a transcription of the trumpet solo and bass accompaniment. In order to show the different underlying cycles used by Carter and Davis, the transcription labels the beginnings of Sections A–C for Carter and Davis throughout (and provides darker barlines at those sectional divisions). The bassist is completely consistent in upholding the 8 + 6 + 8 bar organization of "Dolores." Carter's handling of the harmonic progression projects "Dolores's" harmonic organization fairly consistently. The transcription provides chord symbols at points in which Carter's note choices conform overtly to the harmonies from the head. (See above for the harmonic scheme to the three sections.) Carter is perhaps most consistent in upholding the E♭ major arrival point at the third measures of Sections A and C. For example, compare mm. 3 and 17 (first chorus), mm. 25 and 39 (second chorus), mm. 47 and 61 (third chorus), and m. 83 (fourth chorus).

Carter is generally but not completely consistent in marking the opening harmony of Dmin for Section A, and Gmin for Sections B and C. The list following the transcription indicates Carter's allegiance to the opening harmonies for Sections A-C within all five choruses of Davis's solo.

EXAMPLE 4.2 Continued

Sections	A	B	C
First chorus (opening harmony expressed)	D (m. 1)	G (m. 9)	G (beat 2, m. 15)
Second chorus	D (23)	G (beat 2, 31)	G (37)
Third chorus	X (45)	G (beat 2, 53)	X (59)
Fourth chorus	X (67)	G (75)	X (81)
Fifth chorus	D (89)		

Further, recall that the head to Sections A and C both end with the harmony of D♭9sus4 for their last 2 bars. Carter's accompaniment expresses this harmony to end the first chorus's Section A (mm. 7–8). Carter plays this harmony at the end of Section C during this chorus (at m. 21). The bass provides this harmony to end the second chorus at the conclusion of the C section (mm. 43–44) and again at the analogous place to end the fourth chorus (mm. 87–88).

Elsewhere, at mm. 67–74, Carter relies on a repeated bass figure for 8 bars to express the A section of his fourth chorus. Carter uses variants of this figure on other studio recordings (for example, see the discussions of "Orbits" and "Ginger Bread Boy" in this chapter), and this idiomatic bass figure (beginning at m. 68) implies a grouping of 3 quarter notes that works in conflict with the underlying 4/4 meter.

DAVIS. All this shows Carter's loose but consistent regard for the underlying harmonies and the 8 + 6 + 8 organization of Sections A–C. Davis's solo expresses a form to "Dolores" out of phase with Carter's 8 + 6 + 8 organization. Instead, his trumpet improvisation expresses consistent 8-bar divisions of the form. We should acknowledge that Davis's adherence to the underlying harmonic structure to "Dolores" is more tenuous than Carter's, however. And certainly Davis's phrase organization is free: not all of these phrases overtly articulate 8-bar divisions. (The transcription appears in example 4.2.)

Nevertheless, despite the freedom of the solo, Davis's voice-leading connections, use of melodic paraphrase, and motives respond to those 8-bar divisions. As a result, the trumpet solo offers a compelling study in hearing how Davis asserts these larger formal divisions. It also illustrates how larger harmonic/voice-leading responses transcend individual chord-to-chord progressions, and instead project across the 8-bar sections. The subsequent discussion will examine the sections indicated in the following list in order to examine how Davis asserts the 8 + 8 + 8 form during his four choruses.

Chorus 1   A section (mm. 1–8, :34)
Chorus 2   A section (mm. 25–32, :55): motivic organization
            B section (mm. 33–40, 1:02): melodic paraphrase
Chorus 3   A section (mm. 49–56, 1:16): motivic organization
            B section (mm. 57–64, 1:23): melodic paraphrase
Chorus 4   A section (mm. 73–80, 1:37): motivic organization

Davis does not clearly articulate all formal divisions, but he uses a motivic orientation in his solo at the top of the form—the A sections—during Choruses 2–4, and melodic paraphrase at the beginning of the B sections during his second and third chorus.

The first two A sections offer an interesting comparison. In both cases, Davis relies on a similar voice-leading path. We can hear this path as an abstraction of the harmonic progression from the beginning and ending of each A section, which opens with D minor, and concludes with D♭9sus4 during the last two measures of the section. In those two instances, the uppermost pitches of Davis's Section A (mm. 1–8 and 25–32) create a long-range voice-leading maneuver that moves from A5 to A♭5 across the eight measure sections, reflecting the overarching harmonic motion from D minor to D♭9sus4.

This voice leading happens in a slightly different manner each time. In the first A section Davis overtly expresses the D minor harmony by leading from D5 to A5 at mm. 1–2. He returns to this register at m. 7, following an overall contour descent mm. 3–4 and ascent mm. 5–6. At m. 7 Davis sustains A♭ as the uppermost goal pitch of the previous ascent. (The connection of A5 to A♭5 is shown with a dotted slur in the transcription.) This pitch coincides with the harmonic motion to D♭9sus4. As a result, even while the intervening pitch material does not expressly outline the underlying harmonic organization, the longer range pacing responds to the larger harmonic progression from D minor at m. 1 to D♭9sus4 at m. 7, using the voice-leading move from A5 to A♭5. The result might be described as playing "over" rather than "inside" the harmonic progression: Davis does not painstakingly negotiate all the harmonies of the underlying progression, but the melodic material responds to those harmonies at the beginning and end of the 8-bar section.

Davis offers a related voice-leading path at the beginning of the A section to his second chorus. Here, however, the pacing differs. This chorus begins with a series of related motives at mm. 25–28, indicated as M1a–c in the score. M1a states G5 twice, anticipating the beginning of the chorus. Davis echoes the rhythm of M1a at M1b (m. 26), and this statement alters the original motive in several ways. M1b begins instead with a stepwise ascent (F5–G5), it contains an additional third pitch that repeats G5, and it appears on the metric downbeat rather than mid-measure. M1c (mm. 27–28) further elaborates the motive. The rhythm at m. 28 echoes the three-pitch rhythm heard at 26, but differs both by reversing the contour (A5–G5) and by preceding these pitches with D–G at m. 27.

At m. 29 Davis begins the next phrase by sustaining A♭5. Thus, like the first A section, the voice-leading path expresses A5 to A♭5. Here, however, those two pitches appear in consecutive measures, at mm. 28 and 29, and the A5 emerges through a series of motives that begin with G5 (mm. 25–27) before reaching A5 at m. 28. The longer range pacing places A♭ as a pitch goal to stand for the D♭9sus4. But now Davis attains the pitch goal in the fifth measure of the 8-bar section rather than the seventh. Davis therefore abstracts the harmonic motion in this chorus further, replacing the 6 + 2 bar organization of his first chorus with a 4 + 4 organization in this second chorus.

The passage warrants further observations about Davis's use of melodic motives here. First, it suggests that Davis in this instance launches a series of motives that begin at (or just before) the top of the form, and this projects an underlying 24-bar form. Such motives, which depart from the largely eighth-note orientation of the solo, emerge in this solo at the beginnings of choruses. Although Davis's previous 24-bar chorus did not set up a significant amount of internal formal signposts, nor reflected overtly the harmonic organization, Davis's move to motivic organization highlights the return to the top of the A section. Thus these motives occur not abstractly but against the backdrop of form, appearing at the onset of the chorus.

Second, although this motivic organization appears as something new by departing from the previous eighth-note orientation of the solo, it also emerges as the result of the previous phrase. That is, the overall ascent begun at the end of m. 22 and into m. 23 creates motion that connects stepwise from the F5 of m. 23 to the first pitch G5 of M1a at mm. 24–5. The result may be heard as a phrase overlap (discussed in chapter 2). M1a thus acts out two roles: its opening pitch forms the goal or conclusion of the previous idea, and it launches a series of related motives. Not only does the motive illuminate the top of the form, it emerges from earlier material. This becomes a consistent technique in the solo. Each of Davis's subsequent choruses similarly begins with a series of clear motivic relationships, in which the opening pitches flow from previous material.

The following B section involves a patent paraphrase of the B section melody from the head. This takes place at m. 33, immediately following the previous 8-bar A section, a clear response to the B section.

Davis's third chorus, like the second, relies on a series of related motives begun at the top of the form. Here they begin at m. 49. And as in the previous chorus, the melodic ideas here create an overlap. D5 forms the end of the previous phrase. But that pitch also becomes the central pitch for the subsequent six measures, consisting primarily of a departure/return from and to that D5. M2a consists solely of the pitch D5, heard at the downbeat of the section at m. 49. M2b elaborates that further, by preceding that pitch with F♯, and by stating D5 twice at m. 51. And M2c ascends chromatically to E5 before returning back to D5. Here again the motivic organization establishes the top of the form, and it begins via overlap, concluding the material from the previous phrase.

The subsequent section, like the B section to Davis's second chorus, paraphrases the B section melody, beginning in the middle of m. 57. Again, it marks the form in evident fashion.

And Davis's final fourth chorus (beginning at mm. 73) again uses motivic organization at the top of the form. Here Davis states two motives, related by pitch. M3a (mm. 73–74) embellishes F5 with G5 before returning to F and descending further, to E♭5. Motive M3b telescopes the F–G–F motion at m. 75–76, before altering the pitches further. Here again, Davis reworks a motive to initiate a chorus (his fourth).

And again, this motive emerges from the previous chorus. Yet the link here is attenuated. In this instance, the F–G–F pitch motive of M3a and M3b restates the pitches that concluded Davis's previous phrase at m. 70 (shown with a dashed bracket). In contrast to earlier examples, Davis uses a significant degree of space between the previous phrase and the following motive (M3). Davis does not paraphrase the melody to Section B in this fourth chorus.

All the above suggests a loose interpretation of the form. Yet as described above, the broader outlines of the solo reveal an underlying 8-bar organization for the three sections. Davis uses motivic organization to initiate his 24-bar choruses, and melodic paraphrase to inaugurate the B sections to his second and third choruses. These reveal the specific ways in which Davis's material projects an underlying formal organization of 8 + 8 + 8 bars. Elsewhere Davis's phrasing and pitch material do not mark the form in as clear a fashion, heightening the formal ambiguity.

Further, the conclusion of Davis's solo is ambiguous. It is not clear whether the material following M3a and M3b continues to refer to an underlying form. Davis ends his solo 5 bars into his C section, which begins at m. 89. Carter, who has been hewing to the underlying 8 + 6 + 8 organization, begins the top of his fifth chorus at m. 89. This is to have interesting implications for Shorter's solo that follows.

SHORTER. Shorter's improvisation returns to the 8 + 6 + 8 organization derived from the head for Sections A–C. But his solo begins out of phase with Carter (1:55). A transcription of the opening to the saxophone solo and the bass accompaniment appears as example 4.3. The formal ambiguity at the end of Davis's solo and the overlapping solos (Shorter begins his solo the same measure Davis completes his) causes some slippage in the bass accompaniment. Carter's accompaniment is ambiguous for the opening 6 bars, and he reorients himself to the form by beginning Section B at m. 7 of Shorter's solo. (Thus Carter adds 2 bars to his A section the end of Davis's solo and beginning of Shorter's.)

Within 20 bars, Shorter reorients his place in the form to bring his solo into phase with Carter. This alteration is subtle but reflects serious focused listening and adaptability. Shorter carefully negotiates and expresses the D♭9sus4 harmony that concludes his first A section (mm. 7–8, 2:00). And it is Carter's use of this harmony in the bars following that seems to cue Shorter's reorientation of the form. This occurs at mm.

EXAMPLE 4.3   Mm 1–35 of Shorter's Solo on "Dolores" (1:55)

19–20 (2:10). Here, Carter uses double stops to express the D♭9sus4 harmony, and Shorter responds to this harmony by abandoning his own formal design and reconfiguring it to Carter's. By m. 21 both players are in phase, and both begin the top of a new chorus there.

Eight bars later, Shorter marks the beginning of the B section by paraphrasing the melody (m. 29, 2:19). Like Davis, Shorter marks the form by referring to the B section melody in two consecutive choruses. (The melodic paraphrase in Shorter's second chorus, mm. 51–56, is discussed in chapter 2.) The remainder of the solo is not included here, but the following outlines how Shorter adheres to the 8 + 6 + 8 organization, including his adjustment to Carter's place in the form at mm. 19–20. Shorter plays four choruses.

M. 1   Section A (out of phase with Carter, 1:55)
M. 9   Section B (out of phase with Carter, 2:01)
M. 15   Section C (Shorter foreshortens this section, coming into phase with Carter, 2:07)
M. 21   A (solo now in phase with Carter, 2:12)
M. 29   B (melodic paraphrase of B, 2:19)
M. 35   C (2:24)
M. 43   A (2:31)
M. 51   B (melodic paraphrase of B, 2:38)
M. 57   C (melodic paraphrase of C, 2:43)
M. 65   A (2:50)
M. 73   B (2:57)
M. 79   C (melodic paraphrase of C, 3:02; solo ends in first measure at the top of the next chorus)

Shorter later responded to a question about the basis for improvisation by individual group members for "Dolores": "I think what happened there, I'm pretty sure, is that everyone who played, after the melody and all of that stuff, took a portion of a certain characteristic of the song and—you can stay there. And then you do eight measures of it, and then you make your own harmonic road or avenue with a certain eight measures."[9]

Shorter's comments are intriguing. Although they seem to describe more generally the "time, no changes" approach for "Orbits" rather than the underlying path taken during the improvisations to "Dolores," they may also point to the distinct ways in which each soloist interpreted the form. This discussion of improvisational form began by acknowledging a disparity among different analysts of "Dolores." Yudkin suggested consistent 8-bar phrases, Belden an underlying form of 8/8/6/8. Szwed, relying on Shorter's comments above, suggested no consistent underlying form or harmonic structure. In some ways all are correct, or—more precisely—all point to different features of different solos. Davis's solo and Carter's accompaniment to it both rely on chorus structure but use different hypermetric cycles. Shorter's solo and Carter's accompaniment show the effect of form as a process that requires reevaluation in response to other players since both are relying on the same underlying formal design that begins out of phase. Hancock's solo does not express an underlying chorus structure, but instead provides an example of "time, no changes." All this repudiates common assumptions of form in improvisation and chorus structure, and suggests instead the idea of form as an ongoing process evaluated differently by each soloist.

"ORBITS"

HEAD. The recording of "Orbits" provides one of the primary examples of "time, no changes" for the quintet. The melodic material also seems to have encouraged the soloists to play motivically, and to derive many of their motives from the composition's melody. On "Orbits" the piano avoids comping throughout the recording and Hancock's single-line improvisation thus operates as a third horn. Williams's accompaniment frequently creates a metrical conflict by expressing a level of 3/8 meter, stating dotted quarter notes on the rim of the snare drum. Example 4.4 provides a transcription of the head to "Orbits."

Shorter called attention to the built-in "false start" of "Orbits."[10] The introductory material centers on a pair of related phrases (mm. 1–4) punctuated by bass and drums. Shorter's lead sheet deposit indicates these introductory measures in 6/4. In his analysis to "Orbits," Steven

---

9 Eric Nemeyer, "The Magical Journey: An Interview with Wayne Shorter," *Jazz Improv* 2/3 (1999): 75.
10 Conrad Silvert, "Wayne Shorter: Imagination Unlimited," *Down Beat* 44/13 (July 14, 1977): 58.

EXAMPLE 4.4   Opening Head to "Orbits"

Strunk suggests that the melody pitches in these opening measures alternate F major (with the pitches A–F–B♭–A–G–F) and G♭ major (G♭–B♭–D♭).[11] However, the bass does not imply F major in mm. 1–4 since it twice descends C–A–A♭–G. Only mm. 5–7 more clearly suggest F major as the bass drops out.

Following the introduction, the material of the chorus begins with the pickup to m. 8, but here without consistent bass and drum accompaniment (which begins only at m. 14). The melodic material at mm. 14–15

11   Steven Strunk, "Notes on Harmony in Wayne Shorter's Compositions, 1964–67," *Journal of Music Theory* 49/2 (Fall 2005): 323.

EXAMPLE 4.4   Continued

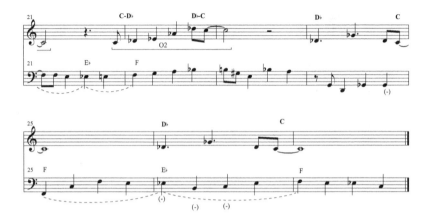

begins as a transposition of that heard at mm. 8–9. One writer describes the melodic material throughout the chorus as setting up a series of "wave" shapes, whose contour alternates ascending and descending motion.[12]

These wave shapes throughout the chorus explore the interval of a perfect fourth in several different ways. This treatment of the fourth differs from that heard in "E.S.P.," which arpeggiated three fixed pitches of that interval. Here instead perfect fourth arpeggiations spiral downward chromatically. At mm. 8–13, following the initial ascending arpeggiation (A–C♯–F–A♭), this perfect fourth wave motion arpeggiates three perfect fourth chords, progressing from G–D–A (descending fourths, m. 9), A♭–D♭–G♭ (ascending fourths, m. 10), to F–C (descending fourth, m. 11). (Brackets indicate these waves in the transcription.) This last could imply continuation to G in order to complete the m. 11 F–C descent, and then on to an ascent of F♯–B–E. However, the sequential pattern is momentarily disrupted (D♯–G♯, mm. 11–12) before recontinuing with F♯–B–E (m. 12).

12 Yudkin, *Miles Davis*, 73.

The conclusion of this section now introduces a crucial component of the melodic design. Rather than maintaining a downward spiral of arpeggiated perfect fourths, Shorter resolves the phrase upward a half step, to F at m. 13. Note that this F echoes that heard 2–3 bars earlier (stated at the end of m. 10). But while F appeared there through downward half-step motion (G♭–F, mm. 10–11), it comes about through upward half-step motion (E–F, mm. 12–13). Both converge on F via half-step motion in either direction.

The melody beginning with the pickup into m. 14 initially transposes mm. 8–9 up a perfect fourth. But the alterations in mm. 8–13 now make C the focal pitch of these measures. Initially it comes about through a similar sort of convergence process that highlighted F in mm. 10–13. Downward half-step motion moves into C (m. 15); upward half-step motion into C (pickup to m. 17).

The continuation of the melody for the final measures (mm. 18–27) preserves C as the focal melodic pitch and D♭ embellishes this C in two different manners. First, D♭4 (at downbeats of m. 18 and 22), preceded by C4, is then projected up an octave through a perfect-fourth arpeggiation (E♭4–A♭4–D♭5), before returning to C, now C5. Second, D♭4 and its perfect fourth embellishment (G♭4, mm. 20, 24, and 26) precede and embellish the C4 arrival at mm. 21, 25, and 27.

The melodic material throughout mm. 14–27 provides the primary motives used in the improvisations. The transcription labels two principal motives as O1 (mm. 20–21) and O2 (mm. 22–23). Subsequent discussion of the solos will use those labels to indicate melodic paraphrase.

The Real Book includes a lead sheet to "Orbits," although the rhythmic design of the melody at mm. 1–13 departs drastically from the way in which the quintet performed it on *Miles Smiles*.[13] Further, the *Real Book* provides a harmonic progression that rarely matches the bass pitches played by Carter on the recording, on either the initial head or the final chorus.[14]

---

13 *The Real Book*, 6th ed. (Milwaukee, Wisc.: Hal Leonard, n.d.), 316. The melody provided by Yudkin matches the *Real Book* melody closely. Yudkin, *Miles Davis*, 71.

14 Many of the chords in the *Real Book* version match the chords to Shorter's copyright deposit lead sheet. Library of Congress Copyright Deposit Eu 982064 (March 1, 1967). The difference between those versions and the recorded version suggests that the group drastically altered the lead sheet version in the studio or did not use that lead sheet version.

Despite the consistent walking bass during mm. 14–27, the harmonic implications of this section are not especially clear.[15] The transcription suggests some possibilities. The opening three measures of the walking bass section (mm. 14–16) perhaps imply C major. The bass at mm. 18–20 perhaps implies G minor, elaborated with D at m. 19. Other harmonic implications revolve around the alternation of F and E♭. The bass implies this progression at the two-beat level (mm. 21–downbeat of 22) and at the measure level (mm. 25–27). The coincidence of F with the melody pitch C at the downbeats of mm. 21, 25, and 27 all support Jeremy Yudkin's claim that the harmonic goal is F.[16] This is true for the opening head statement. However, Carter's bass accompaniment during the out head does not maintain that harmonic goal.

IMPROVISATIONS

For the second quintet, "Orbits" stands as the quintessential representative of motivic improvisation based on the melody to the composition. The improvisations rely on melodic paraphrase and transformations of motives from the head, heard throughout but especially at the beginnings and endings of solos. Given the context of "time, no changes" during the improvisations, the head's perfect-fourth-based motivic structure seems to have invited the soloists to build portions of their solo through that material. These motivic sections alternate with more characteristic eighth-note bop phrasing. There is no piano comping (even during the piano solo, which avoids left-hand chords), adding to the open quality of the performance. The walking bass accompaniment during improvisations is free, and does not adhere to an underlying harmonic framework in the same way that "Dolores" does. Nevertheless, the following discussion will point out how Carter occasionally responds to the motives of the head.

We begin by highlighting the use of motives from the head at the end of Davis's solo, which then motivates the beginning of Shorter's solo. The primary focus is on Shorter's solo, particularly the spontaneous development of motives derived from the melody. The discussion also indicates how the beginning of Hancock's solo emerges from the end of Shorter's. Example 4.5 provides a transcription of the end of Davis's solo, Shorter's solo, the beginning of Hancock's solo, and the bass accompaniment.

15 Carter's accompaniment does not seem to have been motivated by the harmonies from Shorter's lead sheet. Strunk examines the harmonic progression from Shorter's lead sheet and the *Real Book*, but does not examine Carter's bass part from the recording to deduce the harmonies. Strunk, "Notes on Harmony," 323–26.

16 Yudkin, *Miles Davis*, 73.

EXAMPLE 4.5   End of Davis Solo, Shorter's Solo, and Beginning of Hancock's Solo on "Orbits"

EXAMPLE 4.5   Continued

Certainly the practice of initiating a solo by referring to musical ideas stated by the previous soloist was not new to the Davis Quintet, or to jazz practice in general. Chapter 2 discussed these types of motivic links between solos in "Hand Jive." Chapter 3 showed how Hancock began his improvisation on "E.S.P." with material derived from the end of Davis's solo. On "Orbits," the melodic material that begins and ends solos is derived from the composition's melody.

Example 4.5 begins with the last 14 bars of Davis's solo. Davis ends his solo by referring to Motives O1 and O2. (The lead sheet in example 4.4 includes these motivic labels at mm. 20–23.) This includes a truncated version of O1 (m. 68–69, 1:28), now rhythmically displaced from the original, followed by an embellished version of O2 stated via ascending eighth notes at mm. 70–71. (The transcription highlights D♭4–A♭4–D♭5–C5 from O2. Davis's statement does not include the first pitch, C, or the third pitch, E♭4, from O2.) Davis repeats variations of both O1 and O2 again (mm. 72–75), consisting now of a complete statement of O1, and an embellished eighth-note version of O2. Davis's solo finishes with O1.

Shorter's solo features numerous allusions to O1 and O2, as well as other portions of the melody, appearing at mm. 1–5, mm. 29–30, 40–58, and 65–71. These alternate with more standard eighth-note bebop phrases, and other motivic ideas that Shorter uses and develops, typically over the course of 6–8 measures.

Shorter's solo begins (1:37) by alluding to O1, with which Davis ended his solo. Here, however, Shorter transforms the motive by inverting the placement of its first three pitches. Davis's D♭–G♭–D♭–C is now altered to G♭–D♭–G♭–F. Thus the final half-step D♭–C descent from O2 is transferred to Shorter's upper pitch, becoming G♭–F (in m. 1 of Shorter's solo). Here the motive becomes abstracted. The original O2 form as "perfect fourth and half-step embellishment of the lower pitch" (D♭–G♭–D♭–C) now becomes "perfect fourth and half-step embellishment of upper pitch" (G♭–D♭–G♭–F). And we can consider the larger shape of mm. 1–4 as a further abstraction. By widening the opening intervallic boundary G♭–D♭ (m. 1) to C–G (mm. 3–4), the motive now becomes "perfect fourth (D♭–G♭) and half-step embellishment of each pitch."

The second allusion to the O motive in Shorter's solo appears at mm. 29–30. It is set up in a compelling manner. It is preceded by an eight-measure passage (mm. 20–27, 1:54) that explores its own two-note motive. The score numbers each instance of the two-note figure as 1–9. The initial four instances appear mm. 20–24. Note, too, that the initial statement 1 emerges at the ending of a previous melodic idea, forming a phrase overlap (see chapter 2 for a discussion of phrase overlap) at m. 20: C ends the previous gesture and launches the series of nine two-note motives. Shorter playfully answers the first two-note figure, C–B♭ (m. 20) in successive measures with ascending two-note figures: A♭–D♭, B–E♭, F–B♭ (the latter embellished with a chromatic ascent). The following four measures continue these two-note figures, and Shorter states five versions of the ascending two-note idea (indicated as 5–9 on the score) during mm. 24–27. But while Shorter initiated each version of Figures 1–4 on downbeats of each measure, at 5–9 he accelerates the figures, foreshortening the distance between each.

Although Shorter compresses the rhythmic values between Figures 5–9, he expands the intervallic distance. Five spans a minor third, 6 a perfect fourth (notated as an augmented third), 7 a minor sixth, 8 a major seventh, and Figure 9 a minor ninth (notated as D♭4–D5). The overall shape of Figures 5–9 creates a sawtooth motion, with each successive pitch of mm. 24–27 alternating ascending and descending motion. These consistent contour shifts allow Figures 5–9 to be heard as related, despite the rhythmic compression and intervallic expansion that takes place in those measures. Further, Shorter projects Figures 1–9 during the course of eight measures. But as a result of the rhythmic compression and intervallic expansion at Figures 5–9, the effect of this underlying 8-bar section sounds anything but regular or predictable. And the following bar of silence (m. 28) in Shorter's solo creates a dramatic rupture between the previous material and the allusion to the O motive at mm. 29–30.

In addition to these instances of the O Motive, Shorter features an extended allusion to the melody to "Orbits" at mm. 40–58 (2:12). Measures 40–43 paraphrase mm. 9–11 of the melody, consisting of the identical fourth-chord wave motions that descend chromatically: G–D–A (descending), A♭–D–G♭ (ascending; here Shorter does not precisely preserve the fourths), and F–C–G (descending). Measures 44–45 paraphrase mm. 15–16 from the melody, consisting of the pickup D♭ that leads to C–G–D (descending) and C♯–F♯–B (ascending). And as Shorter ends the melodic paraphrase, he continues to pursue the implications of the perfect fourth waves. The brackets in the transcription mm. 46–51 show the ways in which Shorter spins out the wave motions: though fourth chords (mm. 46–47), alternation of perfect fourths and fifths (mm. 48–49), half-step elaboration of the perfect fourths/fifths (mm. 49–50), and finally a perfect fourth arpeggiation (m. 51). All show Shorter's commitment to using the wave motions as an underlying thread throughout the portion of his improvisation.

Shorter continues to derive successive material from O1 and O2, quoting both motives at mm. 53–56 (2:24). He returns to O2 to complete his solo (mm. 65–71), following the 2-bar sawtooth contour of mm. 63–65 (2:33). The use of the contour there is similar to that heard in mm. 24–27. The material exclusively alternates ascending and descending motion, beginning with E3 (m. 63) and concluding with G♭4 (m. 65). Note the relationship of the up/down contour with the three note groupings during the final six pitches at mm. 64–65 (shown with dashed brackets). Despite the consistent up/down contour, the three-note groupings reverse the contour for both sets of three pitches: F♯–D–G (–+) is followed by E♭–A♭–G♭ (+–). (Here + refers to an ascending contour, – to a descending contour.) After the two statements of O2 at mm. 65–67 and 68–69, Shorter transforms the motive to conclude his solo (mm. 70–71).

The emphasis here on motivic improvisation should not detract from Shorter's reliance on bop-oriented phrasing throughout much of the solo. Many of these passages, but by no means all, project a four-flat environment. It is also possible to hear some passages as expressing an underlying harmonic progression in relatively conventional hard bop fashion. For example, mm. 34–35 can be heard to imply A♭Maj7 (m. 34) to A♭min9 (m. 35). Also notable is the use of motivic growth processes, in which successive related motivic ideas appear increasingly lengthened. Chapter 2 examined mm. 12–18, which contain four related motives whose length and intervallic span increases.

A few points about Carter's accompaniment are in order. The term "time, no changes" is perhaps a misnomer, since the bass accompaniment frequently provides "changes" by outlining harmonic progressions in traditional ways. Measures 19–22 (1:54) provide an example of a conventional accompanimental scheme, with each measure expressing roots and fifths of implied harmonies that progress F, E, D♭, and B. Carter's expanded D major accompaniment in mm. 27–30 (2:01) sounds a remarkable backdrop for Shorter's transformation of the O motive. His pitches D♭/C♯, A♭/G♯, and G♭/F♯ of m. 29 sound as major 7th, ♯11th, and 3rd of Carter's D major accompaniment, before the motive then shifts to the minor 7th, C.

But perhaps the most astounding detail about Carter's accompaniment surrounds the places in which the bass accompaniment responds to the O motive. It may be that Carter's downward arpeggiations of perfect fourths, such as at mm. 2 and 6, are conventions of bass accompaniment rather than motivated by the perfect fourth melodic structure of "Orbits." But there are accompanimental passages that outline at the measure level the focal D♭–C motion of O1. And they do this in the immediate context of Shorter's use of the motive in his solo. Not only do the downbeat pitches of mm. 5 and 6 express this D♭–C motion (1:41), but note the downbeat pitches at mm. 53–56 (2:24). In these 4 bars there is a notable coincidence of those downbeat pitches with Shorter's. This suggests several examples in which Carter, even while outlining harmonies in conventional fashion, nevertheless participates in the motivic game by alluding to the D♭–C features of the O motive from the melody to "Orbits."

Hancock's solo begins (2:43) by responding to Shorter's transformation of the O1 motive at mm. 70–71, which alters the pitches of the motive to F♯4–C♯4–F♯3–A3. Shorter's ending pitch of A3 then becomes the focus for the beginning of Hancock's solo, which now transposes O1 to begin with that same pitch. This is an evidently audible response to the end of Shorter's solo, one that reflects concentrated listening on Hancock's part. And Hancock's subsequent phrase makes a more oblique reference to the O1 motive. The final four pitches of his mm. 3–4 phrase (D–G–D–C♯) form another version of the O1 motive. Now, however, the motive begins on D and its rhythm is altered.

In his assessment of "Orbits," Chambers states that the three solos are all "apparently unrelated in mood, style, and melody."[17] On the contrary, the composition is perhaps the primary exemplar of motivic improvisation for the entire ensemble. In particular, the motive becomes an important reference point at the seams between the improvisations. Much as Shorter began his solo in response to Davis's statement of the O motives, Hancock does the same and transposes the motive in response to the end of Shorter's solo. In the context of "time, no changes," all the solos orient themselves to the O motive, and its use in the improvisations decisively links the solos. The motive's consistent recirculation shows the manner in which the quintet regarded motivic improvisation as a fundamental improvisational premise.

"CIRCLE"

In his *Down Beat* review of *Miles Smiles*, Dan Morgenstern described "Circle" as a masterpiece; Frank Tirro regards it as one of the "great performances of the decade."[18] It is hard to disagree with either. In a deeply

---

17 Jack Chambers, *Milestones: The Music and Times of Miles Davis* 2 (New York: Da Capo, 1998), 99. Originally publ. University of Toronto, 1983 and 1985.

18 Morgenstern, Review, 28; Frank Tirro, *Jazz: A History*, 2nd ed. (New York: W. W. Norton, 1993), 54.

dramatic performance, this jazz waltz captures the essence of Davis's (and the quintet's) fragile lyricism and highlights the group's dynamic range and use of space. In superficial ways "Circle" resorts to a convention for Davis. The now-familiar D minor environment recalls earlier Davis compositions, including "So What" (*Kind of Blue*, 1959), and the spate of D minor compositions on his 1957 soundtrack to *Ascenseur pour l'échafaud*—"Nuit sur les Champs-Élysées—Générique," "Florence sur les Champs-Élysées," "Au bar du petit bac," and "Chez le photographe du motel." That key figures in even earlier nonoriginal compositions recorded by Davis, such as "Dear Old Stockholm" (itself the likely model for the "Ascenseur" compositions listed above, *'Round About Midnight*, 1956). Most of these D minor compositions spotlight the plaintive wistful character of Davis's sound.

But in other ways "Circle" reflects many of the second quintet's emerging compositional principles. It continues the group's use of pedal point harmonies, slash chord harmonies, and nonsyntactic harmonies (such as the D(Maj7)/E♭ triad that occurs at m. 5). But perhaps the most unusual aspect to "Circle" takes place during the improvisations. There the players make use of an additive form. That is, the group inserts sections during the improvisation that do not occur during the 22-bar statement of the head. This formal strategy differs from all others done by the quintet on the studio recordings.

HEAD

The head begins with a 22-bar form, consisting of four sections of 6 + 4 + 8 + 4 measures. The group abandons the final 4 bars at the end of Shorter's and Hancock's solos, so employs these measures as a detachable tag. Thus the following diagram designates an 18-bar A section (consisting of A1, A2, and A3) as well as a final 4-bar section T (tag):

A1 (6 mm.)	D–(with E)	Dmin9	Dmin6	B♭Maj7	D(Maj7)/E♭ triad	D7alt		
A2 (4 mm.)	GMaj7/B	CMaj7/B	GMaj7/B	GMaj7/B				
A3 (8 mm.)	GMaj7/F♯	A♭Maj7/G	G/A		F(Maj7)/A	Asus		DMaj7♯11
T (4 mm.)	B♭Maj7♯11		Emin7(♭5) (or E7alt)	A7alt				

The overall D minor tonality established in the first 3 bars gives way to a harmonic progression notable for the nonstandard harmony at m. 5, probably best indicated as a D triad (or, at times, DMaj7) above an E♭ triad. The slash chord harmonies of A2 place this section in the sphere of earlier compositions by the quintet with extended pedal points, such as "Little One," and "R.J." A3 begins with ascending bass motion from F♯–A that returns to D. The Asus harmony in A3 is usually played in a particular fashion by Hancock, almost always with a thin texture, typically a dyad or single note. A3 ends with a return to D, but now with a modal shift to DMaj7♯11. The T section is a harmonic turnaround that propels the harmony back to the top of the form: B♭ Maj7, E7min7(♭5) (or E7alt), A7alt.[19]

During the improvisations, "Circle" takes on heightened formal flexibility with the group's use of sections inserted in between A and T. There are two such inserted sections, designated here as i1 and i2. Each *4 bars* maintains a consistent harmonic progression, so they undoubtedly were provided to the musicians at the recording studio. However, while the insertions consistently appear between A and T, the group is flexible regarding the use of one, both, or neither. Given that degree of uncertainty, the use of inserted sections offers a significant challenge for group improvisation. The result is a departure from typical chorus structure practices, and shows Davis's interest in offering different formal solutions arising through spontaneous challenges.

Insertion 1 (i1) is 4 bars, consisting of chromatic bass motion from G–G♭–F. Hancock typically plays a fourth-chord harmony over the G bass (G–C–F) the first measure, C major/G♭ the second, an F dominant harmony for the final 2 bars. Insertion 2 (i2) consists of the bass motion C–F for 4 bars, with the harmony progressing Cmin9 to F13(♭9). Notice that both insertions conclude with an F dominant chord. Since these insertions appear always between the end of A and the beginning of T, they both lead conventionally to T: the F7 harmony that ends each inserted section progresses to the B♭Maj7♯11 that begins T. Because of this conventional harmonic progression, it is interesting to speculate whether i1 and i2 initially were somehow part of the composition's head, and later omitted from the head and left to be inserted during solos. The insertions during the improvisations alter the underlying 22-bar form stated during the head. The overall form during the composition is as in table 4.1.[20]

---

19 A number of the harmonies provided by Tirro and Yudkin do not correspond particularly well with those used on the recording. See Tirro, *Jazz*, 53–55; Yudkin, *Miles Davis*, 79.

20 Both Tirro's and Yudkin's descriptions of the form are inaccurate. See Tirro, *Jazz*, 55, and Yudkin, *Miles Davis*, 79–80.

TABLE 4.1   Form during "Circle"

DAVIS

Head	First chorus (:29)	Second chorus (1:02)
A (18 bars)	A (18 bars)	A (18)
T (4 bars)	i1 (4 bars)	
	T (4 bars)	

SHORTER

(completes Davis's second chorus)	First complete chorus	Second chorus
(1:24)	(1:39)	(2:11)
i1 (4 bars)	A (18)	A (18)
i2 (4 bars)	i2 (4)	
T (4 bars)	T (4)	

HANCOCK

First chorus	Second chorus	Third chorus	Fourth chorus
(2:34)	(3:02)	(3:35)	(4:14)
A (18)	A (18)	A (18)	A (18)
T (4)	i2 (4)	i1 (4)	
	T (4)	i2 (4)	
		T (4)	

Final head (Davis)

(4:38)

A (18)

Pedal D outro (5:00; Hancock plays harmonic progression of A section over D pedal)

It is likely that the end of each solo was originally predetermined to take place at the end of A. Thus each soloist's final chorus would suppress the tag, with the subsequent solo returning to A. Shorter's and Hancock's solos both do this, and the result is that the DMaj7($\sharp$11) harmony heard at the end of A then links immediately back to D minor at the top of the form, coinciding with the beginning of the new solo. However, Davis's solo differs. It ends at A, but now—rather than returning back to the top of the form—Shorter's solo begins with both inserted sections played successively (i1 and i2). This may have been a deviation from a predeter-mined aspect of the form, since both Shorter's and Hancock's solos are consistent. Both conclude by suppressing the 4-bar tag.

But the use of inserted sections is not generally consistent. Davis's solo includes a statement of i1 (4 bars) in his first chorus. Shorter's solo begins by combining i1 and i2 (8 bars) at the top of his solo, and includes i2 in his first complete chorus. There is no insertion dur-ing Hancock's first chorus, but i2 appears in the second chorus, and the group combines i1 and i2 in the third. Despite this flexibility, the insertions appear seamlessly, and the group negotiates the challenge elegantly.

It is possible that the end of Hancock's solo might not have ended so smoothly in returning to the head; perhaps the group missed a cue or different players moved to a different place in the form. Certainly the recording suggests a splice inserted between the end of Hancock's solo and Davis's return to the head. The accompanying instruments are mixed down here, the drum kick in the final measure of Hancock's solo sounds uncharacteristic, and probably operated as a cue from a different take. Additionally, there is an extra beat inserted between Williams's drum kick and Davis's return to the melody. This drum kick occurs on the third beat during the final measure of Hancock's solo, providing an additional beat that creates a 4/4 bar. Since the time and form here are relatively unambiguous in this portion of the performance, it seems unlikely that the group would add a beat here. The use of an editing splice here would imply that the group negotiated "Circle's" formal challenges up until this point.

The title "Circle," of course, calls attention to its circular nature, and the composition was one of numerous circular compositions that arose during the 1960s. As described in chapter 2, circular compositions are those written in such a way that, following the initial statement of the head, subsequent returns to the top of the chorus no longer sound as if they return to the beginning. Due to harmonic, melodic, or hypermet-ric features, circular compositions contain a formal overlap that camou-flages the return to the top of the form.

What makes "Circle" circular? Certainly crucial are the ever-changing lengths of each chorus, which last, variably, 18, 22, 26, or 30 measures. The absence of consistently regular choruses serves to mask the top of the form. In addition, the six-measure A1 section ensures that at no time does any chorus consistently maintain a 4-bar hypermeter, enhancing the seamless continuity.

But perhaps the clue to the title lies elsewhere. Remarkably, Davis and the quintet assembled the harmonic progression to "Circle" out of fragments of "Drad Dog," a composition he recorded in 1961 (*Some Day My Prince Will Come*). Yet "Circle" bears little resemblance to the earlier model for several reasons. One obvious difference is the meter: "Circle" is a waltz, while "Drad Dog" is in 4/4 meter. Further, "Circle" turns the 16-bar opening form of "Drad Dog" inside out. The quintet reorders the constituent sections, as the following list indicates. The opening mm. 1–6 progression to "Circle" (A1) relates directly to that of the central mm. 11–13 section of the opening head of "Drad Dog."[21] "Circle's" A2 section, with its B pedal point, transforms the model's mm. 14–16, with its arrival on Bmin7(♭5). The inserted sections (i1 and i2) of "Circle" derive from mm. 1–2 and 3–4 of "Drad Dog," and the tag section (T) from mm. 9–10 of "Drad Dog." (The A3 section of "Circle" does not come from "Drad Dog.") Thus "Circle" begins in the middle of "Drad Dog," and the relationship of the two compositions suggests a view of "Circle" as an endless loop. Not only does "Circle" show the quintet creatively reworking earlier materials, but its specifically circular reworking reevaluates the notion of beginning, middle, and end.

contrafact

"DRAD DOG" (OPENING HEAD)	"CIRCLE"
Mm. 1–2 G13 C7♯9 F13	i1 G/C/F C/G♭ F13(9)
Mm. 3–4 Cmin9 F13	i2 Cmin9 F13(♭9)
Mm. 5–8 repeat mm. 1–4	
Mm. 9–10 B♭Maj7♯11 Emin9 A7alt.	T B♭Maj7 Emin7(♭5) A7alt
Mm. 11–13 D–13 Dmin7/C D–/B B♭Maj7	A1 Dmin(Maj7) Dmin7
	Dmin6 B♭Maj7
Dtriad/E♭minor D7alt	D (DMaj7)/E♭ D7alt
Mm. 14–16 Bmin7♭5 G13 Dmin7♭5/G	A2 GMaj7/B CMaj7/B
	GMaj7/B

21 One slight harmonic alteration is the D triad(Maj7)/E♭ from m. 5 of "Circle." In "Drad Dog" Wynton Kelly instead plays a different polychord, with a Dmajor triad above E♭ minor. "Drad Dog" itself offers some unusual formal structures after the opening head is stated. Chambers suggests that Teo Macero subjected it to a high degree of editing and splicing, a "paste-and-scissors job." Szwed indicates the unusual title resulted from a backward spelling of Goddard Lieberson's first name. Chambers, *Milestones* 2, 31; Szwed, *So What*, 218.

Hancock's solo is one of the high points of his output of the decade. It synthesizes salient features of his playing in terms of dramatic pacing, motivic playing, judicious use of space, and textural contrasts. The solo also provides a classic example of continuity and inevitability that Oscar Peterson and Pat Metheny described in relation to Hancock's improvisations, considered as phrase overlap in chapter 2.[22] Further, a number of writers have described Hancock's solo in the context of the lyricism and execution of works by classical European composers (Chopin, Rachmaninoff, and Debussy).[23] No doubt the use of subtle dynamic shadings when moving to linear high points, the careful attention to texture (for example, the penultimate chord of A, indicated as Asus, is usually realized by Hancock as a left-hand single note or dyad), the richness and variety of melodic paraphrase at each of the A2 sections, and the broken chord arpeggios heard throughout i1 and i2 all motivated those writers to link the Hancock solo with classical models.

The broken chord arpeggios of i1 and i2 (mm. 41–44 and 67–74) contribute handily to the overall dramatic pacing of the solo. They form part of larger eighth-note triplet sections that set up dramatic high points that contrast with the solo's sparer and more muted sections. The sections of broken triplet arpeggios usually occur duply grouped, creating a metrical conflict consisting of quarter-note triplets. By now such duple groupings of triplet eighth notes had become a characteristic rhythmic figure for Hancock.[24]

Chapter 2 described the i1 section heard at the end of Hancock's second chorus as an example of phrase overlap. There the broken chord arpeggios concluded with a new motivic idea, one that then launched a series of related motives at the top of the third chorus.

Similarly, Hancock uses the inserted sections in the following third chorus to attain another dramatic high point of the solo, and create a phrase overlap. There he inserts both i1 and i2. A transcription of the passage appears as example 4.6. From mm. 65–70 (3:56) he relies on the

---

22 Interview, *Jazz Profiles*, "Herbie Hancock," National Public Radio (April 2000). Quoted in Yudkin, *Miles Davis*, 80; and Conrad Silvert, "Herbie Hancock: Revamping the Past, Creating the Future," *Down Beat* 44/15 (September 8, 1977): 16.

23 Anthony Tuttle, Liner notes to *Miles Smiles* (Columbia 9401); Belden, Liner notes to *Miles Davis Quintet 1965–68*, 72.

24 Many of Hancock's solos from the Davis *My Funny Valentine* recording, for example, make use of duple groupings of eighth-note triplets. On compositions such as "All of You," such groupings suggest a metrical conflict of 6 stratified over the 4/4 meter.

similar design of eighth-note triplets and broken chord arpeggios. Hancock begins with the final harmony of Section A (mm. 65–6), arpeggiating the upper structure pitches of DMaj7♯11 (G♯, C♯, F♯). Hancock's left hand at m. 67–68 signals to the other players the insertion of i1 here, since he plays its descending chromatic motion at the downbeats of both measures. Broken chord arpeggios at m. 68 articulate C major (over the G♭ bass) and, at mm. 69–70, D major (over the F7 harmony). When grouped duply, they suggest a metrical conflict brought about by a layer of quarter-note triplets (indicated by brackets in the transcription).

EXAMPLE 4.6   Measures 65–82 of Hancock's Solo on "Circle" (3:56)

The ultimate and direct expression of that metrical conflict occurs at mm. 72–75, as the broken arpeggio triplets yield to an ascending line. Now, rather than grouping eighth-note triplets duply, Hancock directly states the quarter-note triplets in both hands (mm. 72–74) in a climactic ascent that tops out at G♭. The dynamics help shape the climax, with the dynamic high point at mm. 73–74 then shading down precipitously over the next eight measures.

As in the previous chorus, this section ends with a phrase overlap. The conclusion of the metrical conflict launches a new series of related motivic ideas that spill over the next two sections, Section T (m. 75–78) and A1 of the fourth chorus (beginning m. 79). This creates an elision between the sectional divisions at i2 and T, as well as between Hancock's third and fourth choruses, at T and A1. We can hear the material mm. 74–76 (beginning with E♭–D–C–A, indicated as M1a) rhymed with material 4 bars later (78–80, beginning with A–G–F–C♯, M1b). Here the motivic correspondence is not exact, but the opening four pitches of each maintain the same contour, and each involves a chromatic slide to the fifth pitch (on the downbeats of mm. 75 and 79). The dynamics and contour correspond throughout these 8 bars: as the dynamic level decreases, the line shapes an overall descent from C6 (m. 75) to D4 (m. 82).

The solo is a significant one for Hancock. Both the end of the second chorus (discussed in chapter 2), and the end of the third chorus (discussed above) create phrase overlap. In both, motivically driven sections begin by overlapping with the conclusion of a previous phrase. These take place during the dramatic high points of the solo at the end of the inserted (i1 and i2) sections, linking the eighth-note triplets with subsequent motivic ideas. All contribute to the sense of continuity, and shape both climactic waves at the end of Hancock's second and third choruses.

As noted above, several commentators have placed the solo in the context of execution and lyricism of classical composers, including Chopin, Debussy, and Rachmaninoff. Jeremy Yudkin has dismissed this perspective by claiming "what makes the solo remarkable is that it is *not* classical."[25] Yudkin is correct in dismissing attempts to legitimize jazz through comparisons to classical music, yet his subsequent comments would seem to invalidate *all* points of comparison between jazz and classical music. In the case of Hancock's solo, this would ignore the musical aspects of the solo that are in some ways indebted to European pianistic techniques, ones that probably invited the comparisons to Chopin, Rachmaninoff, and Debussy in the first place. In particular, the overall

25 Yudkin, *Miles Davis*, 80 n. 9, 139–40.

combination of broken chord arpeggios, attention to textural details, overall legato technique, and subtle dynamic shadings seem not to reflect Hancock's hard bop roots. Instead they show Hancock's ability to absorb and synthesize an astonishing array of influences, place them in the service of highly lyrical and dramatic improvisations, and transcend tidy categories.

Moreover, Hancock's use of broken chord arpeggios, legato touch, and subtle dynamic shadings reflect a larger pianistic trend that began percolating during the decade of the 1960s. Many jazz pianists, particularly those influenced by Bill Evans, cultivated a postbop style indebted in evident ways to classical piano touch and technique. This direction of jazz pianism can be heard overtly in the works of Keith Jarrett and has since become a direction cultivated by many other pianists, including Don Friedman, Fred Hersch, Kenny Werner, Brad Mehldau, Andy LaVerne, Marc Copland, and others. Hancock's solo features a stunning early example of that broader pianistic tradition.

"GINGER BREAD BOY"

"Ginger Bread Boy" is a Jimmy Heath composition, one of the two non-original compositions on *Miles Smiles*. The group transforms Heath's B♭ 12-bar blues into a 16-bar form by adding a 4-bar tag each chorus. Further, the group alters mm. 9–12 of Heath's composition. While Heath's original version groups mm. 9–12 with motives of 5 + 3 + 5 + 3 beats, the quintet alters the melody and groups it as 3 + 3 + 3 + 3 beats at mm. 9–11. Here the bass moves chromatically upward from B♭–D♭ in contrary motion to the D♭–C–B–A motion of the horns. Following m. 12, the group then adds the 4-bar tag.[26]

CARTER AND "GINGER BREAD BOY"

The absence of piano accompaniment throughout the recording enhances the openness and ambiguity of the form. Even so, Carter's bass accompaniment often helps clarify the form, particularly on the arrival points at the downbeats of mm. 1 and 5. The following list shows how Carter accomplishes this: his bass accompaniment typically states B♭ at m. 1 and

---

26 Yudkin makes further observations on differences between Heath's original version and the Davis version. His Example 22 transcribes the head as played by Davis and Shorter, but the chromatic bass motion of mm. 9–11 is incorrectly realized with the chords provided there. See Yudkin, *Miles Davis*, 116–17, esp. Example 22.

E♭ at m. 5 or m. 6. At these places, Carter makes the form clear and adheres closely to the standard blues harmonic structure behind all the soloists (the question marks in the list indicate inaudible bass pitches).[27]

DAVIS SOLO (CARTER'S DOWNBEAT PITCHES)

Chorus 1 (:28)
| M. 1 B♭ | M. 5 E♭ | M. 9 B♭ |

Chorus 2 (:43)
| M. 1 B♭ | M. 5 B♭ M. 6 E♭ | M. 9 F |

Chorus 3 (:57)
| M. 1 B♭ | M. 5 E♭ | M. 9 F |

Chorus 4 (1:11)
| M. 1 B♭ | M. 5 B♭ M.6 E♭ | M. 9 F |

Chorus 5 (1:25)
| M. 1 B♭ | M. 5 E♭ | M. 9 F |

Chorus 6 (1:39)
| M. 1 B♭ | M. 5 G M. 6 E♭ | M. 9 F |

Chorus 7 (1:53)
| M. 1 B♭ | M. 5 E♭ | M. 9 E♭ |

Chorus 8 (2:07)
| M. 1 ? | M. 5 E♭ | M. 9 E♭ |

Chorus 9 (2:21)
| M. 1 B♭ | M. 5? | M. 9 F |

SHORTER SOLO (CARTER'S DOWNBEAT PITCHES)

Chorus 1 (2:35)
| M. 1 B♭ | M. 5 E♭ | M. 9 D |

Chorus 2 (2:48)
| M. 1 B♭ | M. 5? | M. 9 A |

Chorus 3 (3:02)
| M. 1 D♭ | M. 5 G M. 6 E♭ | M. 9? |

Chorus 4 (3:16)
| M. 1 B♭ | M 5? | M. 9 F |

Chorus 5 (3:30)
| M. 1 B♭ | M. 5 A | M. 9 B♭ |

Chorus 6 (3:43)
| M. 1 F | M. 5 B♭ M. 6 E♭ | M. 9 F |

contradict

27 The chart belies Yudkin's claim that each soloist takes 8 choruses. Yudkin, *Miles Davis*, 119.

Chorus 7 (3:57)
M. 1 D   M. 5 E♭   M. 9 F
Chorus 8 (4:11)
M. 1 F   M. 5?   M. 9 F

HANCOCK SOLO (CARTER'S DOWNBEAT PITCHES)

Chorus 1 (4:24)
M. 1 B♭   M. 5 E♭   M. 9 B♭
Chorus 2 (4:38)
M. 1 C♭   M. 5 E♭   M. 9 F
Chorus 3 (4:51)
M. 1 B♭   M. 5 B♭ M. 6 E♭   M. 9 E♭
Chorus 4 (5:05)
M. 1 D   M. 5 E♭   M. 9 F
Chorus 5 (5:18)
M. 1 B♭   M. 5 E♭   M. 9 F
Chorus 6 (5:32)
M. 1 B♭   M. 5 E♭   M. 9 F
Chorus 7 (5:45)
M. 1 F   M. 5 E♭   M. 9 F
Chorus 8 (5:58)
M. 1 F M. 2 B♭   M. 5 B♭ M. 6 E♭   M. 9 F
Chorus 9 (6:12)
M. 1 E   M. 5?   M. 9 F

But it is in the second half of the 16-bar structure where Carter's accompaniment heightens the formal ambiguity. This is due to several factors. First, Carter does not perform mm. 9–12 with a standard harmonic turnaround for these measures of the blues. The bass downbeats at m. 9 occur primarily on F and B♭. Occasionally the bass accompaniment in these measures is consistent. Example 4.7a shows the pitches to Carter's accompaniment at mm. 9–12 of Davis's third and fifth choruses (1:04 and 1:32). Carter plays the first two measures of each consistently. The implied harmony is F (m. 9) to B♭ (m. 10), and the V–I motion at this place in the form cuts against the grain of standard blues progressions by resolving to B♭ at m. 10, one measure earlier than is typical. As example 4.7b indicates, this V–I motion in standard jazz contexts occurs mm. 10–11, often following a ii chord at m. 9. The example also shows how a more traditional blues setting typically features a m. 9 arrival on V (as Carter does in these instances), but the return to I often appears at m. 11, often following motion to IV at m. 10. (This latter describes the bass motion heard on the quintet's "Eighty-One," from *E.S.P.*) Carter's mm. 11–12, especially in Davis's fifth chorus, do set up a more standard harmonic turnaround, implying ii (m. 11) and V (m. 12). In general, however, the formal placement of these mm. 9–12 harmonies do not align with those that typically occur at mm. 9–12 of 12-bar blues progressions. The accompaniment in these measures, unlike those at mm. 1–8, creates a degree of formal ambiguity.

EXAMPLE 4.7a   Carter's Accompaniment, mm. 9–12, to Chorus 3 and Chorus 5 of Davis's Solo

EXAMPLE 4.7b   Measures 9–12 of Standard Turnaround for Jazz and Blues

What happens during the 4-bar tag? The implied harmonies of mm. 13–16 seem freely determined by Carter, and these measures frequently intensify the ambiguity. Carter often relies on pitch sequences during the tag. Example 4.8 transcribes mm. 13–16 from seven different choruses. The upper two systems include both statements of the introductory head. Both times, Carter relies on a descending fifth (or ascending fourth) sequence at the two-beat (half note) level. At mm. 13–15, this sequence progresses F–B♭–E♭–A♭–D♭–G♭, and m. 16 then initiates a new descending fifth sequence that then arrives on B♭ the top of the ensuing chorus (C–F–B♭).

During the solos, Carter further abstracts this sequential motion. Example 4.8 also includes mm. 13–16 from Davis's first and eighth choruses, from Shorter's seventh chorus, and Hancock's third and eighth

EXAMPLE 4.8   Carter's Accompaniment on "Ginger Bread Boy," mm. 13–16

choruses. During Davis's first chorus Carter passes through a descending fifth sequence that begins with A and ends with G♭ (Carter breaks the
sequence with C at m. 16). At m. 14, Carter consistently cycles through
the sequence with dotted quarter notes, setting up a 3/8 metric level in
conflict with the underlying 4/4 meter. He initiates this dotted-quarter
pattern consistently beginning with the second measure of the four-
measure section. This creates a larger 3-bar cycle that allows him to come
out rhythmically at the top of the form.

Several of Carter's mm. 13–16 sequential ideas heighten the metrical ambiguity. During Davis's eighth chorus, Carter states a consistent
rhythmic pattern each measure of quarter note, dotted-quarter, and dotted-quarter. Despite this consistency, something extraordinary occurs.
While Carter's rhythmic pattern consists of three pitches each measure,

the melodic sequence is a four-pitch one that moves down by step. This four-note pattern appears three times during mm. 13–16. It begins with F♯ (m. 13), E (m. 14), and D (m. 15). The final statement that begins with D transposes the motive down a step but alters the intervals of the final two pitches. This four-note pitch sequence challenges the underlying 4/4 metric regularity. It begins on the downbeat of m. 13, on beat 2 of m. 14, and beat 3.5 of m. 15. As a result of Carter's underlying rhythmic pattern, the first motive occupies 5 beats, while the second and third occupy 5½ beats.

During Shorter's solo, Carter's most overt use of sequence occurs during mm. 13–16 of Shorter's seventh chorus. Note that here Carter employs an ascending minor third sequence during each of the four measures (B♭–D♭–E–G). Rather than continuing the sequence into B♭ at the top of the form, Carter instead delays the arrival of B♭ by two beats.

These examples reveal sequence as a general strategy during mm. 13–16 of the head and selected choruses. Even when Carter's sequences challenge the underlying meter, such as during Davis's first and eighth choruses, the sequence and the metrical conflict conclude at the beginning of the next chorus, making evident the top of the form.

But twice during Hancock's solo, Carter's sequences mask rather than clarify the top of the form. In both instances, Carter's sequential ideas spill over into the next chorus, and as a result heighten the formal ambiguity. Both times, rather than arriving on B♭ at m. 1, Carter's sequences continue those begun during the previous 4 bars. For example, at mm. 13–16 of Hancock's third chorus, Carter's accompaniment establishes a four-note pattern that moves sequentially down in whole steps, B♭ (downbeat of m. 13), A♭ (m. 14), G♭/F♯ (m. 15), and E (m. 16). But rather than abandoning the sequence at the top of the form, Carter continues the sequence another four measures into Hancock's fourth chorus, with D (downbeat of m. 1) C (m. 2) and B♭ (m. 3), and A♭ (m. 4). (Measures 2–4 of his fourth chorus are included toward the bottom of example 4.8.) This tactic effectively camouflages the top of the form.

A similar strategy takes place between Hancock's final two choruses. Again, Carter establishes a four-note pattern that descends (B♭–A♭–G♭–F) on downbeats of mm. 13–16. Here, however, Carter breaks the consistent pattern of descending whole steps with the half-step motion from G♭–F (mm. 15–16). Carter advances the pattern 3 bars into the next chorus (E–E♭–D♭). The sequence alternates descending whole and half steps, but the four-note idea that occurs each measure is unmistakable. (Measures 2–3 of Hancock's ninth chorus appear at the bottom of example 4.8.)

The performance refits the 12-bar blues into an overall 16-bar form. Carter's accompaniment typically articulates the first half of each chorus conventionally. But the bass accompaniment interprets mm. 9–16 of each chorus less conventionally, making that half of the form significantly more ambiguous. And Carter frequently makes use of sequence in mm. 13–16, which typically sets up the top of the following chorus. Yet by the latter part of the performance, during Hancock's solo, Carter twice continues those sequences across the beginning of the following chorus, blurring the arrival into the top of the form.

Unlike his contemporaries such as bassists Scott LaFaro and Gary Peacock, Carter maintained a different role during the 1960s. He was an infrequent soloist with the Davis quintet, his accompanimental techniques were often more conventional, and he used the upper registers of the bass more sparingly than LaFaro and Peacock. Yet the techniques described above show how Carter's accompaniment ranges masterfully between formal clarity and ambiguity. Given the absence of piano comping, the bassist's role is crucial for either acknowledging or suppressing the underlying formal cues while maintaining the 16-bar form. What the discussion does not address is Carter's fluid tone and exceptional manner of expressing the time. Lee Konitz colorfully described Carter's—and the quintet rhythm section's—tendency to play on top of the beat as a "false syncopation, to get the beat way up on the top, to give that kind of friction."[28] In live performances the result for the quintet was occasionally an overall tempo acceleration, so that the ending tempo might be faster than the beginning tempo. On "Ginger Bread Boy," the tempo remains consistent (and consistently buoyant) throughout the entire performance, at about 294 bpm.

"FREEDOM JAZZ DANCE"

Along with "Ginger Bread Boy," Eddie Harris's "Freedom Jazz Dance" is the second of the two nonoriginal compositions on *Miles Smiles*. Davis's quintet alters Harris's original 10-bar form into a 16-bar form by inserting several additional measures without melody after each of the three phrases. No doubt the group selected the composition given its melodic foregrounding of perfect fourths. Given the predominance of perfect fourths, the melody is an outgrowth of what Harris referred to as his

---

28 Andy Hamilton, *Lee Konitz: Conversation on the Improviser's Art* (Ann Arbor: University of Michigan, 2007), 124.

"interverlistic" approach, described in his improvisation manual published in 1971.[29] The chromatic transpositions of fourths with a fixed B♭ bass pedal point pose an opposite strategy to that heard in Wayne Shorter's "E.S.P.," which involves chromatic harmonic motion beneath a rather fixed arpeggiation of three perfect fourths. The single pedal point and the straight-eighth feel of the recorded performance provide two musical features that intersect with Davis's later turn to fusion.

STUDIO TECHNIQUES

In the studio, the quintet recorded a series of rehearsal and alternate takes for "Freedom Jazz Dance" prior to the final take. The rehearsal takes, the alternate takes, and the recorded conversation show constant discussion and revision, both of the instrumental roles and the structure of the composition. Much of the commentary is motivated by Davis. The following provides a description of the session reels.

Rehearsal Take A: Davis works with Carter on accompanimental figure, makes suggestions about articulation, harmony, and rhythm (eighth notes). Davis suggests that Carter play "eighth notes off the chord."

Rehearsal Take B: Group plays 10-bar head 2 times (2-bar ostinato in bass, swing feel in drums).

Rehearsal Take C: Davis suggests to Hancock to play chord (rather than phrase with Carter), plays B♭7(♯9/♯11); Hancock plays a doubly diminished harmony.

Rehearsal Take D: Rhythm sections/horns play 10-bar head. Carter moves to 3 eight-note accompanimental figure. Following, Davis has Williams play wood blocks.

Take 1: Horns play 10-bar head, Williams plays wood blocks and hi-hat.

Take 2: Group plays 10-bar head twice, Davis begins solo, cuts off, suggesting Hancock lay out on comping.

Take 3: Group begins to play 10-bar head, Davis flubs third phrase.

Take 4: Group plays 10-bar head one time, Hancock comping on fourth beat of every other measure. Davis suggests he and Shorter divide up the melody.

---

29 Eddie Harris, *The Eddie Harris Interverlistic Concept for All Single Line Wind Instruments* (Chicago: Author, 1971); 2nd ed. publ. by Seventh House, 2006. See also Harris, *The Intervalistic Concept Books I, II, & III* (New York: Charles Colin Music, 1984.)

Take 5: Group plays 10-bar head twice, m. 5 played by Shorter only, m. 6 by Davis only. Performance includes short Davis solo over 4/4 swing feel. Following, Davis recommends expanding Harris's form by including 2 bars of silence after each melodic phrase.

Take 6: Horns play head 6 times, now 16 bars. Hancock comps on beat four, mm. 2, 6, 12.

Take 7: Horns play 16-bar head 6 times, Davis solos, but cuts the group off when Carter goes into 4/4 swing. Tells Carter to instead keep the feel from the head.   mistake

Take 8: False starts, then group plays head 3 times, Davis flubs third phrase.

Take 9: Begins with drum intro, several false starts.

Take 10: Begins with drum intro, Davis cuts Williams off, suggests (eighth-note) triplets. Several false starts.

Master (Released) Take: Begins with false start by Davis. Head is 16 bars (Take 6), Carter plays 3 eighth-note accompaniment (Rehearsal Take D), Hancock comps beat four, mm. 2, 6, and 12 during second head (Take 6); Davis lays out first measure of third phrase (Take 5), and Williams plays eighth-note triplets (Take 10).

All of this highlights the workshop aspect to the quintet's studio processes. The description of the master take shows how it folds in a series of ideas gradually introduced during the previous takes. The insertion of bars of silence between the three phrases (turning the original 10-bar form into a 16-bar form) arises only in Take 6. And the shift to the underlying triplet subdivisions in the drums begins at Take 10. There is no discussion of improvisation on these tracks. Rather they contain an ever-evolving series of ways for working out specific identity roles for the rhythm section instruments, and for ironing out problems of executing the melody. These tracks belie comments that *Miles Smiles* "consists of previously unrehearsed music," and descriptions of Davis as a "one-take" player.[30] Instead, in this instance they reflect a detailed, experimental, and ongoing concern with the final recorded product.

MODE/SCALE ORGANIZATION

Since the composition relies on a single B♭ pedal point in the bass as the harmonic focus, there is no harmonic progression to generate chorus structure. And with the use of the single pedal point, the composition

30 Chambers, *Milestones*, 98. Szwed, *So What*, 264.

reflects the notion of modal jazz defined by static harmonic structures. Yet the use of mode/scales by the soloists is fluid, and considered differently by the three different soloists. Davis's solo relies significantly on the B♭ dorian mode, interspersed with melodic paraphrase.[31] Perhaps as a response to Davis's final two-note phrase, which includes D natural, Shorter begins his solo with the pitches of B♭ mixolydian (mm. 1–10). The motivic correspondences in these opening ten measures come about through the opening pitches: each of these opening ideas initiate with the perfect fourth E♭4–A♭4. Characteristic, too, for Shorter is the role of motivic expansion. The opening two-note idea (mm. 1–2) expands at mm. 4–5, and expands further at mm. 6–8. Following a very loose paraphrase of the melody at mm. 11–15, Shorter then uses the pitches of the mode of F ascending melodic minor, emphasizing E natural, the ♯11 of the harmony. Hancock, in stark contrast, bases his accompaniment and solo on a mode of A♭ harmonic minor, as well as the octatonic (diminished-scale) collection beginning with B♭–C♭. The opening measures to the piano solo use the pitches of the A♭ harmonic minor mode, and project the harmony of BMaj7♯5/B♭ (this same harmony features prominently in Hancock's composition "Madness," released on *Nefertiti*). By the ninth measure, Hancock now alters the collection to express the octatonic (diminished) scale (B♭, C♭, D♭, D, E, F, G, A♭).

The freedom—arising from very different modal interpretations of the B♭ pedal—gives rise to questions regarding musical organization and consistency. The disparity between the pitch choices of Hancock's comping and those of the two horn soloists challenges some fundamental assumptions about the degree of accord between accompanist and soloist. This recording provides instead a wide degree of latitude, allowing for different simultaneous collections above the bass pedal point.

THE CHALLENGES ISSUED TO THE players on *Miles Smiles* allowed any number of unusual solutions in relation to form, the 12-bar blues, motivic improvisation, and static harmony. From the standpoint of form, the use of "time, no changes" ("Orbits") liberated the improvisers from an underlying formal template, allowing a range of possibilities for motivic improvisation based on melodic paraphrase, all in the context of a 4/4 walking bass swing time feel. "Dolores" suggested multiple interpreta-

---

31 My description of Davis's solo is admittedly superficial since many of Davis's lines also include A natural and E natural. See Yudkin, *Miles Davis*, 112–14 for a transcription and motivic analysis of Davis's solo. The transcription is generally accurate, although it does include minor pitch errors at mm. 22–23, 39, and 53.

tions of the form by the three different improvisers, with Davis relying on an underlying 24-measure chorus, Shorter a 22-measure chorus (derived from the three sections of the head), and Hancock moving to "time, no changes" independent of the underlying form. Further, the additive form of "Circle" allowed for additional inserted sections not heard during the head. Both "Footprints" and "Ginger Bread Boy" challenged conventions of the 12-bar blues, the former with an unusual harmonic turnaround, and the latter transformed into a 16-bar form. "Freedom Jazz Dance" provided alternative paths for the soloists to interpret an underlying single tonal center.

The players pulled off these technical challenges subtly and effortlessly. Such challenges reveal an underlying principle for Davis, who said, "That's what I tell all my musicians; I tell them be ready to play what you know and play above what you know."[32] Certainly Hancock's notion of "controlled freedom" is apparent as the group maintained evident ties to their hard bop roots, at the same time acknowledging the work of Ornette Coleman and others. This, as well as the degree of ensemble cohesion, directed listening, rhythm section interaction, and improvisational pacing address—if only partially—why the influence of *Miles Smiles* continues to reverberate.

echo

32 Leonard Feather, "Miles Davis/Blindfold Test Pt. 1," *Down Beat* 35/12 (June 13, 1968): 34.

CHAPTER 5

SORCERER

Witch

HERBIE HANCOCK WROTE THE TITLE track, "The Sorcerer," and dedicated it to Davis, noting "Miles *is* a sorcerer. His whole attitude, the way he is, is kind of mysterious.... His music sounds like witchcraft. There are times I don't know where his music comes from. It doesn't sound like he's doing it. It sounds like it's coming from somewhere else."[1] Wayne Shorter concurred by saying, "it was as if Miles wasn't even playing a trumpet. His instrument was more like a spoken dialogue or like he was a painter using a brush or a sculptor using a hammer and chisel."[2] On the one hand, the album title and its title track show the quintet members perpetuating the mystique surrounding Davis's persona. On the other hand, Hancock's and Shorter's comments show the

---

1 Liner notes to Herbie Hancock, *Speak Like a Child*, reprinted in *Herbie Hancock: The Complete Blue Note Sessions* (B2BN 7243 4 95569 2 8), 45.
2 Dan Oulette, "Ready for Anything," *Down Beat* 76/4 (April 2009): 30.

players bewitched by the ways in which Davis transcended his instrument. Certainly *Sorcerer* reveals Davis's sound and motivic sense fully crystallized, allowing a vast palette of expressive timbres and improvised motives played with such unerring confidence that—even when they do not reflect the underlying harmony—their execution heightens their sense of inevitability.

The quintet recorded *Sorcerer* October 16–17 and 24, 1967. They recorded an alternate take of "Limbo," with Buster Williams on bass, a week earlier in Los Angeles. On the album, the quintet moves away from swing-based rhythmic organization. Only "The Sorcerer" maintains a walking bass 4/4 feel, while most of the remaining compositions rely on straight eighth-note rhythmic organization. *Sorcerer* exhibits the quintet's practice of placing complete or partial statements of the head's melody between or within solos ("Prince of Darkness," "The Sorcerer," and "Vonetta"). This practice originated with "Freedom Jazz Dance" from the previous *Miles Smiles* recording and culminated [climax] in "Nefertiti" (*Nefertiti*), which consists solely of repeated statements of the head without conventional solos by horns and piano. These insertions depart from the strict head–solos–head format of the earlier recordings, and undoubtedly required discussion and preparation prior to recording the master take.

Additionally, the album does not rely on "time, no changes." The quintet instead adheres to chorus structure more regularly during improvisations, even while on several compositions Hancock does not provide harmonic accompaniment beneath the horn solos. Despite the use of chorus structure, compositions such as "Prince of Darkness" use improvisational and accompanimental techniques that challenge but do not abandon the form during improvisations.

Shorter, Hancock, and Williams all contributed compositions to the album. With the exception of "Masqualero," all are single-section compositions. Further, all the compositions share a common detail: each employs a syncopated harmonic progression, typically appearing near the end of the composition's form. This feature operates as a compositional release, one that operates in the absence of standard bridge sections or harmonic turnarounds at the end of the repeating form. The chapter examines compositional aspects of "Vonetta," "Prince of Darkness," "Masqualero," "Pee Wee," and "Limbo." It also describes Shorter's improvisation on "Vonetta," and Davis's and Hancock's improvisations to "Prince of Darkness." The chapter does not examine the title track, although "The Sorcerer" offers compositional goals similar to the other compositions on the recording: it has a 16-bar single-section form, fourth-based melodic structure, and syncopated harmonic progression toward the end of the form.[3] Curiously, *Sorcerer* also included a cut that Davis recorded five years earlier in 1962, entitled "Nothing Like You," with vocalist Bob Dorough.

"VONETTA"

HEAD

"Vonetta" is a fragile lyrical ballad. Its harmonic vocabulary (discussed below) represents an advance for Shorter, and this feature may have been the motivation for Belden's description of "Vonetta" as a tone poem.[4] Tony Williams's drumming throughout is unusual, with militaristic snare drum rolls atypical of ballad accompaniment. Shorter's copyright

EXAMPLE 5.1   Shorter's Lead Sheet to "Vonetta" (more standard harmonic labels heard on recording added in parentheses above Shorter's harmonies)

3   For a transcription of the head and piano solo on Hancock's later 1968 version of "The Sorcerer," see Bill Dobbins, *Herbie Hancock: Classic Jazz Compositions and Piano Solos* (Rottenburg, Germany: Advance Music, 1992), 22–33.

4   Bob Belden, Liner notes to *Miles Davis Quintet 1965–68* (Columbia/Sony 67398), 78.

deposit lead sheet notates "Vonetta" as a 14-bar composition.[5] A transcription of that lead sheet appears as example 5.1. It includes harmonies as notated by Shorter, and I have added above Shorter's chords (in parentheses) more conventional harmonic labels to represent the chords heard on the recording. The composition is in 4/4, with the exception of m. 12, notated in 5/4. Like the other compositions on *Sorcerer*, "Vonetta" includes a syncopated harmonic progression toward the end of the form. In "Vonetta" the syncopated progression appears in mm. 12 and 13, and its appearance in the 5/4 bar creates a degree of metric ambiguity. The quintet alters conventional head–solos–head format to a certain extent. During the piano solo the group alternates piano improvisation (mm. 1–8) with statements of the melody (mm. 9–14). This tactic reveals the quintet's emerging concern with highlighting melody statements between or within improvisations. Further, there is no return to a completed head statement following the piano solo.

The quintet takes some liberties with the lead sheet's melody during the loosely performed head statement (for example, the m. 1 F♯ is played as a quarter note by Davis, and Davis elaborates the melody m. 4). The chords I have added in parentheses above provide further harmonic detail about the group's performance on the recording. They also show that the group alters some of the harmonies, most notably the m. 1 harmony, which is played throughout with C in the bass, and harmonized most frequently by Hancock as B♭/C or Cmin9. (Hancock adds EMaj7♯5 in mid-measure of m. 1 over the C bass during the opening head, during Davis's second chorus, and during his own first chorus. Note how this harmony relates to the m. 1 harmony from Shorter's lead sheet.)

During the improvisations it is possible to hear a circular quality to "Vonetta" by hearing m. 1 of successive choruses as a concluding bar to the previous chorus. This circularity is due to several factors. The 5/4 bar at m. 12 sounds as two foreshortened measures (compare the melody at m. 12 to mm. 1–2 and 5–6). Thus while notated as a single measure 12, it sounds as if forming mm. 12–13. In that event, "Vonetta's" final two measures (following the 5/4 bar) may be heard as mm. 14–15, suggesting an absent 16th bar that is then supplied by m. 1 at the top of the form. Thus the implied 15-bar form helps create circularity by creating a formal overlap.

The circularity of "Vonetta" is also enhanced by the harmony, since the final Cmin9 harmony (or B♭/C) wraps around and continues across into

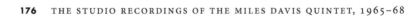

5 Library of Congress Copyright Deposit Eu 42291 (March 13, 1968).

m. 1 of the next chorus, making m. 2 sound like the top of the composition during the improvisations. In addition, Hancock's occasional m. 1 EMaj7♯5 insertion creates the effect of a m. 1 turnaround into m. 2, also making the second measure sound as the top of the form.[6]

To the extent that "Vonetta" is in a primary key, the C minor harmony (or B♭triad/C) that begins and ends the composition provides that key. Yet this creates a conflicted relationship with the melody, which focuses on the pitches of C♯, D♯, E, and F♯, more likely associated with C♯ minor than with C minor.

"Vonetta's" haunting melody is tightly constructed. It contains a series of four related phrases of 4 + 4 + 3 + 3 notated measures. Phrases 1 and 2 (mm. 1–8) consist only of four pitch classes: C♯, F♯, D♯, and E. Phrases 3 and 4 (mm. 9–14) consist primarily of those same pitch classes, but they reorder and develop them further. Phrase 3 begins (pickup to m. 9) echoing the E–D♯ half-step descent initially heard moving into the downbeats of mm. 3 and 7. The following pitches of Phrase 3 (C♯–F♯, mm. 9–10) consist of the two pitches that *began* Phrases 1 and 2, and involve an additional pitch (notated as A♭) before returning to C♯. And Phrase 4 metrically recasts the content of Phrases 1 and 2. Following the additional pickup pitch of A (m. 11), the m. 12 5/4 bar of Phrase 4 duplicates the first four pitches heard in mm. 1–2 and 5–6. However, "Vonetta's" final two measures depart from mm. 3. Rather than the whole-step descent D♯–C♯ heard en route to m. 3, m. 13 descends a half-step E♭–D. Thus the four phrases echo one another in evident ways. Barry Kernfeld suggests the four-phrase construction of "Vonetta" to be a variation on a more standard AABA form. The related Phrases 1 and 2 form the A sections; Phrase 3 an irregular 3-bar bridge, and Phrase 4 a final altered A section.[7]

Yet the accompanying harmonies differ beneath each of the phrases. Because of these harmonic differences beneath the related four phrases, it is tempting to consider "Vonetta" as a study in reharmonization, with each phrase subjected to vastly different harmonic progressions. The progression of "Vonetta" represents in many ways an expansion of Shorter's harmonic syntax, particularly through its exploration of Maj7♯5 (and derivative harmonies) at mm. 2 and 12.

6 This Emaj7♯5 insertion over the C bass sounds as an altered dominant chord. As a result, it creates the effect of a m. 1 turnaround into m. 2.

7 Private communication, January 30, 2010. Kernfeld also indicated the relationship between this mini-AABA form and that of Shorter's more standard 16-bar composition "Fall," recorded on the following quintet album *Nefertiti*.

The use of Maj7♯5 harmonies took root during the 1960s among a number of jazz composers. The origins of the harmony are probably impossible to pinpoint. It is possible that this harmony came about either through the practice of "freezing" the passing tone in a 5–♯5–6 decoration of a Maj7 harmony, or as the result of an upper structure harmony shorn of its lower structure (for example, DMaj7♯5 may form an upper structure to Bmin9(♯7) or to E13(♯11)). *B mm*

Shorter employed Maj7♯5 harmonies prior to "Vonetta" (for example, it appears m. 21 of "Wild Flower," from *Speak No Evil*). But he extends the Maj7♯5 harmony heard at m. 2 in "Vonetta" further. Shorter's lead sheet copyright deposit labels the harmony as A♭+9+. In some ways this harmony recalls the A♭Maj7(nat5,♯5) harmony heard in mm. 7–8 of "Iris" (discussed in chapter 3). The role of the chord is similar to that in "Iris," since that harmony similarly telescopes the melodic motion: in both "Iris" and "Vonetta" the melodic motion involves E and D♯/E♭, and the A♭ harmony includes both those pitches. But in "Vonetta" Hancock's voicing of the chord frequently consists of six pitches, formed by the combination of an A♭ augmented triad beneath a G augmented triad. These six pitches comprise the hexatonic (or augmented) collection, here consisting of the pitches A♭, B, C, E♭, F♭, G.[8] Structurally the "doubly augmented" harmony (A♭+ and G+) that forms this hexatonic (augmented) scale resembles the doubly diminished harmonies favored by Hancock that form the octatonic (diminished) scale.[9] The six-note collection becomes a point of departure for similar hexatonic harmonies heard during the 1960s and later, ones that were to become a staple of more advanced jazz harmonic syntax.[10]

The bass to the A♭Maj7(♯5, ♯9) harmony functions as a chromatic neighbor harmony, resolving upward to the following AMaj7♯11 harmony. And "Vonetta" makes frequent use of such neighboring chords that resolve either chromatically upward or downward. For example, the m. 4 bass to E♭°9 (alternatively realized by Hancock as a fully diminished or as a half-diminished harmony) resolves chromatically downward to D at m. 5. The same chord returns at mm. 10 and resolves chromatically upward to E–11

---

8 Walt Weiskopf and Ramon Ricker, *The Augmented Scale in Jazz* (New Albany, Ind.: Jamey Aebersold Jazz, 1993).

9 For a discussion of the doubly diminished harmony, see Mark Levine, *The Jazz Theory Book* (Petaluma, Calif.: Sher Music, 1995), 88.

10 Chick Corea's "Song of the Wind" uses several related hexatonic harmonies, such as E–(maj7)/G♯. See a transcription in *Piano Improvisations*, trans. Bill Dobbins (Rottenburg: Advance Music, 1990).

at m. 11. Further, even the final harmonic progression at m. 13 makes use of a chromatic neighbor harmony, but above a fixed bass pedal point. Here, the bass remains on C, while the upper structure progresses from B major to B♭ major (B/C to B♭/C).

SHORTER'S SOLO

Shorter's solo on "Vonetta" is exceptional in its dramatic passion, expansive lyricism, and recollection of the melody. Example 5.2 contains a transcription of it. Shorter recalls similar pitch material at analogous points in each chorus. One clear pitch path occurs at mm. 1–2 of each chorus (mm.

EXAMPLE 5.2   Shorter's Solo and Bass Accompaniment on "Vonetta" (2:32)

EXAMPLE 5.2   Continued

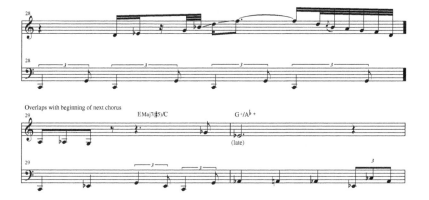

1–2 and 15–16; 2:32 and 3:15), which traces the motion from C4 upward to
Gb, before descending to Eb. This Gb to Eb motion recalls the melody, and
it even recurs at the end of Shorter's solo, which responds to "Vonetta's"
circularity by spilling over two measures into the next chorus.

Measures 5–7 of both choruses (mm. 5–7 and 19–21; 2:44 and 3:27)
elaborate a motion from C#5 to D#5, before then stating E to D#. These
pitches echo the principal material from the melody to "Vonetta" at mm.
5–7 (although avoiding the m. 5 F# from the melody). And Shorter's subsequent treatment of the Gb13(#11/b9) harmony at mm. 7–8 (mm. 8 and
21–22; 2:53 and 3:34), while not related to the melody, in each chorus
superimposes and elaborates C major (the latter initiated with A minor
before superimposing C major).

In many ways the half-step E–D#, appearing in all four phrases of
"Vonetta's" melody, forms its expressive core. Measure 9 in each chorus
(mm. 9 and 23; 2:57 and 3:40) refers to the melody by subtly recalling that
E–D# motion. In Shorter's first chorus, this motion merely initiates Shorter's continuing start-and-stop phrase. At m. 23 (in Shorter's second chorus) he restates the pitch pair three times before the phrase continues.

Finally, Shorter's treatment of mm. 26–27 (3:48) paraphrases the melody. The pitches C#–F#–D# from the 5/4 bar of the melody now appear with
the first two pitches in different octaves, creating an overall ascending
line, and each treated to expressive smears. Shorter's continuing phrase
highlights the Eb–D motion (from m. 13 of "Vonetta's" melody) at m. 27.

The discussion of Shorter's solo on "Pee Wee" suggests a cavalier attitude toward its final harmony of F/Db (DbMaj7#5) since Shorter was fairly
consistent in avoiding A natural. However in "Vonetta," Shorter expresses
the m. 2 "doubly augmented" harmony (Ab–C–E–G–B–Eb) carefully. This
is particularly evident in the second chorus. Note that Shorter's downward

arpeggiation at m. 16 (3:19) outlines five of the six pitches of this harmony (E♭–B–G–E–C) before then descending chromatically. This is something of a magical moment during the performance, as Hancock's accompaniment and Shorter's solo both delicately express this doubly augmented harmony.

One feature of the solo not captured by the transcription is its dramatic and dynamic range and its relationship with the accompanying instruments. There are quicksilver motions between quiet lyricism and intense abandon, particularly within the second chorus, such as at mm. 21–24 (3:32). Here Shorter's dynamic intensity sounds as a response to the accompanying instruments, such as Hancock's octatonic realization of the mm. 21–22 harmony (G♭13♭9(♯11)) as well as Carter's rhythmic grouping in m. 22, whose quarter-note triplets group duply, implying triple meter against the 4/4 measure. (Carter frequently uses this level of rhythmic conflict during the G♭13 harmony behind the other soloists.)

The harmonic language, the circular form, and the metrical challenge of the 5/4 measure all suggest a significant reconsideration of what constitutes a jazz ballad. Extended Maj7♯5 harmonies (G+/A♭+) provide harmonic avenues explored by later jazz composers, such as Chick Corea, Richie Beirach, and others. Further, the unusual aspects of the drum accompaniment (according to Hancock, Davis in the studio asked Williams to play a "Rat Patrol" sound, referring to the mid-1960s military-themed television show)[11] give additional evidence of the quintet deliberately thwarting conventions of jazz ballad playing, and affixing a unique personality to the composition. Shorter's negotiation of all these features in his improvisation puts on display several crucial facets of his playing, particularly his expressive vocabulary and wide dramatic range.

"MASQUALERO"

Of the Davis studio recordings, perhaps "Masqualero" has drawn the greatest critical attention. The recording displays careful listening and response between soloists and rhythm section, liberal use of space, underlying straight eighth-note organization, and a flexible interpretation of the form. The features of heightened interest to jazz historians and analysts are the slow harmonic rhythm (the entire composition consists of three primary harmonies) and the slowly unfolding mysterioso melody. Both the slow harmonic rhythm and fragmentary melody place

11 Bob Blumenthal's liner notes to Davis's album *Directions* (ca. 1981) quoted in Jack Chambers, *Milestones: The Music and Times of Miles Davis* 2 (New York: Da Capo, 1998), 105. Originally publ. University of Toronto, 1983 and 1985.

"Masqualero" some distance away from most of Shorter's earlier quintet compositions, which reflect Shorter's hard bop roots through faster harmonic rhythm and more apparent motivic relationships. However, "Masqualero's" fourth-based arpeggiation in the melody links it to Shorter's "E.S.P.," and the chromatic elaboration of that arpeggiation (progressing downward B♭–F–C–B, mm. 5–6) is similar to that used in "Orbits."

Both Todd Coolman and Mark Gridley examine "Masqualero" extensively.[12] Gridley's analysis highlights its contrast and drama, and invokes written classical music in order to validate the recording's quality and variety. "The result," he writes, "is an extemporaneous work that takes the listener through significant changes in loudness, melody, texture, and rhythm, showing almost as much internal contrast and development as we might find in a prewritten symphonic piece. In some respects, it even evokes the drama we expect of an opera."[13] Coolman regards it as one of the quintessential Davis quintet studio recordings, using a set of criteria that includes tempo, number of measures (16 or more), tonality/modality, duration, and order of solos. For Coolman, form is the only criterion not represented by "Masqualero," since it is not a single-section composition.

The form to the head is ABA. The 8-bar A sections and 6-bar B section comprise a 22-bar chorus structure. The A section of "Masqualero" consists of a single primary referential harmony. Shorter's copyright deposit lead sheet indicates the A section harmony as Dø7, but on the recordings the focal pitch in the bass is G rather than D. Lead sheet renditions of "Masqualero" typically designate the A section harmony as G phrygian. As a result, many analysts consider the composition as exemplary of modal jazz.[14] Here the referential harmony is decidedly more unstable and less syntactic than compositions deemed modal whose primary harmony (and modal/tonal center) is minor (such as "So What" or "Agitation").

The G phrygian primary harmony places "Masqualero" within a broader tradition of phrygian jazz compositions. It may be useful to understand this tradition as representing two general directions. On

12 Todd Coolman, "The Miles Davis Quintet of the Mid-1960s: Synthesis of Improvisational and Compositional Elements" (Ph.D. diss., New York University, 1997), 86–120; Mark Gridley, *Jazz Styles*, 10th ed. (Upper Saddle River, N.J.: Pearson Education, 2009), 278–83.

13 Gridley, *Jazz Styles*, 278.

14 A noncopyrighted fake book, *Jazz Ltd.*, contains a lead sheet, p. 218. Scott Reeves describes "Masqualero" as a phrygian composition in *Creative Jazz Improvisation* (Englewood Cliffs, N.J.: Prentice Hall, 1989), 90–91.

the one hand are those compositions, such as "Masqualero," that use a phrygian sonority as the primary harmony. On the other hand are those compositions that use a I–♭II–I (or ♭III–♭II–I) harmonic progression (for example, the fourth section of "Flamenco Sketches," "Nardis," "Speak No Evil," "La Fiesta"), but that use more standard major or minor harmonies on the I chord.[15] For the latter group, "phrygian" refers not to the harmony, but to the upper half-step motion in the bass.

Coolman suggests a more complex view of the A section's harmony and modality than that of G phrygian, however. In discussing the two-measure figure played by the bass in the introduction, he notes that the bass alternates G and C on successive downbeats. He concludes that C is ultimately the priority pitch, and G functions only as a pedal point in C minor.[16] Likely Carter's use of C to alternate with G (rather than the more conventional upper fifth, D) motivated Coolman's observation. His point raises a number of interesting analytical issues regarding modal/tonal center and priority. Is the piece in G or C? In other words, does C elaborate G, or does G elaborate C? Certainly it is possible to regard the G phrygian harmony as a type of dominant harmony in C. However G, not C, operates more evidently as a point of harmonic arrival. G appears on the stronger measures (1, 3, 5) of the two-measure units, and C is avoided at downbeats to m. 8 of the 8-bar sections.[17]

The harmony played by Hancock that begins the B section is most frequently an E7alt harmony. The general structure of that chord above the bass (A♭/G♯–C–D–G) is cognate with the G phrygian harmony of the A section. At m. 13 of the B section the bass moves from E to F, providing a syncopated harmonic progression (each of the compositions on *Sorcerer* similarly relies on syncopated harmonic progressions at or near the end of the form). At m. 13 Hancock typically relies on FMaj7 (often with a ♯11) for both bass pitches of E and F.

The form during improvisation for both the released and alternate tracks appears in table 5.1. There are some decided similarities. In both, Davis's solo ends and Shorter's solo begins within the final A section of Davis's solo (during Davis's fourth chorus on the released take, and Davis's third chorus on the alternate take). The released track differs, however,

---

15 See Reeves, *Creative Jazz Improvisation*, 90.
16 Todd Coolman, "The Miles Davis Quintet of the Mid-1960s: Synthesis of Improvisational and Compositional Elements" (Ph.D. diss., New York University, 1997), 88–89.
17 The role of modality in the solos is even more complicated, since the different improvisations interpret the harmony differently. Davis does not strictly adhere to a G phrygian foundation, and relies on B natural rather than B♭ for much of the trumpet solo.

TABLE 5.1   "Masqualero," Form on Released Take

	A	B	A
Head	:14	:28	:39
Davis 1st chorus	:54	1:08	1:19
2nd chorus	1:33	1:47	1:58
3rd chorus	2:12	2:26	2:37
4th chorus	2:51	3:05	3:16 (Shorter begins during this section, at 3:22)
Shorter 1st chorus		3:31	3:42
2nd chorus	3:56	4:10	4:21
3rd chorus	4:35	4:49	5:00
4th chorus	5:14	5:28	⟵ 10s here
5th chorus	5:38	5:52	6:03 (Carter: only four bars; Hancock begins A at 5:56: 8 bars)

	A	A	B	A
Hancock 1st chorus	6:10	6:24	6:38	6:49
2nd chorus	7:03	7:17	7:31	7:41
Head	7:55			

"Masqualero," Form on Alternate Take

	A	B	A
Head	:14	:29	:40
Davis 1st chorus	:54	1:09	1:19
2nd chorus	1:34	1:48	1:59
3rd chorus	2:14	2:28	2:39 (Shorter enters during this section, at 2:49)
Shorter 1st chorus	2:54	3:08	3:19
2nd chorus	3:33	3:48	3:59

	A	A	B	A
Hancock 1st chorus	4:13	4:28	4:41	4:52
2nd chorus	5:06	5:20	5:34	5:45
Head	6:00			

flow of the time disrupted

since—following this point of overlap—the group omits a subsequent return to a following A section, and moves directly to the B section.

Hancock's solo departs from the ABA form of the head, and moves instead to AABA form. For Coolman, this alteration to the form is a "random accident," and both Coolman and Gridley suggest that it highlights the group's flexible ability to spontaneously override the formal design of the head during improvisation.[18] Both Coolman's and Gridley's analyses preceded the release of the alternate take, however. There the form during Hancock's solo is also AABA. Because of that similarity, it is probable that the group decided in advance to alter the form during Hancock's solo, rather than determined it spontaneously during performance.

The focal point for formal ambiguity occurs during Shorter's fourth and fifth choruses on the released track. Hancock ceases piano comping during these choruses, and the rhythm section interaction further makes the form ambiguous. Both Coolman and Gridley each regard these sections differently, and the group's loose performance during these measures does make hearing the underlying form difficult here. The group jettisons an A section at the end of Shorter's fourth chorus (5:38) as Shorter continues to spin out a motive begun the previous B section (5:28). As Hancock returns to comping (at 5:56) he and Carter are out of phase: Hancock begins comping two measures into Carter's B section, but playing as if at the beginning of an A section.

Despite the formal looseness of the released track performance, there are decided events that help the group orient themselves within the form. The first is the E to F syncopated harmonic progression from the B section to the head (m. 13) that the group largely maintains during the improvisations. Further, Hancock's comping is significantly more downbeat oriented than in other compositions, and he frequently places harmonies squarely at the beginnings of formal sections, clearly marking their onset.

Another idea that emerges during the improvisations is Carter's frequent move to A♭ in the bass at mm. 7–8 of each A section, which is then used to cue the B section or the top of the form.[19] Hancock's comping is generally consistent during mm. 7–8 of the A sections, shifting the referential sonority a minor third above G phrygian (m. 7), and a half step above G phrygian (m. 8). These minor third and minor second transpositions that Hancock generally plays during mm. 7–8 then link

18 Coolman, "The Miles Davis Quintet," 95–96; Gridley, *Jazz Styles*, 278–83.

19 Coolman describes the moves to A♭ in the bass as well as the E–F harmonic progressions as "signals." See Coolman, "The Miles Davis Quintet," 97–100.

both phrygian traditions discussed above: not only does "Masqualero" use the phrygian harmony as a referential sonority, that harmony itself becomes elaborated with ♭III–♭II motion.[20] Perhaps most notable about this rhythm section accompaniment—particularly Carter's and Hancock's role in mm. 7–8 of each A section—is how the players elaborate the underlying phrygian sonority, creating the sense of harmonic activity within a static harmonic context. Such elaborations of extended individual harmonies provided the players transcendent ways to interpret compositions with slow harmonic rhythm.

"PRINCE OF DARKNESS"

HEAD

"Prince of Darkness" is a single-section 16-bar composition whose melody is dominated by a four-note rhythmic motive. This motive operates as a long upbeat, anticipating the composition's 2-bar divisions. The harmonic rhythm of the opening 8 bars supports those 2-bar divisions. Following a discussion of the harmonic structure to "Prince of Darkness," the analyses of Davis's and Hancock's solos will highlight the ways in which the improvisers used those 2-bar divisions during mm. 1–8 to project crucial motives.

The mm. 1–8 harmonic progression (Gmin7 Dmin7 B♭min7 Gmin7) arpeggiates the tonic triad using parallel minor seventh structures on each member of the G minor harmony.[21] all from G min

The harmonic progression to mm. 9–16 appears as follows:

m. 9   m. 11   m. 13   m. 14   m. 15
G♭Maj7(♯5) B♭Maj7(♯5) BMaj7 A♭Maj7(♯11) G♭Maj7(♯11) E♭min7 Dmin7
                                                            (CMaj7/D)

20 These additional ♭III–♭II elaborations of G phrygian may be considered in a number of ways: B♭ phrygian to A♭ phrygian, D♭13 to B13, or G7alt to F7alt. The first pair label makes clear the half-step harmonic motion to G phrygian at the top of the form, and the final pair makes clear the half-step harmonic motion to E7alt at the beginning of the B section. At times Hancock omits the first harmony of the pair, and states only the ♭II harmony. Coolman calls attention to one such statement and describes it as unexpected. However, it operates instead as a generally consistent signal throughout the performance. See Coolman, "The Miles Davis Quintet," 94.

21 This point is drawn from Steven Strunk, "Notes on Harmony in Wayne Shorter's Compositions, 1964–67," *Journal of Music Theory* 49/2 (Fall 2005): 309. The lead sheet to "Prince of Darkness" in *The Real Book*, 6th ed., contains a number of errors in the harmonic labels (p. 332).

minor vs Major

There are several points to make here. First, notice that the mm. 9–13 harmonies all support Maj7 (or Maj7#5) harmonies. Chord quality therefore plays into the composition's formal design, with the minor harmonies of mm. 1–8 (and 14–16) contrasting with the Maj7 harmonies mm. 9–13. Additionally, the mm. 9–13 harmonic progression moves afield from the bass's arpeggiated G minor (Gmin7 Dmin7 B♭min7 Gmin7) of mm. 1–8. The overall motion from mm. 9–13 implies a departure and return from G♭Maj7. The bass notes occurring between both statements of G♭ (B♭, C♭/B, A♭) suggest an elaboration of G♭ through its first four scale degrees. Rather than supporting harmonies strictly diatonic to G♭ major, these harmonies share a consistent Maj7 structure. The final two harmonies (E♭min7 Dmin7 (or Cmaj7/D), mm. 14–15) support a chromatic progression that returns to the minor sonorities that characterize of mm. 1–8. The syncopated harmonic rhythm at mm. 11 and 13 recreates the technique that appears on all of the quintet compositions on *Sorcerer*, since each includes a similar syncopated progression near the end of the form.

During the improvisations, the group maintains the underlying form. Yet it offers a case study in how the quintet creates challenges to the 16-bar regularity: the improvisations and the ambiguity of accompaniment often mask the formal divisions. Further, the almost complete absence of piano comping heightens the ambiguity, although—as the following will show—Hancock steps in once to clarify a discrepancy.

DAVIS'S SOLO

The discussion of Davis's solo on "Dolores" in chapter 4 described how Davis frequently turned to clear identifiable motives at the top of the form. In "Dolores," this comes about through phrase overlap: a repeated motivic statement begun at the top of the form arises by concluding a longer phrase from the previous chorus. A similar process occurs at the beginning of Davis's solo on "Prince of Darkness." Example 5.3 contains a transcription to the beginning of Davis's solo and the bass accompaniment (:31). Note how M1a anticipates the beginning of Davis's first chorus by an eighth note, and emerges from the eighth-note lead-in figure begun 2 bars earlier. Each M1 motive appears every two measures, recurring at the downbeats of mm. 3, 5, and 7. All share the same rhythmic profile (with the exception of M1a's opening pitch). Most share the same pitches of G♭5, F, E, E♭, and C (M1c repeats E♭, rather than continuing to C). M1c develops the motive by leaping to A♭4 (m. 6), with the ensuing rising line creating a lead-in to M1d at m. 7.

EXAMPLE 5.3   Davis's Solo and Carter's Accompaniment on "Prince of Darkness," mm. 1–52 (:31)

EXAMPLE 5.3   Continued

Since M1 returns every 2 bars, it makes clear the underlying 8-bar section and its 2-bar harmonic rhythm. And since Davis lays out mm. 2 and 4, he further sets the motives in high relief. However, a significant aspect of M1 is its independence from the underlying harmony. Here Davis forgoes the harmonic progression (Gmin7 Dmin7 B♭min7 Gmin7), and superimposes the repeated motive. The motive may perhaps be heard as

elaborating a C diminished triad, or A♭7 at mm. 5–6. By dint of its repetition and 2-bar placement, the motive takes on potency, and exhibits
Davis's ability to shape memorable motives independent of the underlying harmony. (Note, too, that Carter at mm. 5–6 abandons the B♭– harmony heard during the head and beneath other improvised choruses.)

It is possible to hear these 8 bars as shaping a larger level of musical
organization to which the following bars respond. Davis's move to G–F–
E♭–C at mm. 9–10 (:40) provides a response to the M1 motive. It creates a
larger voice leading maneuver that sends the upper pitch of M1, F♯, up a
half-step to G at mm. 9–10, before retracing the same general path downward through F–E♭–C. The overall motion from M1 mm. 1–8 to mm. 9–10
can be heard as a trope on a blues lick in C minor, with ♯4 progressing
to 5. It also helps explain how the sustained G at m. 9, independent of
the underlying G♭Maj7 harmony, sounds convincing. Measures 1–10 also
indicate how Davis shapes longer musical spans that need not require
absolute fidelity to the underlying harmonic progression, but still generally support the 2-bar divisions of the harmonic rhythm.

The mm. 9–10 idea continues to generate subsequent material. The 4-bar
section at mm. 9–12 shapes a rhythmic motive as it unfolds, M2. The transcription brackets the two versions of M2 (mm. 9 and 11) in order to show
how they offer the same rhythmic profile. Thus throughout these opening
bars Davis spins out a series of ongoing motivic relationships, based not
only on pitch and rhythm (M1), but also solely on rhythm (M2).

A comparison of the beginning of Davis's third chorus (m. 33ff.; 1:03)
with the first reveals some interesting overall similarities. The first 8 bars
(mm. 33–40) rely primarily on elaboration of a single motive, initially
heard as three statements of the same pitch C (M3a), before becoming
elaborated with E♭ (M3b) that precedes the three statements of C. Davis
elaborates M3c even further, and notice here how the melodic line *does*
carefully project the underlying harmony (B♭min7) in a way that M3a–b
do not. In contrast to M1, however, the M3 motives do not as clearly
support the underlying 2-bar harmonic rhythm. Instead, M3 displays
motivic expansion, with each consecutive idea appearing longer and
developed more fully. A comparison of mm. 8–10 with 40–42 show some
consistent moves: the motion upward to the sustained G at the midpoint
of the form (over the same G♭Maj7 harmony), and the following motion
down through F, E♭, and C (the line at m. 43 continues upward to D♭).[22]

Davis's second chorus (m. 17ff; :48) departs drastically from the motivic
orientation, and there are a number of factors that obscure the underlying

22 Davis undertakes largely the same path at the midpoint of his sixth chorus as well (1:56).

form here. One of them is Carter's use of half-note triplets to stratify triple meter within the 4/4 meter. Carter begins stating the conflicting meter at m. 11 of Davis's solo, and maintains it throughout the second chorus.

In addition, Davis's gestures cut across the 4- and 8-bar groupings of "Prince of Darkness" in his second chorus. There occur three larger gestures here. The 6-bar descending line, expressed with sustained pitches at mm. 17–22, extends over two octaves and ultimately outlines an A♭ minor harmony m. 22. The eighth-note line of mm. 23–26 reverses the overall contour. Despite the gradual ascent, note how tightly compact are some of Davis's eighth-note constructions: m. 24 spans only a minor third as the line turns on itself. The entire phrase straddles the downbeat of m. 25, blurring the midpoint of the 16-bar form. (Notice too Carter's harmonic alteration at mm. 25–26, which replaces the G♭ harmony with a more functional progression that moves C–F. This reharmonization creates an evident harmonic arrival at B♭ at m. 27.) Finally at mm. 27–31 occurs a largely descending line that accelerates as it progresses, and its pitch material retraces some of the material heard during the mm. 17–22 descending line (shown by dashed slurs at mm. 18–22 and 26–29).

The sense of underlying meter becomes attenuated here, to the extent that the group is out of phase with one another moving into Davis's third chorus (1:03). The asterisks in the transcription illustrate what happens. As Carter departs from the triple groupings at the beginning of this next chorus, the bass accompanimental pattern strays from the others. Carter begins an eighth note behind Williams and Davis (asterisks show where Carter interprets the downbeats at mm. 33–36). At m. 35 Carter adjusts, but he adds an eighth note, and now lags a beat behind Williams and Davis. The lack of metric clarity here induces Hancock—who has provided no accompaniment during Davis's solo up until now—to participate and help shore up the meter. At m. 37 Hancock plays a single dyad on the downbeat of the measure. Two measures later (m. 39) he plays again on the downbeat, now stating a single pitch, and two dyads at mm. 40–41. Hancock's cues are sufficient to clarify the meter, and he ceases playing. Carter's accompaniment moves back into metrical phase with the other players by m. 38. Here the pianist steps in momentarily to help clarify the metrical discrepancies.

As Carter moves back into metrical phase, he departs from the underlying harmonic progression and inaugurates a sequence that progresses by whole step downward from F to G mm. 43–48. At m. 51 he returns to overtly expressing the underlying harmonic progression.

Noteworthy at the beginning of Davis's fourth chorus (1:18) is Motive M4. M4a emerges at mm. 48–49 as the endpoint of a longer line, creating a phrase overlap. M4b focuses on the pitches of G♭5–F5 before continuing and outlining a G♭Maj7 harmony. Typical for Davis is the use of a clear motive, one that emanates from a previous line, and one used to mark the top of the form. With Davis's implied G♭Maj7 harmony, M4, like Davis's other motives in "Prince of Darkness," are strongly memorable while largely independent of the underlying harmony.

HANCOCK'S SOLO

Like Davis's solo, much of Hancock's solo pursues overt motivic relationships. Hancock's solo is often ruthless in its pursuit of motivic integrity, and—during these motivic sections—Hancock eliminates nearly everything extrinsic to these motives. Unlike Davis, who establishes here pitch-specific motives, Hancock's motives are based instead upon rhythm, contour, and interval. During these motivically driven sections (such as at mm. 1–8, 17–24, 81–88), Hancock is consistent about expressing motives in four 2-bar units. These appear in the first halves of their choruses, and uphold the 2-bar divisions of the harmonic rhythm. Elsewhere, such as at mm. 27–31 and 75–79, Hancock pursues similar motivic relationships within the second half of the chorus.

The analysis will focus on those motivic sections and show how they contrast with other portions of the solo in which Hancock obscures the form and challenges the underlying 2-, 4-, 8-, and 16-bar regularity. Certainly Davis's return to the head 1 bar early suggests Hancock's success in obscuring the form. Hancock uses his left hand sparingly, further enhancing the openness and ambiguity. Example 5.4 is a transcription of the piano solo.

EXAMPLE 5.4   Hancock's Solo on "Prince of Darkness" (4:03)

EXAMPLE 5.4   Continued

The opening to Hancock's solo (4:03) uses four two-note descending motives (P1a–d) that delineate the 2-bar harmonic rhythm and the 8-bar first half of the composition. Each begins mid-measure. Each express descending fourths save for P1b, a descending fifth. Each consecutive motive is lower than the previous, with the first pitch of each motive expressing C–A–F–D, an upper structure harmony of the overarching G minor tonality.

The second half of this first chorus (4:11) departs from the evident motivic orientation. It relies more regularly on eighth-note phrasing, although mm. 9–12 preserve some of the underlying 2-bar organization heard in mm. 1–8. The left-hand harmony at mm. 10–11 corresponds to the BMaj7 harmony of m. 12 from the head. Thus here Hancock suppresses the B♭Maj7(♯5) harmony from the head at m. 11, and anticipates the m. 12 harmony by 2 bars, linking the G♭Maj7 (m. 9) with BMaj7 (mm. 10–12). Hancock avoids the m. 11 B♭Maj7(♯5) throughout the solo, therefore this harmonic deletion becomes a consistent feature. Its motivation may have been to make the improvisation more seamless, given the closer harmonic relationship between G♭Maj7 and C♭/BMaj7.

By the end of the first chorus, at mm. 15–16 (4:16), Hancock recalls the descending two-note motives heard in mm. 1–8. The first, B–G (mm. 15) outlines not a fourth but a major third. Note that the upper pitch B is attained through ascending half-step voice leading (B♭, end of m. 14, to B, beginning of m. 15). This upward voice-leading takes place in counterpoint to the half-step descending harmonic progression of E♭min7 to Dmin7. (Hancock undertakes a similar technique in his third chorus.) The second descending two-note motive, A–E (mm. 15–16), returns the descending fourth that dominated mm. 1–8.

Similar to the first chorus, the first half of Hancock's second chorus (mm. 17–25; 4:18) sets out four 2-bar motives that corroborate the underlying 2-bar harmonic rhythm (P2a–d). Here the motive is a six-pitch figure. It consists of a three-pitch ascent, a descent that retraces those steps, and a downward leap to the final pitch. The rhythmic identity of each motive differs somewhat, and the subtle rhythmic changes to each P2 motive create a remarkable oratorical effect. And, as in mm. 1–8, each motive descends relative to the previous one. The opening pitches of each motive express C–A–G–F.

As with the second half of the first chorus, mm. 25–32 abandon the earlier motive. Hancock states a new motive at m. 27 (4:28), which becomes the primary focus of the remainder of the chorus. P3a–d consistently span a descending fourth (mm. 27–31). A chromatic lead-in precedes P3b–d. The first two motives (P3a–b) span 6 beats, and P3c–d appear on downbeats (mm. 30 and 31), creating a process of rhythmic contraction with the final two motives. Further, Hancock transposes each successive fourth down by whole step: E♭5–B♭4 (m. 27), D♭5–A♭4 (mm. 28–29), B4–F♯ (m. 30), A–E (m. 31). This transpositional scheme overrides the underlying harmonic progression, a technique to which Hancock returns during the fourth and fifth choruses.

Hancock's third chorus (m. 33ff.) becomes the flash point for metrical and harmonic ambiguity, beginning at m. 39. At mm. 37–38 (4:37) Hancock's elaboration of B♭–11 becomes the launching point for a series of five downward arpeggiations, P4a–e. Here these motives do not uphold the composition's 8-bar formal divisions. Nor do they corroborate the meter. Measures 39–40 suppress the harmonic change to G minor. Measure 39 maintains the same pitch material heard in m. 38, and this then initiates a sequence in which each motive appears every three beats. The resulting metrical conflict creates a layer of 3/4 at mm. 39–42. The sequence consistently maintains a five-flat environment as Hancock effectively links the B♭–11 of mm. 37–38 with the G♭Maj7 of mm. 41–42, bypassing the G minor harmony of mm. 39–40. As P4a–e carry across the midpoint of the form, the motives, the metrical conflict, and the consistent five-flat environment all conspire to blur the midpoint of the form at m. 41.

By the end of this third chorus Hancock hews more closely to the harmonic progression. Nevertheless, he retains a hint of metric ambiguity through subtle accentual shift. For example, the second half of m. 46 (4:46) arpeggiates the chromatic neighbor harmony of E♭min9, and Hancock continues this arpeggiation into the downbeat of the following measure. The C♯–D motion m. 47 moves the voice-leading chromatically upward, as the harmonic progression moves chromatically downward from E♭min7 to Dmin7, effecting a move similar to the one that appeared in Hancock's first chorus (mm. 14–15). But here Hancock moves to Dmin7 on the second beat of the measure, creating an accentual shift. The D– arpeggiation at mm. 16 outlines D–6/9 here, and Hancock carries the sixth of the harmony, B, into the beginning of his next chorus, thwarting the G minor harmony at the top of the form.

Hancock's fourth and fifth choruses continue to challenge the underlying form, and further depart from the underlying harmonic progression. Measures 60–65 (4:58) set up a series of motives that arpeggiate a perfect-fourth based harmony. P5a–e emerge through phrase overlap, with P5a concluding a previous line and initiating a series of motives. The motives descend successively in whole steps, beginning with G♭5 (m. 60), E5 (m. 62), D (mm. 62–63), C (mm. 63–64), and B♭ (mm. 64–65). As in his second chorus, the transposition downward by whole step here superimposes a harmonic structure largely independent of the underlying harmonic progression of "Prince of Darkness." Note the rhythmic flexibility of these motives, and P5d–e create metrical conflict by expressing a layer of 3/4 above the 4/4 meter.

In Hancock's fifth chorus, he returns to a similar transpositional scheme at mm. 75–79 (5:12), again superimposing it over the underlying harmonic progression. P6a–e occur rhythmically regularly, appearing on consecutive downbeats save for P6e, which begins a beat earlier. The opening pitches of each move downward by whole step, with each motive spanning a third.

Hancock's final chorus returns to clear motivic construction during both halves, and this clarifies the underlying form. Measures 81–88 (5:17) revert to a descending two-note motive, and the four statements of this 2-bar motive underscore the 8-bar section of the form. Measures 89–92 establish a dotted quarter-note/eighth-note pattern.[23] Measures 93–94 reverse the rhythmic pattern of the previous 4 bars, and now appear within an eighth-note/dotted quarter pattern.

The tight motivic construction of Hancock's improvisation is striking. It shows the extent to which motivic improvisation becomes an underlying premise on some of the quintet recordings. Many of these motives clearly support 2-, 4-, and 8-bar formal divisions. But at other moments the solo thwarts the underlying meter, harmonic progression, and form. All of this offers ways for hearing motivic solutions that range widely between clarity and ambiguity. Although not discussed above, certainly critical to all this is the role of the other members of the rhythm section. The latitude between clarity and ambiguity allows all the players to make astonishingly pliable the highly regular underlying 16-bar form.[24]

"PEE WEE"

"Pee Wee" is one of three compositions that drummer Tony Williams contributed to the Davis quintet studio recordings. The haunting composition exhibits a memorable melody and harmonic progression, and is notable for the absence of Davis on the recording. The composition has enjoyed an extended shelf life due to its inclusion in fake books (such as *The Real Book*) but despite the rigorous challenges of its 21-bar form and unusual harmonic progressions.[25] Yet *The Real Book* lead sheet contains a number of harmonic labels inconsistent with the performance on the recording. Example 5.5 contains an annotated lead sheet. The group plays the chromatic progression at mm. 5–6 as Ebmin9(b5) to Emin9(b5) (this progression could also be realized as B13(#11)/Eb to C13(#11)/E rather than Eb7(#9) to E7(#9), as indicated in *The Real Book*. And Hancock plays the following (mm. 7–8) harmony as Db13, with Carter playing Gb in the bass against it. Here *The Real Book* indicates the harmony as GbMaj7(#11), and the rationale for that error is clear. The melody at m. 8 includes C natural, a note theoretically incompatible with the Db13 harmony (which suggests Cb rather than C natural). This is perhaps why Hancock usually voices the chord more strongly in m. 7 than m. 8.

---

23 Although the rhythm is altered, the pitches at mm. 89–90 are identical to those heard at mm. 9–12.

24 However, the group does collectively drop two beats during Davis's final chorus.

25 "Pee Wee" has now been omitted from the sixth edition version of *The Real Book*.

EXAMPLE 5.5   Annotated Lead Sheet to "Pee Wee."

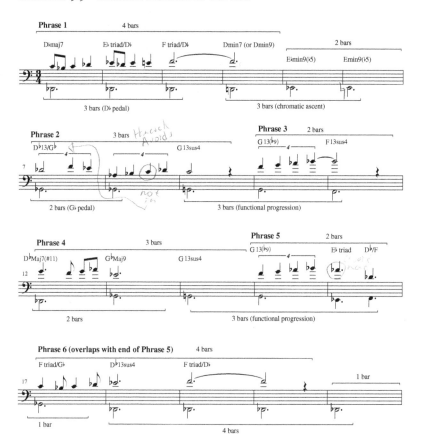

Additionally, *The Real Book* realizes the m. 16 downbeat harmony—
with its melody pitch of A♭— as F–11. Ron Miller indicates this same harmony differently, as E♭6/9.[26] In fact, the group plays this harmony at the
downbeat of m. 16 as neither, but instead as an E♭ triad (or E♭Maj7 during
the improvisations). Again, the melody pitch here probably explains this
confusion, since the use of A♭ as the sole melody pitch above the root

26 Ron Miller, *Modal Jazz: Composition and Harmony*, vol. 1 (Rottenburg Germany: Advance
   Music, 1996), 74.

of the E♭ triad contradicts jazz theory strictures that consider the fourth above the root of a triad or major seventh chord as an "avoid note."[27]

The haunting melody of "Pee Wee" is, with the exception of the single E natural passing tone in m. 2, exclusively diatonic to a four-flat environment. Example 5.5 identifies and numbers six melodic phrases. These six phrases are tightly knit, and the pitches for each span a stepwise fourth, fifth, or sixth. Phrase 1 spans B♭3–F4, Phrase 2 increases Phrase 1's melodic span by a step, forming a sixth (A♭3–F4). Phrase 3 begins with the upper pitch of the first two phrases, and spans a fourth (F4–B♭4). Phrase 4 frames a fourth, now down a step from Phrase 3 (E♭4–A♭4). Phrase 5 expands that span by a step in either direction, forming a sixth (D♭4–B♭4). Phrase 6 recalls the identical opening fifth span of Phrase 1 (B♭3–F4), but note the decided phrase overlap between Phrases 5 and 6. The consistent use of such tight intervallic spans filled out stepwise allies "Pee Wee" with other compositions the quintet recorded: compare, for example, the stepwise phrase structure to Shorter's "Prince of Darkness."

In Ron Miller's list of attributes for the composition, he suggests that "it seems to have been composed purely by intuition, without much pre-planning."[28] Williams himself acknowledged that he began only with the opening phrase, and Davis coaxed him into completing the composition.[29] But the phrases host a number of astounding melodic relationships. The six phrases reflect and refract one another as if through a prism. Some of these interior relations are overt. Others are less so. The following chart illustrates the more evident relationships:

Phrase 1   A
Phrase 2   B
Phrase 3   C
Phrase 4   D
Phrase 5   C'
Phrase 6   A'

The chart shows how earlier material is brought back later in the composition. The final Phrase 6 clearly echoes Phrase 1, and Phrases 3 and 5 begin identically. Additionally, there are other reflections at work. Phrase 2 ends with C4, the same pitch that began Phrase 1. And Phrase 4 rhymes

---

27 See Levine, *The Jazz Theory Book*, 37, for a discussion of the fourth as an avoid note over major seventh harmonies.

28 Miller, *Modal Jazz*, 74.

29 Zan Stewart, "Miles Lives," *Down Beat* 59/9 (September 1992): 20.

with the opening Phrase 1: note that although the rhythms are changed, m. 12 precisely transposes the intervals of m. 1 upward by a fifth. Additionally, there is a rhythm and contour relationship between mm. 8 and 10: both rely on a stepwise four-note ascent with the identical rhythmic grouping. (The melody provided is taken from the opening head statement played by Shorter on the recording).

These interior mirrored relationships among the different phrases seem to contradict Miller's notion that the piece relied on minimal preplanning. To be fair, Miller does not consider the melodic structure of "Pee Wee" in his analysis, which focuses exclusively on harmonic structure. And the harmonic structure is certainly more elusive than the melodic design. At the very least, we can acknowledge that the harmonic organization of "Pee Wee" maintains aesthetic ties with quintet compositions written by other group members. These shared techniques include the use of extended pedal points with shifting triadic structures above them (i.e., slash chord harmonies), chromatically ascending dominant harmonies (such as at mm. 5–6—compare with mm. 5–8 of "E.S.P.," which also uses ascending chromatic dominant-type harmonies, rather than the more common downward chromatic progression of dominant sonorities), and the merging of nonfunctional progressions with occasional reliance on more functional progressions.

The more functional progressions appear at mm. 9–11 and at mm. 14–16. In both the overall motion initially moves from G13sus4 to G13(♭9). These harmonize similarly the related Phrases 3 and 5, making the relationship between Phrases 3 and 5 even clearer. The chord following the G13(♭9) differs in both instances, with the group playing F13sus4 (or E♭Maj7/F, m. 11), and E♭ (or E♭Maj7, m. 16). Yet despite the difference in bass pitch at mm. 11 and 16, the upper structures remain consistent. And Carter's bass substitutions often interpret the overall progression in an even clearer functional way. Behind Shorter's initial two solo choruses at mm. 9–11, he substitutes D for G at m. 9 (resulting in Dmin9), and C for F at m. 11 (resulting in Cmin9), creating the progression Dmin9 G13(♭9) Cmin9. These harmonic progressions at mm. 9–11 and 14–16 stand out in the context of the less functional progressions throughout much of "Pee Wee." The subsequent discussion will consider those three-chord progressions as "functional" in a provisional sense, ones that conspicuously transform a progression that links pre-dominant to dominant to tonic function chords.

As a 21-bar composition, "Pee Wee's" hypermetric structure is unusual. There are some compositional features that might suggest Davis's input: the transitional-sounding 2 bars without melody at mm. 4–5, the melodic syncopation at the end of m. 10 that seems to make m. 11 sound as an inserted bar (for example, note how the m. 10 melody links convincingly to m. 12 without m. 11), and the final m. 21 that sounds in some ways as an extra inserted bar.

Perhaps the most beguiling aspect of the composition involves the ways in which the melodic structure and the harmonic structure create conflicting measure groupings. The two dimensions of melody and harmony crosscut one another in unusual ways. Example 5.5 shows how melody and harmony operate out of phase with one another. For example, the composition opens with the melody of Phrase 1 establishing a clear 4-bar grouping, followed by 2 bars without melody. This results in a grouping of 4 + 2 measures. But the harmonic progression cuts against this grouping. In the harmonic dimension, the progression suggests two 3-bar groupings. Measures 1–3 consist of a fixed pedal point D♭ below upper triadic structures that ascend from D♭–E♭–F. This is followed by a 3-bar chromatic ascent (Dmin7 E♭min9(♭5) Emin9(♭5), mm. 4–6) that undercuts the 4-bar melodic structure.

Similarly, the interior Phrases 2–5 house melodic and harmonic groupings out of phase with one another. The melodic structure to Phrases 2 and 3 consist of 3 + 2 measures. Similarly, the melodic structure to Phrases 4 and 5 consist of 3 + 2 groupings (with the melodies to Phrases 3 and 5 intimately related, as discussed above). However, the harmonic structure cuts across those groupings, and instead creates groupings of 2 + 3 measures. The single harmony D♭13/G♭ (2 bars, mm. 7–8) then yields to the functional harmonic progression of G13sus4 G13(♭9) F13sus4 (3 bars, mm. 9–11). The functional progression initiates a 3-bar metric grouping. Measures 12–16 operate analogously to mm. 7–11, with the melodic grouping of 3 + 2 bars crosscutting the harmonic grouping of 2 + 3 bars, the latter formed by D♭Maj7(♯11) to G♭Maj7 (mm. 12–13) that appears prior to the functional harmonic progression (at mm. 14–16).

Finally, Phrase 6 (mm. 17–21) lasts for 5 bars, and it is possible to hear this in a manner similar to Phrase 1. Phrase 1 is a 4-bar melodic phrase, followed by an additional 2 bars without melody, creating a 4 + 2 grouping for mm. 1–6. Phrase 6 consists of a 4-bar melodic phrase, followed by a single additional bar, creating a 4 + 1 grouping. (This unusual 5-bar grouping may have been the catalyst that caused Hancock to add an additional bar at the end of his second improvised chorus.) But in Phrase 6, the bass works against this 4 + 1 grouping. Notice that the arrival of D♭ occurs at m. 18, and the bass remains on D♭ for 4 bars. This creates a 1 + 4 grouping for the accompaniment. However, it is important to acknowledge that the melodic and harmonic structure of mm. 17–21 is ambiguous. The melody begins by overlapping with the end of Phrase 5, before Phrase 6 provides a varied repetition of Phrase 1. And the degree to which the harmony provides a grouping of 1 + 4 is certainly open to question—other listeners may hear this entire progression as simply a 5-bar group.

The tonal center of "Pee Wee" relies on the opening and closing D♭, and this bass pitch supports a number of shifting harmonies above it in mm. 1–3 and mm. 18–21. Note that while the harmonization at Phrase 6 differs from that of the related Phrase 1, a clearer harmonic relationship emerges at the 3rd bar of both phrases. Both m. 3 and m. 19 rely on the same harmony of F(triad)/D♭. The resultant Maj7♯5 harmony appears in a number of compositions on *Sorcerer*, including Shorter's "Vonetta" and "Prince of Darkness." (However, Shorter's solo on "Pee Wee" remains rather indifferent to the ♯5—A natural—of this harmony. Shorter much more consistently relies on A♭, rather than A natural, while improvising over this harmony.)

Heard against the backdrop of standard jazz compositions, "Pee Wee" offers radically different compositional solutions. It contains a forward-looking harmonic vocabulary characteristic of the Davis quintet, and an unusual 21-bar structure. Standard jazz compositions frequently rely on a consistent 4- and 8-bar hypermeter, and the two dimensions of melody and harmony typically work in tandem with one another. But the melodic and harmonic dimensions of "Pee Wee" do not operate in phase with one another in the same manner. The six phrases reflect and respond to one another in differing ways, and the metric groupings of these six melodic phrases do not consistently align with the groupings created by the harmonic structure. These out-of-phase melodic and harmonic groupings supply much of the elusive intrigue of the composition.

"LIMBO"

Shorter notated the copyright deposit lead sheet to "Limbo" as an 8-bar composition in 6/4.[30] It includes two harmonies per bar for most of the composition, save for four harmonies at mm. 12–13, which provide the syncopated harmonic progression that appears in all of *Sorcerer's* compositions. In addition to the released take to "Limbo," the group recorded an alternate take (with Buster Williams on bass in place of Ron Carter). On both takes, the group elongates m. 4, altering the notated 6/4 into a

---

30 Library of Congress Copyright Deposit Eu 42290 (March 13, 1968).

TABLE 5.2   Harmonies Played on Released and Alternate Takes of "Limbo"

Released Take (indicated below as 17-bar form in 3/4)

[handwritten: 8 bar original]

M. 1	2	3	4	5	6	7–8	9
E♭min9	D♭min9*	C7(♭5)	F13sus	B♭13sus	D(triad)	A♭°9	B♭13sus
10	11	12	13	14	15	16	17
G♭Maj9	D♭min7*	BMaj7(♯5) E7alt	E♭min9 D13 *[handwritten: (♯4)]*	D♭min7	A7alt	E♭min9	(DMaj7*: first time only)

[handwritten below BMaj7(♯5) E7alt: A D, G]

*These harmonies included only in the rhythm section introduction (introduction on released take is 18-bar form: m. 9 extended into two bars).

Alternate Take

M. 1	3	5	7–9
E♭min9/A♭	C7/G♭	B♭13sus	C13/G** or A♭°9
10	12	13	14	16–17
G♭Maj9	BMaj7(♯5) E7alt	E♭min9 D13	D♭min7	E♭min9

** A♭°9 occasionally played m. 7

9/4 measure. For clarity, the following discussion will regard "Limbo" in 3/4, rather than 6/4. With this, the composition is a 17-bar form in triple meter.[31]

In many ways the two takes are similar. Both begin with the rhythm section playing an introductory two choruses, which yields to more aggressive accompaniment during the head. But there are differences between the two versions. One notable difference is due to the accompanying harmonies. Table 5.2 lists the harmonies played by the group on the released take and the alternate take.

There is an ongoing series of harmonic deletions. First, note that for the released take, the two-chorus introduction includes harmonic changes at m. 2 and 11 (indicated with asterisks). These harmonies were part of Shorter's original lead sheet, but become deleted for the head statements and improvisations. (The rhythm section also provides an additional DMaj7 harmony the final measure in the first chorus of the introduction.) Further, a comparison between the two takes shows that on the alternate track the group makes further harmonic deletions, eliminating the harmonies at mm. 4, 6, and 15. This alters the harmonic rhythm significantly. In addition, there are some subtle differences in the harmonies that remain. For example, the upper structure of the harmony remains similar, but the bass pitch differs at mm. 1 and 3, relative to the released track. Further, the group realizes mm. 7–9 differently in both takes. The differences between the two versions indicate deliberate alterations to Shorter's compositions.[32]

Measures 12–13 provide the syncopated harmonic progression to "Limbo," with the two harmonies per measure interpreting the triple meter duply. Throughout the performances, Hancock's voicings here typically plane down chromatically, rather than systematically adhere to the underlying chord progression (the mm. 12–13 progression shown above is drawn from Shorter's lead sheet). During the introduction of the released track, for example, he plays the four chords at mm. 12–13

---

31 Shorter notated a number of his compositions in 6/4, including compositions more commonly considered in 3/4, such as "Wild Flower" and "Dance Cadaverous."

32 This point counters the view that arises from Coolman's interviews with the quintet members. Both Shorter and Hancock make the point that Shorter's compositions were among the only ones unedited by Davis. Perhaps Davis did not alter Shorter's compositions to the extent he did those by others, but certainly the alternate take to "Limbo" reflects evident harmonic deletions. See Coolman, "The Miles Davis Quintet," 24 and 30. It is important to acknowledge, though, that the more altered version was the earlier alternate take, while the less altered version, closer to Shorter's original lead sheet version, was the later released take.

as chromatic descending fourth chords in the left hand, beginning with A–D–G. In this way, the final fourth chord, F♯–B–E, aligns with the bass D (forming a D6/9 harmony), before both bass and piano resolve to the D♭–9 harmony at m. 14. Within the first statement of the head, Hancock uses the same descending fourth-chord voicing, but now elaborated to a two-hand voicing, beginning with A–D–G–C♯.

The slower harmonic rhythm of the alternate take might suggest that the group would treat the form more freely on it than on the released track. Yet the opposite occurs. The group clearly maintains the form on the alternate take, and with Hancock's comping during the solos the quintet preserves the form consistently. However, although the group maintains the general formal outlines, they do not precisely maintain the form on the released track. The absence of Hancock's comping behind the horn solos, and the free interactive bass and drums, create a high degree of formal elasticity on the released take. For example, Shorter's second, third, fourth, and fifth choruses (3:07–4:09) each last 16 bars rather than 17 bars. And Hancock's solo begins with the syncopated progression of mm. 12–13 (4:46), and his following chorus (4:52–5:06) eliminates mm. 14–17.

Another significant difference between the two takes relates to the metric strategy during solos. The alternate take maintains the triple meter throughout. But on the released track Williams changes the meter once the solos begin. This metric modulation relates to one of two types discussed in chapter 2. The 3/4 to 4/4 shift in "Limbo" preserves the pulse while expanding the measures. The quarter note value remains consistent. (In contrast, the metric modulation in "Footprints" moves from 6/4 to 4/4. It preserves the measure, but decelerates the underlying pulse.)

The melody to "Limbo" consists of a series of related phrases, particularly in the opening 11 bars. For example, mm. 1–2 and 10–11 rely on the same melodic motion, and mm. 5–6 varies this motion slightly. All begin with F4, and all end with G♭. The craggy melody supports a wavelike contour during the opening 11 bars with each ascending gesture preceding a descending one. This contour offered some interest to Shorter: the contour of the opening melody to "Prince of Darkness" is strikingly similar to that of "Limbo." Example 5.6 contains the opening measures to both. "Prince of Darkness" expresses its contour through stepwise motion, while "Limbo" expresses it primarily through skipwise motion. The underlying contour of both is nearly identical. For "Prince of Darkness," the contour segment is (+ + + + − − +), for "Limbo" it is (+ + + + − − − +). (The designation + refers to an ascending contour among adjacent pitches, − to descending contour.)

EXAMPLE 5.6   Comparison of Melody Contour to "Prince of Darkness" and "Limbo"
(+) = Ascending Pitch; (−) = Descending Pitch

Structurally, both phrases are remarkably similar. Both include an initial motive of four ascending pitches, followed by a related motive that steps higher, descends, then reverses the contour at the end. They differ in that "Prince of Darkness" begins with a four-note upbeat figure (anticipating m. 1), while "Limbo" begins with a four-note afterbeat figure (beginning in m. 1). These types of contours—whether stepwise or arpeggiated—explain in part some of the more questionable claims about scalar organization and modality. Chambers describes "Limbo" as "simply a unison run by the trumpet and saxophone up the minor scale and back down it." Certainly even the first four measures of the melody contained in example 5.6 show "Limbo" to be much more intricately conceived than Chambers's scalar description.

For Chambers this scalar/modal view fuels a negative assessment of many of the second quintet compositions. "Nondescript themes," he writes, "as in 'Limbo' and 'Pee Wee,' and on 'Orbits' from *Miles Smiles,* slip past without asserting any distinctive mood, leaving behind only an expanse of improvisation on minor scales." He continues by describing these compositions as providing "themes for modal improvisation."[33] Elsewhere he suggests that Shorter's second quintet compositions "consist of brief, melodic catch-phrases...that get repeated arbitrarily in the opening and closing ensembles. The point of the catch-phrase is to encode the scale that is available to the improviser." As chapter 2 suggested, the picture is significantly more complex. Most of the second quintet improvisations rely on far more than single—or even multiple—minor scales, and most of the compositions do not maintain the slow or

---

33 Chambers, *Milestones* 2, 103, 105, and 99.

static harmonic rhythm characteristic of works considered modal jazz. With some clear exceptions ("Agitation," "Freedom Jazz Dance," "Masqualero"), the second quintet compositions offer less in terms of modal scales and static harmonic rhythm, and more in terms of modal harmony: faster harmonic progressions with absent or limited functional moves (such as V–I or ii–V–I) and the use of nontraditional harmonies.

IN CONTRAST TO THE EARLIER *MILES SMILES*, *Sorcerer* remains more detached from the hard bop tradition by largely abandoning the walking bass swing feels heard on the earlier recording. "Vonetta" indicates further developments in Shorter's harmonic vocabulary in the context of a circular tune. On "Masqualero" the quintet molded the slow-moving harmonic progression, highlighted by the phrygian orientation, into a deeply dramatic performance. Davis's and Hancock's solos on "Prince of Darkness" show the improvisers firmly committed to motivic improvisation, while still offering significant challenges to the underlying regularity of the 16-bar single section form. "Pee Wee," an unusual 21-bar form, supported a melodic structure and harmonic structure frequently operating independently of one another. And the two takes to "Limbo" show remarkably different approaches to the same composition: the alternate take removed a number of harmonies and maintained the underlying triple meter; the released track involved a more intricate harmonic progression, and shifted to 4/4 as the solos began. The group recorded their first three studio albums with substantial time between each. They began work on their fourth album, Nefertiti, only a month after Sorcerer.

CHAPTER 6

NEFERTITI

DID THE TITLE TRACK TO *Nefertiti* mark a watershed moment for
the second quintet? The group took the decisive and unusual step of
performing "Nefertiti" without improvisations by trumpet, saxophone,
and piano. Instead, the recording consists of repeated statements of the
melody, with shifting accompaniment provided by the rhythm section,
effectively reversing the standard roles for horns and rhythm section.
For many reasons—the absence of standard horn/piano improvisations,
the floating melody consisting of three related phrases, the harmonic
progression, the mercurial rhythm section accompaniment—Shorter's
composition "Nefertiti" represented for many an important point of
departure. For pianist Josef Zawinul, "Nefertiti" was emblematic of the
"new thinking." Michelle Mercer writes "'Nefertiti' was the harbinger of

a new period for Miles, one in which improvised solos became second-ary to mood and fragmented riffs."[1]

Yet it may be more accurate to consider the quintet's decision to record "Nefertiti" only with repeated statements of melody as evolving out of a continuing practice, one that thrust compositional melody further into the foreground. On earlier recordings the quintet began returning to the composition's melody between and within the improvisations ("Free-dom Jazz Dance," "Vonetta," "The Sorcerer," and "Prince of Darkness"). This posed an alternative to standard chorus structure, which typically relies on the compositional melody stated merely at the beginning and the end of the performance. However, with "Nefertiti," the quintet takes the decisive step by making statements of the melody the central event of the composition, replacing standard improvisation by horns and piano.

It seems that by 1967 Davis had been chafing under the limitations of the head—solos—head format for some time. In a 1959 interview, Can-nonball Adderley described Davis as already expressing dissatisfaction with those limitations. "He's tired of tunes," said Adderley. "You know he says, 'You play the melody, then everybody blows, and you play the melody, and the tune is ended, and that's a jazz performance.'"[2]

Elsewhere *Nefertiti* features unusual techniques. "Fall" also blurred conventional distinctions between melody and improvisation: it begins with the trumpet improvisation and ends with the bass improvisation, and only fragments of the melody are heard during those two improvisa-tions. The improvisations in "Riot" move down by half step with each new solo. Yet the quintet also returns to some improvisational and accompa-nimental strategies heard earlier on *Miles Smiles* but largely absent from *Sorcerer*. The group applies the technique of "time, no changes" in the context of 4/4 walking bass on "Madness" and "Hand Jive."

"HAND JIVE"

HEAD

Like Shorter's "Pinocchio," Tony Williams's "Hand Jive" is an 18-bar com-position. But whereas the two sections of "Pinocchio" comprise 8 + 10

---

1 Zawinul quoted in Jack Chambers, *Milestones: The Music and Times of Miles Davis* 2 (New York: Da Capo, 1998), 109, originally publ. University of Toronto Press 1983 and 1985; Michelle Mercer, *Footprints: The Life and Work of Wayne Shorter* (New York: J. P. Tarcher/Penguin, 2004), 123.

2 Ira Gitler, "Julian 'Cannonball' Adderley" (Part 2), *Jazz: A Quarterly of American Music* 4 (1959): 291.

bars, "Hand Jive" comprises 11 + 7 bars. (Example 6.1 contains the melody to "Hand Jive.") The initial 11-bar section contains a single measure (m. 11) without melody, and the unusual grouping of 11 bars arise from metric deletion—that is, the three measures of mm. 9–11 sound as if comprising a foreshortened 4-bar segment.[3] For the second section of "Hand Jive" the unusual grouping of bars arises from the presence of 3 bars without melody that follow a pair of 2-bar phrases (2 + 2 + 3). (Williams's 21-bar composition "Pee Wee," discussed in chapter 5, contains similar metric and phrase groupings.)

Like "Pee Wee," "Hand Jive" also contains several melodic correspondences among its different phrases that echo earlier-heard material. (Example 6.1 also numbers the opening eleven pitches in order to facilitate comparison with Davis's solo.) The opening ascending fourth (Ab4–Db5) at m. 1 returns twice, each time transposed. It appears 4 bars later within a larger phrase, at m. 5 (transposed to E4–A), and again at m. 8 (F#–B). Further, there is a clear correspondence between the mm. 6–7 gesture (Bb4–D5–F–F#), and the one heard at mm. 14–15 (Bb4–Db5–F–Gb). Another facet underlying mm. 5–7 is the half-step voice leading heard on the downbeats of each of those three measures: the E4 (m. 5) links to F (m. 6), and—through octave displacement—to F#5 (m. 7). This chromatic voice leading enhances the melody's sense of direction during these measures.

EXAMPLE 6.1   Melody to "Hand Jive"

3   There are other ways to hear mm. 9–11, naturally. Hearing the 3-bar phrase as a foreshortened 4-bar phrase comes about through hearing it against the backdrop of more traditional 4-bar phrasing of standard jazz compositions.

The group recorded three different versions of "Hand Jive." Perhaps due to the unusual measure groupings at this tempo, each take involves "time, no changes" for all three solos. However, Hancock does end his solos in each take by alluding to the harmonic progression of the head (the second alternate take includes an entire 18-bar chorus at the end of his solo, at 7:07). It is interesting to speculate why the group elected to record three different complete takes. On the first released take, there is a slight confusion at the beginning of Davis's solo, when Shorter also begins to play. Additionally, the execution of the out head on the second alternate take is somewhat ragged. But these glitches are no less glaring than other takes that the quintet released. However, the improvisations improve exponentially with each successive take. The improvisations on the final take offer a higher degree of motivic improvisation based upon melodic paraphrase. There is also a heightened degree of continuity between solos, as motivic ideas that end solos then launch successive solos. In the following discussion I regard the beginning of Davis's solo from the released take and examine several features: Davis's abstraction of motives from the melody, his use of registral connections, and the overall 8-bar orientation of mm. 1–32. I then turn to the way in which Shorter links the beginning of his solo to the end of Davis's.

DAVIS'S SOLO

Example 6.2 contains a transcription to the opening of Davis's solo (:38). It exemplifies Davis's ability to effortlessly improvise 8-bar phrases with immediate lyrical relationships. For example, mm. 1–8 consist of two 4-bar ideas that relate in an integral manner. Measures 5–8 rhyme with mm. 1–4 in elaborated fashion. Measure 5 consists not of a repeated pitch, as does m. 1, but of an ascending line that moves to D♭ at m. 6. Measure 6 varies m. 2. The stepwise descent from D♭ to B♭ at m. 6 transposes down a whole step the initial three pitches of m. 2. The remainder of the phrase, at mm. 7–8, continues the whole step transposition but it is rhythmically displaced, with G♯–A transposing the B♭–C♭ of mm. 2–4. (Example 6.2 uses dotted slurs to show the whole step transpositional relationship between mm. 2–3 and 6–7.) The opening of the solo uses a pair of 4-bar ideas in evident relationship to one another. And characteristically for Davis, the related 4-bar ideas are played in a manner that avoids rote repetition.

This relationship of mm. 1–4 with mm. 5–8 exhibits one facet of Davis's lyricism. Further, the opening bars of the solo abstract the opening melody to "Hand Jive" in a particular manner. Example 6.1 numbers

EXAMPLE 6.2   Measures 1–32 of Davis's Solo on "Hand Jive" (released take, :38)

the opening pitches of the melody, and Example 6.2 includes the pitch ordering to show how Davis's opening gesture begins with the second pitch of the melody (D♭), repeating that pitch before continuing with the following two melodic pitches (E♭–D♭, m. 2). Following two intervening pitches (C–B♭, m. 2), Davis ultimately moves to the fifth melodic pitch (C♭, mm. 3–4). Throughout these opening 4 bars, Davis recalls the opening of the melody, but abstracts that melody by altering its rhythm and by beginning on its second pitch.

A similar process of melodic abstraction occurs during mm. 25–30, to which I turn after briefly considering the intervening material. Measures 9–24 are notable for Davis's careful attention to longer range registral pacing. For Davis, such registral pacing arises by returning to uppermost pitches stated earlier. For example, mm. 9–11 create a general ascent to E♭5 at m. 12, and here he returns to the highest pitch heard so far during the solo (stated originally at m. 2). And Davis returns again to this pitch at m. 22 (notated as D♯), before ascending another half step to E. These uppermost pitches at mm. 12 and 22 can be heard as melodic goals not only because they return to registral peaks, but also through longer duration (m. 12), or as phrase endpoints (m. 22). Further, nested within the registral peaks at mm. 12 and 22 appears another example of registral pacing: the dotted slurs at mm. 16–20 show a departure and return to C♭ during those measures. These registral connections show a specific technique of Davis for shaping longer improvised spans.

Up until m. 24, the solo has progressed in largely eight-measure sections, and Davis maintains that orientation for an additional 8 bars, through mm. 25–32 (1:02), where he again abstracts the melody. Notice that during mm. 25–26, Davis uses the same opening rhythm as that of "Hand Jive." But a comparison between those measures with example 6.1 indicates a difference. The pitch numbers added to the score show that Davis omits the first pitch of the melody, and instead states its second and third pitches (D♭–E♭, rather than A♭–D♭). Measure 27 states pitches 4–7 of the melody. And mm. 29–30 distill the pitches from the melody at m. 4. Throughout these 8 bars, Davis abstracts and transforms the melodic motives.

All this points out the use of melodic abstraction and registral pacing within improvised phrases, and these phrases generally maintain an 8-bar orientation. The discussion is not intended to suggest that Davis's use of this underlying 8-bar orientation during the opening measures of the solo is somehow superior to other types of phrase groupings. Instead it suggests that—in the opening 32 bars of this solo at least—Davis relies on an intuited general framework consistent with many of the jazz compositions he would have improvised on during his career, and that this framework guides the opening bars of the solo. Certainly as the solo develops, this underlying organization evaporates, although Davis continues during the solo to rely on using successive 2-bar motives.

A comparison of the opening measures of this solo with the first alternate take to "Hand Jive" shows that Davis abandons an underlying 8-bar orientation during the alternate take. Nevertheless, he paraphrases the melody at a very similar place. In the alternate take it begins at m. 24, rather than at m. 25 of the released take. In comparison with the released take, then, Davis's solo on the first alternate take forgoes the underlying 8-bar design but maintains a similar structural design and sense of pacing.[4]

Example 6.3 contains a transcription of the end of Davis's solo (3:04) and the beginning of Shorter's solo from the released take. Here Davis again paraphrases a portion of the melody. This happens at m. 153, which recalls m. 3 of the melody, and it appears after an ascending half-step gesture of E♭–F♭ (mm. 151–52). Davis ends his solo with those same pitches E♭–F♭–E♭ (mm. 158–59), and this half-step move then forms the opening gambit for Shorter's improvisation. The opening of Shorter's solo subjects that half-step motive to a series of upward transpositions. They are bracketed and indicated in the score as 1–7. Shorter uses rhythmic transformations to elasticize the half-step idea and regard it from a number of different viewpoints, highlighting his ability to seemingly float free of the pulse and meter.

EXAMPLE 6.3   End of Davis's and Beginning of Shorter's Solo on "Hand Jive" (3:04)

4   Different takes of earlier Davis works likewise offer such structural designs, with similar melodic material placed at analogous places. On both the released and alternate take of "Milestones" (*Milestones*), Davis plays B natural—the raised eleventh of the underlying F major harmony—at m. 17 during each initial chorus, just prior to the B section.

Thus Davis's final motivic idea becomes Shorter's opening one, which is then treated to further rhythmic and transpositional alteration. Shorter's and Hancock's solos are similarly linked. (That section is transcribed and discussed in chapter 2.) Like many of Shorter's other "time, no changes" quintet solos, his solo on "Hand Jive" balances evident motivic ideas with more characteristic eighth-note bop phrasing. But Shorter's solo also betrays a more direct link to the jazz avant-garde through the use of sound-based improvisation and nontempered pitches (for example, hear the passages beginning at 4:51). In this way, Shorter's solo contrasts distinctly with the lyrical and more coolly cerebral pacing of his solo in "Pinocchio."

It may be that the unusual 11 + 7 organization of the head proved inhospitable for chorus structure improvisation, motivating the use of "time, no changes" for all three of the solos. All the soloists developed a host of sophisticated strategies for metrical conflict, irregular metrical groupings, and accentual shift in the context of up-tempo improvisation over 4-bar and 8-bar hypermetric divisions. But perhaps odd-numbered measure groupings posed some challenges for up-tempo improvisation. The earlier "R.J." (*E.S.P.*) revealed some evident problems with improvisation over 5-bar sections. The group did maintain odd-numbered measure groupings and chorus structure with ballads ("Mood," "Vonetta," and "Pee Wee")—and occasionally preserved 6-bar groupings and chorus structure with improvisations over faster works (for example, "Masqualero," Shorter's solo on "Dolores," and Hancock's solo on "Pinocchio"). But it is possible that up-tempo chorus structure over sections of odd-numbered measures impeded the creative flow and freedom sought by the quintet.[5]

"NEFERTITI"

The decision to release "Nefertiti" as a series of repeated statements of the melody without standard improvisation by horns and piano was a novel one for the quintet. Yet, as discussed at the beginning of the chapter, it is possible to regard that strategy as one that emerged out of a continuing practice of highlighting compositional melody on the recordings. Further, the alternate takes for "Freedom Jazz Dance" (discussed in chapter 4) described the group's technique of stating the melody repeatedly as

5 However, "Limbo" (*Sorcerer*) is an exception, since it largely preserves a 17-bar chorus structure.

a means for rehearsing ensemble execution. There the horns repeated the melody as many as six consecutive times during a single take. This is also the genesis for repeated melodic statements on "Nefertiti." On the unreleased rehearsal take for "Nefertiti" the group similarly rehearses repeated melodic statements, then—mirthfully—makes the decision to omit the horn and piano improvisations completely. The horns interpret the melody freely and loosely during the repeated melodic statements on the released track.

"Nefertiti" is a 16-bar single section composition. Shorter's lead sheet copyright deposit is unusual because it does not indicate all the accompanying harmonies with traditional chord symbols. It instead provides notated three- and four-note voicings at certain points in the lead sheet. The harmony to m. 1, for instance, appears as A♭3–D4–G4 beneath the first melody pitch of C; the harmony to m. 2 as A♭3–D♭4–G♭4. Shorter also provides notated voicings at mm. 10–12.[6]

There is a circular quality to "Nefertiti's" melody, which consists of three related phrases. Its melodic circularity may also have been a catalyst for the decision to perform it without horn and piano improvisations. Example 6.4a provides a lead sheet for "Nefertiti." It shows that the final two phrases initiate an ascending stepwise sequence. This occurs as the result of the opening pitch of each phrase. Phrase 2 (m. 9) begins on G#/A♭. Phrase 3 (m. 11) begins with B♭. The return to the top of the form at Phrase 1 begins with the pitch C. Phrase 1 thus continues the ascending stepwise sequence begun by Phrases 2 and 3. This allows Phrase 1 to sound as a continuation of the previous phrases, creating a compelling formal overlap, and giving the work its continuous quality.

This continuation creates a circularity that is supported by the development and duration of these phrases. The melody to "Nefertiti," like that to "Pinocchio," differs from Shorter's earlier compositions in its approach to motivic organization. In compositions such as "E.S.P.," "Dolores," "Prince of Darkness," and "Limbo," the rhythmic span of repeated motives is generally consistent, usually recurring each 2 bars. However, the three related phrases of "Nefertiti" differ, and rely on motivic expansion and contraction. Phrase 2 is the shortest phrase, and Phrase 3 expands the phrase further. Phrase 1, as the longest of the three phrases, may be heard

---

6   Library of Congress Copyright Deposit Eu 42288 (March 13, 1968).

EXAMPLE 6.4a   Lead Sheet to "Nefertiti"

Wayne Shorter

as a consequent to Phrases 2 and 3. Thus both the sequential nature of "Nefertiti's" three phrases, as well as the additive phrasing, contribute to its circularity.

Example 6.4b isolates the first pitches from Phrases 1–3, using a slur to show how that ascending sequence creates the circularity. While the above discussion (and that slur) might suggest that listeners hear Phrase 2 as the "beginning" of the composition, certain musical factors stitch Phrase 1 to Phrase 2. These are also included in Example 6.4b, which shows the half-step resolution from A (end of Phrase 1) to A♭/G♯ (beginning of Phrase 2), and the deeper retrograde relationship of A♭/G♯ (m. 6–7), A (m. 7–8), and A♭/G♯ (m. 9). These factors enhance the perpetual and seamless quality of the composition.

Chapter 2 offered three possible conditions for circularity in jazz compositions: melody (the opening phrase of the composition sounds

(Top of form)

Phrase 1   2   3   1

as a continuation of the previous phrase(s)); harmony (the opening harmonic progression continues a sequence begun at the end of the form);
and hypermeter (irregular metric groupings suggest a continuation into
the top of the form). The above discussion indicates how melody is the
decisive factor in creating "Nefertiti's" circularity.

Yet circularity is not the only feature for understanding the significance, appeal, and intrigue of "Nefertiti." Certainly the expanding and
collapsing motivic design of the three phrases, all related by their opening chromatic descent (C–B–B♭ m. 1, G♯–G–F♯ m. 9, and B♭–A–A♭ m. 11)
and descending arpeggiation (B♭–F–C m. 2, F♯–D–A m. 10, and G♯–E–B
m. 12) is critical. All three phrases end similarly (with the pitch A). Yet
that pitch—and other factors—work to undermine the larger sense of
an A♭ tonality suggested by the opening A♭ harmony and the E♭7 harmonies that close Phrases 1 and 3. And despite the ambiguity of key, the
harmonic progression relies significantly on traditional bass motions,
progressing primarily through descending fifth and chromatic motion
characteristic of functional harmonic progressions. Even while it is possible to enumerate these motivic, melodic, and harmonic factors, in
many ways "Nefertiti" remains strikingly elusive and enigmatic.

"MADNESS"

REHEARSAL TAKE

The complete studio recordings of the Davis Quintet contain three versions of "Madness": a rehearsal take, an alternate take, and the released
take. Comparisons between the rehearsal take and the other two reveal
a radical change to "Madness" that took place in the studio. On the
rehearsal track, the group performs "Madness" as a slow impressionistic waltz, consisting of two sections. However, on the other two takes,
the group performs "Madness" in 4/4, at a rapid tempo, and consisting
merely of the second of the two sections heard on the rehearsal track.
Presumably the rehearsal track shows Hancock's original intent for
the composition. And the other two tracks reveal studio processes that

allowed for reconstituting many of the original principal structural features to "Madness." The difference provides the starkest evidence of the group's willingness to alter and redevelop compositions while recording in the studio.

The following diagram outlines the form heard on the rehearsal track. It begins with an 8-bar section (indicated as A) that repeats. There is a slight flub and hesitation within the B section. Keeping the tempo, the group returns to another statement of the 8-bar A section. The following B section consists of six distinct harmonies. The fifth harmony repeats continuously, and during this section the horns play a six-note descending motive (F♯–F–E–B–B♭–G). This B section lasts 22 bars, and the rehearsal track ends following another statement of the 8-bar A section.

REHEARSAL TRACK

A (:01): 8 bars, saxophone melody
A (:17): 8 bars, saxophone melody
B (:32): Flub, starts over
A (:43): 8 bars, saxophone and trumpet melody
B (:57): 6 different harmonies, 22 bars
A (1:35): 8 bars, trumpet/saxophone melody

RELEASED TAKE: HEAD

Between the time the group recorded the rehearsal track and the released track, "Madness" underwent a drastic makeover. Example 6.5 transcribes the bass and piano from the opening head. For the head of the released track, the quintet jettisoned the composition's A section, and retained only the B section. Moreover, the slow 3/4 meter from the rehearsal track is struck, replaced initially by a 4/4 meter at a significantly faster tempo. By m. 7 the group effects a metric modulation, shifting from a quarter note pulse to a dotted quarter note pulse. Since the underlying eighth note remains constant, the effect is one of a slight deceleration. The group returns to the original 4/4 and quarter note pulse the beginning of Davis's solo, at m. 42. All these alterations to the rehearsal track version speak to a highly fluid and flexible notion of the composition.

What is retained from the rehearsal track is the melodic and harmonic structure from its B section. Hancock is relatively consistent in realizing these same six chords during the heads to the B section of the rehearsal track, the alternate take, and the released take. The harmonic progression consists of six harmonies, from Cmin13 (voiced in fourths) to D♭Maj7 (mm. 1–2). He realizes the third chord both as Emin9 (F♯–G–B–D) and

EXAMPLE 6.5   Rhythm Section Accompaniment to Head of "Madness"

E13sus (A–C♯–D–F♯) on the different takes of the head. (Carter moves from E to G mm. 3–4 on this released track.). The fourth harmony is a pedal point harmony, perhaps best indicated as C♭Maj7♯11/B♭.

The fifth chord secures the metric modulation (notated here as 3/8) by repeating insistently the dotted quarter note pulse. Above it, the horns create a layer of 3/4 by playing the six-note descending motive (F♯–F–E–B–B♭–G) in quarter notes. This fifth harmony is the least traditional and not referable to a single typical jazz harmony. I will refer to it here as the "Madness" chord. It appears over a B♭ bass pitch, with the left hand pitches of A3–C4–E♭–A♭, and the right-hand pitches of B–D–D♯–E/F♭. There are perhaps a number of different methods to consider this harmony. It seems related to many of Hancock's doubly diminished harmonies, in this instance sharing most of its pitches with G#°7 over A°7, derived from the octatonic (diminished) collection. However, the upper pitch of E/Fb stands outside this collection, as does the bass note Bb. The harmony might also be represented by the combination of the lower structure A°, and the upper structure cluster as EMaj7/b7. Its use here shows the problems that arise with standard harmonic nomenclature. Like the "Riot" chord, the dissonant structure of the "Madness" chord was likely intended to symbolize themes of social alienation and unrest highlighted by the composition's title. Note that the combination of its pitches, along with the six-note melody stated by the horns, nearly exhausts the chromatic collection, forming 11 of the 12 chromatic pitches.

The sixth harmony returns to the one heard prior to the Madness chord, CbMaj7#11/Bb. Hancock changes the upper pitch of this harmony during the latter part of the head to include Ab (mm. 28–30) and G (CbMaj7#5/Bb, mm. 36–38). We may indicate the six harmonies as follows.

1. Cmin13
2. DbMaj7
3. Emin9 (E13sus)
4. CbMaj7#11/Bb
5. Madness chord
6. Cbmaj7#11/Bb

HANCOCK'S SOLO

Hancock's solo is an improvisational tour de force. It is an example of a solo in which the players abandon consistent hypermeter and meter. It is also one of the rare instances on the studio recordings in which the rhythm section players extensively abandon their typical timekeeping roles. This freer interactive section lasts for about half the piano solo, before the rhythm section then recoups their regular timekeeping role. Example 6.6 provides a transcription of the piano solo.

Among the many remarkable qualities of this solo is its freedom and interaction among the players, and this seems to reflect a high degree of spontaneity. However, the solo nevertheless reflects Hancock's notion of "controlled freedom" (discussed in chapter 2). The freedom in this solo arises from its departures from regular hypermeter and meter. The transcription suggests that the group preserves an underlying sense of pulse, while the meter is fluid. (It is therefore notated with a consistent quarter note pulse, but with measures that expand and collapse.) Thus, the rhythm section adheres to what chapter 2 described as "Level 1"

EXAMPLE 6.6   Hancock Solo on "Madness," mm. 1–74 (4:57)

EXAMPLE 6.6   Continued

(preserves pulse, but abandons consistent meter and hypermeter). The control in the solo comes about from some profound and deep-seated relationships to the head of the composition, particularly the harmonic structure.

The six chords of the head are indicated above. Despite the freedom of this portion of the solo, Hancock nevertheless preserves and expresses precisely this harmonic progression during his solo. The transcription numbers and labels the appearance of each of the six chords, showing how Hancock consistently cycles through them during this portion of his solo. Thus, even while abandoning consistent hypermetric and metric groupings, Hancock maintains the progression of the six harmonies, expanding and contracting the harmonic rhythm at will. The following discussion will point out how that portion of the solo adheres to the harmonic progression.

The solo opens (4:57) by outlining the fourth-based C minor harmony (m. 1, C–F–B♭), before yielding to the D♭Maj7 harmony. Hancock's subsequent voicings and melody express both versions of the E harmony from the head (E13sus and Emin9, mm. 2–3). Hancock's voicing for the fourth (and sixth) harmony appears consistently as G–A♭–C♭/B, indicated in the transcription as C♭Maj7♯5 (m. 4).[7]

The turn to the Madness chord, Chord 5, occurs in m. 7. Throughout the solo, Hancock preserves this harmony longer than the others. (Its initial appearance occurs at mm. 7–13.) The discussion above called attention to its relation to harmonies derived from the D/E♭ octatonic

7   This harmony may also perhaps be realized as A♭min9♯7/B♭.

collection, and Hancock's use of this harmony typically appears in the left hand as A°(♯7) (m. 7), or merely as A° (m. 10–12). Hancock's improvisational material over the Madness chord uses the octatonic collection. But it does not express that of the D/E♭ collection. Instead, Hancock uses consistently the octatonic collection based upon C♯/D.

The use of that C♯/D octatonic collection with Hancock's left-hand A° voicings strongly calls into question a general principle of improvisation, one that suggests some degree of coincidence between accompanying harmony and improvisational line. Here the question is even more acute, since it is the same player—Hancock—who is projecting both harmony and line via left and right hands. Rather than using right-hand pitch material that conveys the left-hand harmony, Hancock instead here uses an octatonic collection that does not interact with the left-hand harmony. The net result is very nearly the chromatic aggregate, formed by the left-hand pitches A–C–E♭ (A♭), and the right-hand octatonic collection, formed with G–A♭–B♭–B–C♯–D–E–F (only A♭ is common to both). This degree of chromaticism is fitting, and perhaps—like the Madness chord itself—is intended to symbolize the title of the composition. Whatever the motivation, the result here provides a consistent strategy at odds with traditional chord/scale precepts, which instead require a higher level of congruence between accompanying harmony and improvised line.

The second cycle through the six chords of "Madness" begins at m. 20 (5:17). There the absence of left hand makes the relationship to the opening two chords more abstract, but Hancock corroborates the move to Emin9 with the left-hand voicing at mm. 24–25. Again, the shift to the Madness chord (at m. 31) is set up by the C♯/D octatonic collection in the right hand (at m. 29). The phrase at mm. 29–33 gives evidence of one of Hancock's many elaborated octatonic routines. Here Hancock embellishes the collection with chromatic pitches that either surround the octatonic pitch, or serve as chromatic passing tones. The transcription shows the pitches that elaborate the underlying octatonic collection with an asterisk.

The following phrase, beginning at m. 36, continues the Madness chord. Here, note that the right hand arpeggiates the uppermost pitches (EMaj7/♭7) as played by Hancock during the head before yielding again to the octatonic material, now stated with the sixth chord (mm. 40–43).

The third and final cycle through the six chords (prior to the rhythm section returning to 4/4 with walking bass) occurs at m. 46 (5:41). Again, the scarcity of left-hand voicings make more abstract the relation to the first two harmonies, but the pitch material at m. 46 expresses C minor

(Chord 1) and at m. 47 D♭Maj7 (chord 2), before the left hand participates in expressing Chord 3 (mm. 48–49). Note that Hancock rhymes the motive heard with Chord 3 (mm. 49–50) with the one heard with Chord 4 (mm. 51–52). And again with the return to the "Madness" chord, Hancock returns to the C♯/D octatonic material, expressing repeatedly—if not obsessively or madly—the descending octatonic passage beginning with E5 at mm. 55–60. During the final statement of Chord 6, the group accelerates into a regular tempo with walking bass.

Despite the metrical freedom of the passage examined above, the analysis shows Hancock maintaining the underlying harmonic progression to "Madness," since he cycles through the composition's six chords. Thus, this portion of the solo preserves the harmonic structure while abandoning the metric structure. It provides an alternate strategy to "time, no changes." Instead, Hancock performs the changes while the time is freer (described in chapter 2 as Level 1a). Because the rhythm section does not keep a consistent underlying meter present, this portion of Hancock's solo moves perhaps most decisively toward the jazz avant-garde than on any of the previous quintet studio recordings.

RHYTHM SECTION AND IMPROVISATIONAL STRATEGIES

What is the role of Carter and Williams during this opening portion of the Hancock solo? Carter maintains a loose relationship with the underlying harmonic progression. His accompaniment is not included in the transcription, but it is possible to hear him returning to the top of the form when providing bass pitches of C and D♭ (Chords 1 and 2) at particular places during Hancock's solo: mm. 1–2 (4:57), mm. 36–37 (5:31), and again at mm. 51–53 (5:46). Except for the opening, these instances are not in phase with Hancock's choruses. Yet in the final instance, beginning at mm. 51, Carter and Williams are in phase with each other, generally preserving the rhythm and the harmonies heard during the head (see example 6.5). This now includes the repeated B♭ pedal (m. 57, 5:51), and the players recreate the same metric modulation from the head, accelerating into the 4/4 walking bass (m. 68, 6:03).

At this point the group returns to more traditional timekeeping techniques, shifting the formal strategy. And for the remainder of the solo the group preserves the meter and Hancock maintains the harmonic structure, but with an elastic harmonic rhythm, exhibiting Level 2a. The alternate take maintains the same Level 1a to 2a shift during Hancock's solo. There, as in the released track, the rhythm section plays more freely the first half of the piano solo (preserving pulse, but not consistent meter or hypermeter) before moving to a 4/4 accompaniment with walking bass. And there, as in the released track, Hancock preserves the harmonic progression during both portions, cycling through the composition's six chords consistently. In contrast, the horn solos on both the released and the alternate take maintain the Level 2b ("time, no changes") technique. Thus although the quintet reworked the composition thoroughly between the rehearsal track and the later two tracks (by eliminating the A section and altering drastically the meter and tempo), the later alternate and released tracks are both constructed similarly and rely on a similar set of improvisational principles for each soloist.

Of the four Hancock compositions recorded and released by the Davis quintet, "Madness" is the only one that he did not record elsewhere. This may have had to do with the alterations made to his composition in the studio. Perhaps the tempo and meter changes, as well as the amputation of the entire A section—itself a lovely waltz whose melody and harmonic progression were entirely representative of many other quintet compositions—resulted in a decapitated version too far removed from the composer's original conception. The *Miles Davis Quintet: 1965–1968* also included rehearsal takes of two other Hancock compositions, "Speak Like a Child" and "I Have a Dream," but Davis's quintet never went on to record further or release those compositions.

"PINOCCHIO"

The quintet recorded two versions of "Pinocchio," the released take and an alternate take. The released track is the more standard version, consisting of statements of the head as well as trumpet, tenor saxophone, and piano solos. The horns restate the melody between each of the solos, advancing the technique of returning to melodic statements within the performance. In contrast, the alternate take consists only of repeated statements of the head, performed at a much slower tempo than the released track. This alternate take resembles the performance of "Nefertiti," which similarly excludes improvisations by trumpet, tenor saxophone, and piano.

HEAD

The melody to "Pinocchio" offers a different approach to motivic organization. Like "Nefertiti," it represents a change from Shorter's earlier compositions. Many of Shorter's earlier quintet compositions rely on motives (formed by contour, rhythm, and/or pitch) that are metrically consistent.

For example, "E.S.P.," "Dolores," "Prince of Darkness," and "Limbo" begin with motives that recur regularly, usually every 2 bars.

In contrast, "Pinocchio" relies on motivic expansion. Example 6.7 contains a transcription of the head to "Pinocchio." At mm. 1–8, rather than appearing in regular intervals of two measures, the related motives group into 1 + 2 + 5 measures during the opening eight-measure section, with each successive motive expanding the previous one. The first motive consists of four notes. This pentatonic subset forms a melodic idea whose pitches would not be out of place in the context of a blues in the key of F. The second motive continues similarly (mm. 2–3), and note that the additional pitch (B natural) could also operate as a blue note in that same F context. However, the final pitch of this motive, G♭, moves outside that blues scale context, and now these mm. 2–3 pitches—save for the B natural—outline expressly the opening E♭min6/9 harmony. Yet the harmonic change at m. 3 places the final two pitches (B♭ and G♭) in a new harmonic environment, and they are now heard supporting the D♭min6/9 harmony. The third motive expands the previous one. It begins similarly, and at m. 5 the Bmin9(Maj7) harmony provides yet another harmonic environment for B♭/A♯ and G♭/F♯ before the motive expands further.

A similar process takes place at mm. 9–18, but with further transformations. The motive at m. 9 inverts the contour of the m. 1 motive. Measures

EXAMPLE 6.7   Head to "Pinocchio"

9–11 duplicate the growth process heard at mm. 1–3, with mm. 10–11 transposing mm. 2–3 by whole step. Measures 13–18 host a six-measure phrase, with the melodic material here forming a release by departing from the earlier motives. Thus in mm. 9–18, the groupings occupy 1 + 3 + 6 bars.

These processes of motivic expansion formed an ongoing feature of Shorter's improvisations (see chapter 2). It is significant that they now appear as structural features of Shorter's compositions, and this represents a compositional breakthrough for Shorter. Both "Pinocchio" and "Nefertiti" use recurring motives that expand and collapse. In contrast to compositions that rely on motives that recur at regular 2-bar intervals, the motivic growth processes heard in "Pinocchio" create a different relationship between melody and underlying metrical structure. The resultant expandable and/or collapsible motives are frequently unmoored from the underlying 2- and 4-bar hypermeter. Note that with "Pinocchio" this provides a melodic flexibility as the motives cut across those 2-bar or 4-bar divisions, such as at m. 3 (2-bar division), m. 5 (4-bar division), and m. 11 (2-bar division). This metric flexibility works alongside other instances in which the melody supports the hypermeter, such as at m. 9 (8-bar division) and m. 13 (4-bar division).

Since "Pinocchio" is an 18-bar form, the question of hypermeter is crucial. Along with the irregularly appearing motives described above, the final 6-bar phrase undercuts the underlying 4-bar and 8-bar regularity that appears earlier. The result makes "Pinocchio" circular as a result of this final 6-bar phrase. For listeners expecting 4- and 8-bar phrases characteristic of jazz composition, the 6-bar phrase may be heard as "missing" 2 bars, which creates a formal overlap with the top of the form. Yet the circularity of "Pinocchio" does not seem exceptionally strong. The discussion of "Vonetta's" circularity in chapter 6 indicated that it similarly arose from hypermeter. But with "Vonetta" the formal overlap was enhanced, since the same C minor harmony appears both at the end and the beginning of the form. With "Pinocchio" the circularity appears weaker, probably because of the harmonic change appearing between the final measure and the return to the top of the form. (However, note that the horns cut off Hancock at the end of his solo by returning to the melody 3 bars after he arrives at the top of his third chorus. This was perhaps a response to "Pinocchio's" circularity: by adding 2 bars to the final 6-bar phrase, the horn players inadvertently square the 6-bar phrase into an 8-bar phrase.) It is interesting to speculate whether the circularity to "Pinocchio"—like that of "Nefertiti"—may have contributed to the decision to record the alternate take only as repeating statements of the melody, without improvisations by trumpet, saxophone, and piano.

The *Real Book* includes a lead sheet to "Pinocchio," although a number of the harmonies depart from the harmonies and bass pitches included on the studio recordings. Several published analyses to "Pinocchio" rely on *The Real Book* lead sheet.[8] The rhythm section plays the harmonies during the head to "Pinocchio" most generally as follows:

M. 1	2	3	4	5–6	7–8
Ebmin6/9	Amin9	Dbmin6/9	Amin9	Bmin9(Maj7)	Gmin9(Maj7)

9	10	11	12
C13	Bmin9	Ebmin6/9	

13	14	15	16	17–18
F#13sus	Emin9	F13(#11)	C7alt(Gb13)	Gbmin9(Maj7)/B13(#11)

The Real Book indicates the m. 1 and m. 11 harmonies as Ab13, and the m. 3 harmony as Gb13. Certainly the upper structures of those harmonies are cognate with the Eb–6/9 and Db–6/9 harmonies played by the quintet at those measures, but do not generally reflect Carter's bass accompaniment. Additionally, *The Real Book* indicates the intermediate harmony at m. 2 as G13 (leading to Gb13 at m. 3), and at m. 10 as A13 (leading to Ab13 at m. 11). Those harmonies are understandable since they conform to the standard harmonic practice of dominant harmonies that resolve downward by half step.

However, the harmonies played by the group at those measures differ. These harmonies at m. 2 (Amin9, resolving to Dbmin6/9) and m. 10 (Bmin9, resolving to Ebmin6/9) do not immediately appear to be as functional as the G13 and A13 harmonies supplied by *The Real Book*. Nevertheless we may understand them as deriving from more standard harmonic progressions. To do so requires two levels of substitution. The first substitution is indicated in example 6.8. First, it requires that we hear and consider these Amin9 and Bmin9 harmonies as ii chords that *substitute* for V chords of a ii–V pair. Thus, within a ii–V pair Amin9 to D13, the Amin9 of m. 2 substitutes for the V chord, D13.[9] The second level of substitution is the more common one that allows for tritone substitution of dominant chords. Here the implied D7 (or D13) substitutes for Ab7, effecting

8   *The Real Book*, 6th ed., 328; other analyses that seem to rely on the incorrect *Real Book* version include Rick Helzer, "Two Compositions by Wayne Shorter: 'Pinocchio and Dolores,'" *Jazz Improv* 2/3 (1999): 210 (see also lead sheet, p. 84); and Steven Strunk, "Harmony," entry in *The New Grove Dictionary of Jazz*, ed. Barry Kernfeld, 2nd ed. (London: Macmillan, 2002), 168.

9   For a discussion of such substitutions, see Steven Strunk, "The Harmony of Bop: A Layered Approach," *Journal of Jazz Studies* 6 (1979): 4–53.

the move to D♭min6/9. The exact substitutions obtain at m. 10, merely transposed up a step. Bmin9 (m. 10) substitutes for E13, which itself forms the tritone substitution for B♭7, effecting the resolution to E♭min6/9.

These two harmonic progressions therefore derive from more standard progressions. However, like many of Shorter's compositions, the larger harmonic motions do not support functional harmonic progressions. The opening measures consist entirely of minor-derived sonorities whose roots initially progress downward by whole step every two measures (E♭–D♭–B) before then tracing a longer path downward by major thirds, from B (m. 5) to G (m. 7), and then returning to the initial harmony of E♭ (m. 11). (This interpretation bypasses the intermediate harmonies of mm. 2, 4, and 10, as well as the C13(♯11) harmony of m. 9.)

EXAMPLE 6.8   Harmonies at mm. 2–3 and 10–11 that Substitute for More Functional Harmonic Progressions

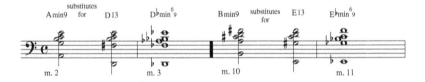

SHORTER'S SOLO

The improvisational strategy for the two horn solos is that of "time, no changes," Level 2b. It is likely that this strategy was not determined beforehand. At the beginning of Shorter's solo, Hancock provides harmonic accompaniment, suggesting an assumption of chorus structure on the pianist's part. Yet as Shorter's solo continues to depart from the underlying form and harmonic structure, Hancock's accompaniment becomes sparser and more tentative. By the 16th bar of Shorter's solo, Hancock ceases accompanying altogether, and the saxophone and rhythm section move into "time, no changes."

Hancock's solo itself, in contrast, does rely on chorus structure by adhering to "Pinocchio's" underlying harmonic and 18-bar formal framework. This change in improvisational strategy further suggests that the group did not work it out in advance. The resultant clash that occurs as the horn players return to the melody 3 bars into Hancock's third chorus

Others could not tell

also suggests that the players may have been unaware that—unlike their own solos—Hancock's solo maintained the underlying form.

A transcription of Shorter's solo (2:31) appears as example 6.9. I have divided the solo into five sections, labeled 1–5 in the example. Each of the first four sections occupies eight measures. Thus, in these four sections, Shorter establishes consistent and regular metric groupings. Even in the absence of a regularly repeating chorus structure and within a remarkably creative solo, Shorter relies on comfortable 8-bar hypermetric schemes, which here enhance the lyricism of the solo. The fifth and final section occupies 16 bars.

Each section is clearly delineated by a move to a new motivic idea. Section 1 begins and concludes with G#/A♭3. This is the same pitch heard at the end of the head statement. In mm. 3 and 6, he embellishes this

EXAMPLE 6.9   Wayne Shorter's Solo on "Pinocchio" (2:31)

G#3 with A♮3. These two pitch classes are restated up an octave in m. 5, notated as A4 to G#4.

The phrases of sections 2, 3, and 4 are remarkably lyrical. Their phrase design is related, contributing to the lyricism. Each in different ways alludes to a phrase design known as "sentence structure." This refers to a phrase consisting of constituent 2 + 2 + 4 ideas, and this design organizes any number of jazz and popular song melodies.[10] Sections 2 and 3 form what I label in the score as an "incomplete sentence," a 2 + 2 grouping without a completing 4-bar phrase. Sections 2 and 3 differ in the ways in which this incomplete sentence is realized. In Section 2, the 2-bar motive of mm. 9–10 precedes a related 2-bar motive in mm. 11–12, shown in the example with dotted slurs. The final 4 bars of mm. 13–16, rather than having a concluding 4-bar response, consist only of Shorter's single pitch of A♭4 at m. 15.

Section 3 is similar to Section 2 since it has a 2-bar motive (mm. 17–18) followed by a related 2-bar motive (mm. 19–20). However, Sections 2 and 3 differ in their second halves. In Section 2, the 2 bars of silence in mm. 13–14 dissociate the single pitch of A♭4 (m. 15) from the first half of the section at mm. 9–12. In contrast, Shorter *links* the two halves of Section 3. The C♭5 at mm. 20–21 binds the preceding material with the material at mm. 21–23. Thus the incomplete sentences of Sections 2 and 3 have similar 2 + 2-bar openings, but differ in their conclusions.

Section 4 more closely resembles a complete 2 + 2 + 4 sentence structure. A 2-bar motive at mm. 25–26 precedes a related 2-bar motive, begun with the eighth-note pickup to m. 27. Shorter's material in the second half of the section (mm. 29–31) lasts 3—rather than 4—bars, but continues and concludes mm. 25–28.

The use of sentence structure as a way of describing Sections 2–4 allows a somewhat more nuanced view of Shorter's motivic improvisation. It points out not only how the opening 2 + 2 organization of those sections rely on motivic repetition at some level, but it further shows how concluding 4-bar sections respond to and further the opening 4

---

10 Sentence structure typically appears with groupings of 1 + 1 + 2 or 2 + 2 + 4 measures. For example, such 1 + 1 + 2 phrasing provides the organization for the opening 4 bars of "Blue Monk," "Dat Dere," "Tenderly," "Ain't Misbehaving," "Darn That Dream," and "Memories of You." The same proportion applies in 2 + 2 + 4 organization for the opening 8 bars of compositions such as "Yesterdays," "The Very Thought of You," "Willow Weep for Me," "Over the Rainbow," "My Funny Valentine," "Cottontail," "If You Could See Me Now," and "When I Fall in Love." Arnold Schoenberg uses the term sentence structure to describe occurrences in Western European classical musical examples in his *Fundamentals of Musical Composition*, ed. by Gerald Strang and Leonard Stein (London: Faber and Faber, 1967), chapter 5.

bars of each section. As Shorter moves through Sections 2–4, he impro-vises 8-bar phrases that approach a songlike phrase organization. All this makes vivid Shorter's lyricism.

Sections 1–4 each preserve regular underlying 8-bar metric group-ings, established by the introduction of new motivic material every 8 bars. Yet despite Shorter's use of new motivic material, not all of these sections are unrelated to material just heard. Indeed, the pitch material that concludes Sections 2 and 3 motivate the pitch material that initiates Sections 3 and 4. For example, at the end of Section 2 Shorter articu-lates the pitch A♭4 (m. 15). This pitch then provides the opening pitch for each 2-bar phrase of Section 3, at mm. 17 and 19, as Shorter improvises a blues-related idea in A♭. These motives at mm. 17 and 19 emerge from the previous A♭ heard in m. 15, creating a pitch connection that cuts across the two sections.

Similarly, Section 3 ends with the pitches C/B/G♯/E. These four pitch classes provide all the pitch material for the next three measures (mm. 25–27, shown by the brackets). Although mm. 25–27 are heard as a new motivic idea, the pitch material emerges from the pitch material conclud-ing the previous section. As Shorter initiates new motivic ideas every 8 bars, the pitch material at Sections 3 and 4 emanates from the pitches stated just previously. This illustrates a compelling improvisational tactic in which events flow out of preceding material and suggests that solo-ists establish musical relationships and continuity not only from overt motivic correspondences, but also from pitch relationships that then launch new motivic ideas.

Chapter 2 discussed Section 5, presenting it as an example of the use of motivic cell improvisation. Here, the recurring four-note descending motive relates to the opening gesture from the melody to "Pinocchio." Although the intervallic arrangement differs, the relationship of these motives heard in mm. 33–45 to the melody of "Pinocchio" is unmistak-able, and the final motive at mm. 44–45 duplicates the opening four pitch classes (F–E♭–C–B♭) of the melody. Note that the rhythm through-out most of these statements differs from the head statements played by the horns. The rhythm used by Shorter here is that which appears on his copyright deposit lead sheet. That rhythm appears at the bottom of example 6.9.[11]

Shorter's solo is startlingly economical. With its clear motivic orga-nization and ample use of space, there appear no wasted or throwaway notes. The discussion above called attention to further features that put

11 Library of Congress deposit Eu 42286 (March 13, 1968).

Shorter's lyricism on display, particularly the sentence structures that show Shorter improvising phrases that share features with standard jazz composition melodies. Subtler are the pitch connections that link Sections 2–3, as well as Sections 3–4, enhancing the continuity even as the motives themselves shift. Finally, one aspect of the performance that should be acknowledged is the role of drummer Tony Williams, whose interaction during the silences of Shorter's solo, particularly during Section 5, engenders a remarkable dialogue.

"RIOT"

"Riot" is one of two Hancock compositions that appear on *Nefertiti*. Like "Madness," "Riot" features a nontraditional harmony resistant to a standard chord label. Likely the Madness chord and the "Riot" chord were intended to be emblematic of the mid-1960s themes of social unrest and alienation suggested by the composition titles. Hancock also recorded "Riot" some nine months later on his own Blue Note recording, *Speak Like a Child*, in a more arranged setting for piano trio, bass trombone, alto flute, and flugelhorn.

Example 6.10 provides the first two measures of the introduction to "Riot" from the *Nefertiti* recording. The introductory bass riff revolves around a tonal center of E. The grouping of the bass pattern suggests a subtle metrical conflict, with a grouping of three quarter notes, since the first motive (E–B–A–E) returns three beats later in varied form (E–B–A–F♯). The Riot chord is the opening cluster harmony of B–C–D♯–F♯–G. This nonstandard harmony may perhaps best be represented as Emin9(♯7,♭13).[12] This harmony returns at the end of the second measure, with the harmony of C7 preceding it. As we will see, these two harmonies of i (the Riot chord), and ♭VI7 (C7) have significant implications for the improvisations.

EXAMPLE 6.10   Opening to "Riot"

12 On Hancock's later version of "Riot" he removes the upper pitch G from the Riot chord. This chord may best be represented as Btriad(♭9)/E.

The melody following the 4-bar introduction is brief, and it consists of two sections. The first is a 5-bar phrase. The second is a four-measure phrase in mixed meter, in a grouping of 3 + 3 + 3 + 4 quarter notes. Shorter's improvisation begins following a return of the 4-bar introduction.

While the setting of Hancock's improvisation on the *Speak Like a Child* version of "Riot" largely maintains a 4/4 swing feel, the rhythm section on *Nefertiti* maintains a straight-eighth note feel during the improvisations. Williams's accompaniment provides significant commentary on the tom-toms, and he moves to a quarter-note hi-hat pattern during portions of Davis's and Hancock's solos. Carter's accompaniment is freer and more loosely tied to the beat.

The improvisations on "Riot" sound free-flowing and thus, perhaps, unplanned. Yet there is an unusual tonal organization for the improvisations that must have been predetermined. The first solo, Shorter's saxophone solo, is based on a tonal center of E, the same tonal center as the head to "Riot." Davis's trumpet solo, the second solo, uses a tonal center of E♭, while Hancock's solo relies on a tonal center of D. Thus for each consecutive solo the tonal center migrates down a half step, an unprecedented technique for this quintet.

The improvisations—while maintaining these tonal centers—move nearly consistently in 8-bar sections. This is due to Hancock's accompaniment, which provides a harmonic shift each 8 bars. This harmonic shift derives explicitly from the harmonies of the introduction provided in the example above. Heard during the introduction, Emin9(♯7, ♭13) and C7 appear as successive harmonies within the opening 2 bars (see example 6.10). But during the initial improvisation the two harmonies alternate every 8 bars. Thus the accompaniment to Shorter's solo consists of the following:

Mm. 1–8 (:16)	Emin9(♯7, ♭13) (Riot chord)
9–16	C13/E
17–24 (:31)	Emin9(♯7, ♭13) (Riot chord)
25–32	C13/E (accompaniment also uses pitches from C/C♯ octatonic collection)
33–40 (:47)	Emin9(♯7, ♭13) (Riot chord)

This provides a general outline of the harmonic progression, although Hancock's accompaniment is somewhat free, such as during mm. 37–40 (during which he plays F♯min7♭5). (The 8-bar alternation of an extended E minor harmony with C13 also provides the organization for the piano solo for Hancock's *Speak Like a Child* version of "Riot.")

Davis's solo moves down a half step, to the tonal center of E♭. The following diagram of the harmonic organization to Davis's solo indicates that Hancock changes the complexion of the opening harmony, first to E♭min9 (mm. 1–8), then to C♭Maj9(♯11)/E♭ (mm. 17–24 and 33–40). During Davis's final eight measures (mm. 49–56) the accompanying harmony returns to the quality of harmony heard during the head and Shorter's solo by transposing down a half step most of the "Riot" chord, now played as B♭(♭9)/E♭ (B♭, C♭, D, F). The alternating harmony is performed generally as either C♭13/E♭ (a half-step transposition of C13/E heard in Shorter's solo), or as the cognate harmony G♭min9(♯7)/E♭. Thus this solo, like Shorter's, progresses in 8-bar sections, and maintains the i–♭VI7 organization from the introduction.

Mm. 1–8 (:54)	E♭min9 (but accompaniment mm. 1–3 begins with C7, as if continuing the progression from Shorter's solo)
9–16	C♭13/E♭ and G♭min9(♯7)/E♭
17–24 (1:09)	C♭Maj9♯11/E♭
	25–32 C♭13/E♭ and G♭min9(♯7)/E♭
33–40 (1:25)	C♭Maj9♯11/E♭
41–48	C♭13/E♭ and G♭min9(♯7)/E♭
49–56 (1:40)	B♭triad(♭9)/E♭

The diagram also indicates how the harmonic accompaniment at the opening of Davis's solo begins initially with C7, as if continuing the progression from Shorter's solo. By the 4th bar of Davis's solo, however, the harmonic accompaniment shifts to E♭min9. This holdover C7 harmony thus masks the underlying 8-bar organization consistently present behind Shorter's and Davis's solos.

A similar event takes place at the beginning of Hancock's solo, which now begins with G♭min9(♯7), continuing the progression from the end of Davis's solo. But at the beginning of Davis's solo, Hancock's subsumed the holdover C7 harmony within the 8-bar section. For his own solo, however, Hancock continues this harmony for 6 bars before advancing to the D tonal center and the 8-bar alternation of Dmin9 and B♭13. Again, the holdover harmony makes more seamless the connection between the two solos.

Mm. 1–6 (1:47)	G♭min9(♯7)
7–14 (1:53)	Dmin9
15–22	B♭13/D
23–30 (2:09)	Dmin9

31–38	B♭13/D
39–46 (2:24)	Dmin9
47–50	B♭13/D (Davis returns to head at m. 49)

Despite the accompanimental and improvisational freedom during the solos of "Riot," the improvisations adhere to some clear organizational principles. The tonal center of each successive solo moves down by half step, from E (Shorter), to E♭ (Davis), to D (Hancock). Clearly this overall strategy of descending by half step for successive solos must have been predetermined—the rhythm section players and the soloists are in general accord during the performance. Moreover, with the exception of Hancock's opening 6 bars to his solo, each of the solos preserve an underlying 8-bar organization, established by Hancock's harmonic progression, which alternates versions of i and ♭VI7 every 8 bars. This harmonic progression reflects the opening two harmonies stated successively during the introduction to "Riot."

Unlike the half-step modulation among consecutive solos, it is possible that the 8-bar divisions formed by that harmonic progression were not predetermined. The diagrams above show that neither Shorter nor Davis ends their solo at a conclusion of a two-chord cycle. And since Davis returns with the melody to "Riot" three measures into one of Hancock's 8-bar sections—one of several studio compositions whose abrupt exit strategy conflicts with the end of a Hancock improvisation—it may be that those 8-bar divisions formed by the harmonic accompaniment were not discussed in advance.

"Riot" was recorded on July 19, 1967, two days after the bloody Newark race riots had ended leaving 26 dead and scores injured. The Newark riot was one among over one hundred race riots that erupted during 1967 in reaction to urban blight, discrimination, unemployment, and simmering civil rights issues. Hancock's "Riot" is one of the only Davis second quintet titles that responded to contemporary political issues. Certainly its mixed meter (heard during the head) and extended harmonies were intended to depict an urban landscape whose ongoing unrest and turbulence seemed, in mid-1967, omnipresent.

THE PERFORMANCE OF "NEFERTITI," with its endlessly repeating melody, justifiably figures as a signal event for the group. Yet in other ways it emerged from earlier quintet practices, and reflects Davis's growing disinterest if not boredom with the head/solos/head template. The quintet recorded Nefertiti only a month after Sorcerer. The four June 1967 sessions produced not only Nefertiti, but also an additional 22 minutes of music that Columbia would later release in 1976 as part of the album *Water Babies*.

And Davis's restlessness is in effect with some of his ensuing recording projects at the end of 1967 and the beginning of 1968, some of which
Columbia later released on *Directions* and *Circle in the Round*. On these
recordings Davis augmented the quintet with a guitarist (Joe Beck,
Bucky Pizzarelli, and George Benson performed on different tracks),
and he induced Hancock to play celeste, electric harpsichord, and the
Wurlitzer electric piano. On several of these compositions, Davis uses
the guitarist to double the bass part, at times as part of an underlying
groove riff ("Water on the Pond"). Probably the most unusual work from
these studio tracks is "Circle in the Round." It shows the studio processes
on which Davis would soon rely. The group recorded it in thirty-five
segments, which were then spliced together into a single version. Two
different versions now exist. The segments were spliced together for the
1979 release of *Circle in the Round*. More recently discovered was the
version that producer Teo Macero spliced together in 1968 as a thirty-
three-minute track; that version is included on *Miles Davis Quintet:
1965–68*. The composition relies on a set of three melodic statements of
nine, eight, and nine measures, its exoticism enhanced by the repeated
guitar droning and the celeste trills throughout.[13]

13   Carl Woideck, "Miles Davis's 'Circle in the Round': Composition, Performance, and
      Recording Process," unpublished ms.

CHAPTER 7

MILES IN THE SKY AND FILLES DE KILIMANJARO

detailed

Less ~~analysis~~

tallest mountain

(Girl of White Mountain (Africa))

THE SECOND QUINTET'S LAST TWO studio albums have yet to be thoroughly assessed. *Miles in the Sky* (recorded January 16 and May 15–17, 1968) and *Filles de Kilimanjaro* (May 21, June 19–21, September 24, 1968) differed qualitatively from the earlier recordings, and marked an important turning point for the group. Some of the differences were patent. For example, the move to electric piano and electric bass, the use of single extended tonal centers for improvisation, and the importation of rock-based straight-eighth rhythms all adumbrated an imminent shift to jazz-*represent* rock fusion. But there were subtler but no less drastic changes on these final quintet recordings. One change involved retooling and rethinking conventional attitudes toward chorus structure and jazz composition. And this took place as Davis became the primary composer, writing or cowriting six of the ten compositions on these last two albums.

Lawrence Kart has written perceptively on these last two recordings, both in a 1968 *Down Beat* review of *Miles in the Sky* as well as in the 2002 liner notes for the CD rerelease of *Filles de Kilimanjaro*.[1] In the former, he described the influence of the jazz avant-garde on the quintet, particularly the "Coleman-Coltrane revolution" and their "assault on popular song." This attempt to link Davis with the avant-garde posed for Kart a challenge, given Davis's well-known dismissals of Coleman and other avant-garde players. Yet as earlier chapters have shown, this connection was an ongoing part of *Down Beat*'s critical reception of the Davis studio recordings since *E.S.P.* In the latter writing, Kart positioned *Filles de Kilimanjaro* along the path from the earlier postbop recordings through Davis's later fusion recordings *In a Silent Way* and *Bitches Brew*.

It is both tempting and necessary to acknowledge *Miles in the Sky* and *Filles de Kilimanjaro* as significant predecessors for Davis's later fusion work, with the use of rock rhythms, pedal point improvisation, and a harmonic language somewhat sparer than earlier quintet recordings. The fusion of jazz with R& B, gospel, and rock was already firmly in place by the early 1960s, appearing in funky jazz works such as Lee Morgan's "Sidewinder" and Herbie Hancock's "Watermelon Man." Hancock even later claimed he deliberately included a straight-eighth note composition on each of his 1960s Blue Note recordings.[2] The second half of the 1960s continued to witness individual fusions of jazz with rock, funk, and popular music—through gospel-tinged piano (Ramsey Lewis's "The 'In' Crowd"), covers of popular rock groups like the Beatles and the Mamas and the Papas (Wes Montgomery), the use of electronic devices to alter the sound of an acoustic instrument (Eddie Harris), and the use of guitar feedback and distortion (Larry Coryell). Critics even lobbed the same criticisms they would hurl at fusion artists a decade later. For example, the review following Kart's *Miles in the Sky* review dismissed Eddie Harris's R & B-based *Plug Me In*, suggesting that Harris's motivation was commercial gain. The term "soul jazz" eventually replaced "funky jazz" when Riverside Records used it to promote the recordings of Cannonball Adderley, and Adderley's quintet provided a significant influence for Davis around this time. Adderley's 1966 soul jazz hit "Mercy, Mercy, Mercy" featured pianist Josef Zawinul playing Wurlitzer electric piano, and Zawinul's use of the Wurlitzer and the Fender Rhodes electric piano

---

1 Both essays reprinted in Lawrence Kart, *Jazz in Search of Itself* (New Haven: Yale University, 2004). The review of *Miles in the Sky* originally appeared *Down Beat* 35/20 (October 3, 1968): 24.

2 Ben Sidran, *Talking Jazz: An Oral History*, expanded edition (New York: Da Capo, 1995), 268.

was a catalyst for Davis's turn to electric keyboards. Davis's second wife Betty Mabry, whose picture appears on the cover of *Filles de Kilimanjaro*, kindled his interest in the music of Jimi Hendrix and Sly and the Family Stone.[3]

But a view of these two Davis recordings solely as transitional, emerging between the twilight of postbop jazz and the dawn of fusion—or, alternatively, in light of the jazz avant-garde—does not address substantively their achievement and novelty. Likely it was these recordings that Hancock described when he said, "We were always trying to create something new. It became more and more difficult. Like trying to make conversation never using any words you used before."[4] And the designation on the cover to *Filles de Kilimanjaro*, "Directions in Music by Miles Davis," reflects a self-conscious attempt by Davis to call attention to the recording's newness, its further departures from postbop conventions as well as, perhaps, his own enhanced role as composer.

Certainly on these recordings appear much more involved compositional structures. "Stuff" begins as a 40-bar form, whose later head statements expand and contract the internal sections, and whose melodic fragments return altered with each reappearance. "Tout de Suite" is an elaborate 70-bar form. "Filles de Kilimanjaro" is a series of seven melodic ideas, several of which are fragmentary, many of which appear in different metric identities with each restatement. These compositions reevaluate the relationship of compositional melody to improvisations: multiple head statements postpone the improvisation until three or four minutes into the recording—with "Stuff," improvisations are withheld until after nearly six minutes of head statements. For both "Stuff" and "Filles de Kilimanjaro," the alterations made to successive melodic statements create a sense of shifting perspective upon recurring melodic objects.

Davis's "Country Son" exhibited yet another challenge to conventional notions of jazz composition by *removing* melody from the composition, which consisted of three contrasting sections, without any overt melody head statements. The group determined the length of two of those three sections spontaneously during performance. And the head to "Paraphernalia" used melodic statements with intervening sections of freely

---

3   Further, Leonard Feather wrote in Davis's June 1968 *Down Beat* blindfold test that Davis had in his room albums and tapes by pop artists James Brown, Dionne Warwick, Tony Bennett, the Byrds, Aretha Franklin, and the Fifth Dimension. Leonard Feather, "Miles Davis: Blindfold Test Pt. 1," *Down Beat* 35/12 (June 13, 1968): 34.

4   Jack Chambers, *Milestones: The Music and Times of Miles Davis* 2 (New York: Da Capo, 1998), 140. Originally publ. University of Toronto, 1983 and 1985.

determined length played by the rhythm section. These two compositions maintain an elastic harmonic framework liberated from a consistent underlying hypermeter. With the self-imposed challenge of flexible harmonic rhythm, the quintet relies on spontaneous musical cues to advance the harmonic progressions.

Jack Chambers and John Szwed have discussed the participation of Gil Evans on these recordings, particularly *Filles de Kilimanjaro*, its title a reference to Kilimanjaro African Coffee, a coffee importing business in which Davis had invested. (The French titles of its compositions were purportedly a result of Davis's last-minute desire to translate all the titles into French.) The extent of Evans's role is unclear. Writing in 1977, Dan Morgenstern noted that it was not widely known that the recording date "was largely written and arranged by Gil." Szwed indicates that Evans was involved in arranging bass lines, voicing horns, and was the uncredited co-composer for "Petits Machins."[5] It is likely that the intricate counter-lines by saxophone, electric piano, and bass heard against the melody of "Tout de Suite" are indebted to Evans. Whatever Evans's specific role, his participation clearly indicates the fertile ongoing collaboration with Davis that—by this point—had flourished for nearly two decades.

Filles de Kilimanjaro included three compositions recorded by the original quintet, done in May and June. The second recording date in September included two other compositions, "Frelon brun" and "Mademoiselle Mabry." By this second date Davis had fired Hancock, who missed the session because he had contracted food poisoning while on his honeymoon in Brazil. Davis replaced Hancock with Chick Corea. Hancock would continue to appear on various Davis studio recordings through 1972. British bassist Dave Holland took the place of Ron Carter.

"COUNTRY SON"

In many ways, "Country Son" departs most radically from other studio recordings done by the quintet. It does not include a melody statement,

5   Chambers, *Milestones* 2, 131; John Szwed, *So What: The Life of Miles Davis* (New York: Simon & Schuster, 2002), 272–73. Evans was listed as co-composer on his album *Svengali*, where "Petits Machins" was retitled "Eleven." Szwed includes a recollection by saxophonist Steve Potts that Davis (not Gil Evans) wrote the melody to "Filles de Kilimanjaro" on an African thumb piano. Regarding the May 17, 1968 sessions that produced "Paraphernalia," Martin Williams quotes Gil Evans as stating that he "midwifed a couple of these pieces." Martin Williams, "Recording Miles Davis," essay in *Jazz Masters in Transition* (New York: Macmillan, 1970), 273.

but instead consists of three alternating sections, each with a contrasting rhythmic identity. On the alternate take to "Country Son" (recorded after the released track), the group plays the first section (Section A) in a loose triple meter (consisting of two statements of five harmonies), the second section (Section B) with a straight-eighth rock feel, and the third (Section C) with a 4/4 swing feel. Transitional harmonies link the B and C sections (T1) and the C and A sections (T2). With the absence of a given melody to "Country Son" and the solos determined by a single cycle through the constituent sections, the compositional organization here invites comparison to Davis's 1959 "Flamenco Sketches" (*Kind of Blue*), which shares those features. Yet with "Country Son" the individual sections last significantly longer. The distinct rhythmic identities of the three sections also set "Country Son" apart from "Flamenco Sketches."

Section A, in slow triple meter, consists of a repeated section of 8 bars consisting of five harmonies. The group ceases the fixed triple meter briefly at the end of each 8-bar section. The first four harmonies involve a G pedal in the bass, before the bass falls to F♯. Hancock's harmonic rhythm is flexible, but the harmonies appear generally as shown in the following list. Notice that the harmony that appears at mm. 7–8 is a nonstandard harmony, consisting of the pitches G–C–F♯–B over the F♯ bass. It may be useful to consider this harmony modally, derived from an underlying F♯ locrian collection. In this case the F♯ locrian collection shares the same pitch collection as G major, allying it with the G bass of the preceding six measures.

HARMONIES FOR SECTION A

m. 1	2–3	4	5–6	7–8
Gmin11	G13sus	G13(♭9)	GMaj7(#11)	G–C–F♯–B/F♯

Both Sections B and C use the same tonal center of D, and the length of both those sections is determined spontaneously during performance. Each solo by trumpet, tenor saxophone, and piano lasts through one cycle of each of the three sections. Two transitional harmonies link Sections B and C (Bmaj triad (♭9/♯9) and D♭7♯9), and a single harmony links Section C with A (Dmin13/E).[6] During the alternate take the form is as follows. The diagram indicates Sections A–C, as well as the two transitional sections (T1 and T2) for the alternate take.

6   This D-13/E may also be considered modally as an E phrygian sonority.

[handwritten: triple st feels]   *[handwritten: swing]*   *[handwritten: Transition]*

Davis	A (:00) B (:46) T1 (1:57)	C (2:08)	T2 (4:06)
Shorter	A (4:13) B (5:03) T1 (7:00)	C (7:16)	T2 (8:55)
Hancock	A (9:07) B (9:50) T1 (11:15)	C (11:34)	
Davis	T2 (13:27) A (13:36)		

On the released track, the group modifies the organization discussed above somewhat. The timings and organization are as follows:

Davis	*[handwritten: 1:23 talking]*		C	T2 (1:02)	A (1:12; 8 bars played once only)
Shorter	B (1:34)	T1 (2:37)	C (2:59)	T2 (4:34)	A (4:56, 8 bars)
Hancock	A (5:20, 8 bars)	B (5:48)	T1 (6:56)	C (7:15)	T2 (9:09)
Davis	A (9:15)	B (9:58)	T1 (11:26)	C (11:39)	T2 (13:16)
	A (13:23, 8 bars)				

On "Country Son," it is important not to understate the role of Williams who was "starting to play in a consistently dramatic way, pushing the drums to a new level of accompaniment."[7] "Country Son" is unique to the quintet studio output, given the absence of a melody to provide the head to the composition. It provides an example of what chapter 2 described as Level 2a since it preserves an underlying harmonic structure but allows for flexible harmonic rhythm during the B and C sections, with the players relying on cues for subsequent sections.

It is possible to read "Country Son" as depicting Davis at a crossroads. The composition is a hybrid, melding in a single composition the straight-eighth rock feel (highlighted by the D major and C major triadic comping in the piano) of Section B, and the 4/4 swing feel of Section C. Thus it links Davis's upcoming fusion concerns with his prior postbop ones. It suggests, perhaps, a failed possibility of a détente between them. Save for "Black Comedy," this is the last quintet studio recording to use walking bass and conventional postbop swing roles for the rhythm section. Perhaps "Country Son" indicated that those two positions were irreconcilable. Soon Davis opted for one path and abandoned the other.

But there are other readings of "Country Son." Its swing-feel C section effectively co-opted John Coltrane Quintet's extended improvisations over a single focal bass pedal point, and the improvisations on "Country Son" move inside and outside the prevailing tonal center in ways that recall Coltrane's quartet. Many of Coltrane's canonic modal jazz compositions—even when retaining an underlying 4/4 swing

---

7   Bob Belden, Liner notes to *Miles Davis Quintet 1965–68* (Columbia/Sony 67398), 98–99.

feel—led decisively to jazz-rock fusion of the following decade: through straight-eighth improvisation, pentatonics, ostinato and pedal point, and a slow-moving harmonic rhythm that allowed for clear inside/ outside improvisational strategies. In the same way, the swing feel and the straight-eighth sections of "Country Son" illustrate—in a single composition—a link between Coltrane's postbop innovations and those of jazz-rock fusion. Rather than two irreconcilable positions, the two share many of the same musical concerns.

"PARAPHERNALIA"

The performance of "Paraphernalia" includes George Benson on guitar. Benson was one of several guitarists (including Joe Beck and Bucky Pizarelli) that Davis included in his studio recordings between December 1967 and February 1968. Recorded in January 1968, "Paraphernalia" took place several months earlier than the mid-May sessions that produced the remainder of *Miles in the Sky*. The recording suggests deliberate accompaniment decisions made for specific instruments, contributing to the overall identity of the performance. These include Williams's focus on the hi-hat, Benson's use of octaves, and Hancock's strict use of the midrange of the piano for comping.[8]

By these last two Davis quintet recordings (*Miles in the Sky* and *Filles de Kilimanjaro*) Shorter's participation as primary composer for the quintet receded. "Paraphernalia" is Shorter's only composition on these recordings. This seems not to represent any flagging compositional activity on Shorter's part. Shorter's *Schizophrenia*, recorded the previous year (March 1967), contained five Shorter compositions, elaborately arranged for three horns, providing instances of funky jazz ("Tom Thumb"), a phrygian-based composition with some resemblance to "Masqualero" ("Go"), aggressive postbop ("Schizophrenia"), a jazz waltz ("Miyako"), and free jazz ("Playground"). Shorter's lead sheets show him at times departing from lead sheet conventions: "Playground" consists only of melody without chord symbols, "Go" merely contains the instruction "Bb sound" with the notated melody.

Shorter's Library of Congress copyright deposit of the lead sheet to "Paraphernalia" is dated July 10, 1968.[9] It continues the trend begun

---

8   According to Martin Williams, who attended the session, Davis deliberately requested to Hancock during the rehearsal that he avoid the upper register of the piano when comping. Martin Williams, "Recording Miles Davis," 276.
9   "Paraphernalia" Library of Congress Copyright Deposit Eu 62584 (July 10, 1968).

with Shorter's earlier lead sheets to "Pinocchio" and "Nefertiti," which alternate standard chord symbols with written-out harmonies with no attendant chord symbols.[10] Shorter's written harmonies for "Pinocchio" and "Nefertiti" consist of three- and four-note midrange chords, usually with no bass pitch indicated. The written harmonies for "Paraphernalia" include bass pitches along with harmonies consisting anywhere from three to seven pitches. In addition, relative to "Pinocchio" and "Nefertiti," the proportion of written harmonies to chord symbols drastically increases with the lead sheet to "Paraphernalia." "Pinocchio" and "Nefertiti" use only a handful of notated harmonies that alternate with twice as many standard chord symbols. In contrast, "Paraphernalia" includes only five standard chord symbols amidst fourteen notated harmonies. Many of these notated harmonies appear during the final 3/4 section of the composition. Likely Shorter's notated harmonies suggest a desire for specific voicings, a number of which pair an upper structure triad above a bass note. Their progression creates a rising line formed by the upper pitches of those chords, a line that Hancock consistently maintains during the 3/4 section.

Shorter's lead sheet to "Paraphernalia" indicates it as an 18-bar composition. It is notated primarily in 4/4, but includes two metric shifts to 3/4, at mm. 9–11 and 15–18. The performance on the recording alters this organization significantly. These alterations made to Shorter's lead sheet, also described by Martin Williams—who attended the recording session—do provide evidence that the group altered Shorter's compositions in the studio and contradict some of the recollections of the quintet members.[11] For the recording, the group reduces the composition to two alternating sections. Section 1 is in 4/4, and Section 2 in 3/4. The group consistently plays the second 3/4 section as a 9-bar section over three pedal points of F, B♭, and D♭. This 3/4 section provides a metrical shift near the end of the form.

While the group plays the 3/4 Section 2 consistently by maintaining its 9 bars throughout the head and solos, the players interpret Section 1

---

10 And Shorter's lead sheets for the compositions to his 1965 recording *The All-Seeing Eye* contain no chord symbols at all. Instead, the lead sheets for "The All Seeing Eye," "Chaos," "Face of the Deep," and "Genesis" contain melody and specifically notated voicings.

11 Martin Williams describes those studio alterations Davis made to the "Paraphernalia" lead sheet in "Recording Miles Davis," 276. Hancock and Shorter claimed that Shorter's compositions remained unedited: see Todd Coolman, "The Miles Davis Quintet of the Mid-1960s: Synthesis of Improvisational and Compositional Elements" (Ph.D. diss., New York University: 1997), 24 and 30.

more freely. They do this during the head by detaching and dissociating each of the five melodic phrases from one another. In between each of the melodic phrases, the rhythm section continues to play, but the group determines the length of these intermediate sections freely during the performance. Thus while on Shorter's lead sheet the 4/4 Section 1 consists merely of 8 measures, it instead lasts 25 bars during the recording's first head statement (initiated with the melody). On this first head statement, each of the five melodic phrases appear 6 bars apart, with the fifth of these melodic phrases lasting merely 1 bar, linking to the 3/4 Section 2. And during the recording's second head statement, Section 1 lasts 29 bars. Undoubtedly, the two horns relied on visual cues for each successive phrase. The enhanced use of space between each phrase places each one into heightened relief.

The freely determined lengths of Section 1 provide an example of what might be called a "mosaic" technique, consisting of ordered phrases played by the horns, but with intervening accompanimental sections of spontaneously determined length. During the head statements Carter's bass accompaniment perpetuates a start and stop feel, accomplished by walking beneath the melodic phrases, but moving to a more static accompaniment between them.

The group maintains this overall formal strategy during the improvisations (with the exception of the guitar solo: there the group does not move to Section 2). Section 1 (4/4) is of flexible length, and Section 2 (3/4) is consistently 9 bars. During the improvisations Hancock largely adheres to the harmonic progression stated during the head, but determines the harmonic rhythm of Section 1 freely. The flexibility of harmonic rhythm operates as a self-imposed challenge for the quintet.

Shorter's lead sheet indicates "D pedal" for Section 1, and Carter's bass accompaniment generally supplies that D tonal center during that section. It is interesting to compare "Paraphernalia" with "Country Son" since both use the D tonal center as one of the primary structural features. They differ in that "Paraphernalia" yet maintains a loose but consistent harmonic progression over this tonal center, during both the head and the solos. Hancock typically realizes this harmony at the top of each chorus as a D7 harmony with alterations of ♭5 and ♯9. (Shorter's lead sheet indicates the first harmony as D+9.) Since the group freely determines the length of Section 1, Hancock's subsequent harmonies (E♭Maj7♯11/D, B♭Maj7♯11/D, A♭Maj7♯5/D, and B♭Maj7♯11/D) follow the cues that the soloists provide, cues that during the solos typically arise through melodic paraphrase.[12] Thus paraphrase both regulates the harmonic progression for Section 1 and cues Section 2.

The quintet's use of melodic paraphrase during the improvisations shows how the players address ensemble challenges that arise when performing a work with flexible harmonic rhythm. These challenges require a high degree of ensemble communication. With "Paraphernalia," the stakes are elevated since the move to Section 2 in each chorus involves a change in meter from 4/4 to 3/4, requiring all the performers to move simultaneously to that section. As a result, the players collectively determine the formal outlines during the course of the performance. This may explain why Benson does not cue or move to Section 2 during his solo. Perhaps for Benson—not a regular member of the quintet—that level of ensemble communication did not have sufficient time to flourish. On the other hand, the regular quintet members had by now cultivated a sophisticated level of rapport in response to these spontaneous challenges.

"BLACK COMEDY"

Tony Williams's "Black Comedy" is the most metrically ambitious of all the quintet's studio recordings. The group recorded an alternate take as well as the released take. On the released track, the metric scheme of the 16-bar form is as follows:

6 against 4	4 mm.
4/4	2
5/4	1
4/4	3
6 against 4	4
5/4	1
7/4	1

The alternate take maintains the same metric organization, save for the final measure, played in 6/4 rather than 7/4. The composition is in two sections. The first section occupies the first 10 bars, with the second 6-bar section (mm. 11–16) forming a varied reprise of mm. 1–6.

Throughout the composition, the harmony of mm. 8–10 is played as G♭Maj7 E♭min9 D♭Maj7♯11. On the released track, Hancock during these measures of his improvisation alters the harmonic progression slightly,

---

12 Hancock also occasionally states G♭Maj7/D during the third and fifth melodic phrases.

and he reharmonizes those measures with a more functional harmonic progression. Example 7.1 shows these measures from each of Hancock's four choruses. Note the left-hand harmonies during these three measures in the first chorus (4:41), which correspond to E♭min9 A♭7alt D♭Maj13, with one harmony expressed per measure. The right hand material corresponds to the A♭7(alt) harmony within m. 8, thus Hancock elasticizes this harmony to enter earlier in the right hand than in the left. However, the voice-leading to the D♭Maj13 chord is paced to resolve directly to

EXAMPLE 7.1   Measures 8–10 of Hancock's Solo on "Black Comedy": Reharmonization and Hard Bop Voice Leading

F on the downbeat of m. 10. The eighth-note pitches on the third and fourth beats of m. 9 drive the voice-leading, with A♭ (beat 3) to G♭ (beat 4) propelling the resolution to F.

In the second chorus (5:02), the left-hand harmonies again correspond to E♭min9 (m. 8), A♭7(alt) (m. 9, mid-measure), and D♭Maj13 (m. 10). Here the right-hand material corresponds closely to the harmonic shift each measure. Measure 9 outlines a D major triad that begins and ends with D, and this D resolves to E♭ the downbeat of the following measure, before the line continues, expressing the D♭Maj13 harmony. Similarly, during the third chorus (5:21) the left-hand harmonies express the harmonic shift each measure. Here at mm. 8.5–9.5 appears a characteristic Hancock device—a fixed pitch (A♭) off the beat elaborates the chromatic voice-leading on the beat (F–E–E♭–D). The right-hand material then yields to the harmonic shift (with a similar D major orientation as the second chorus) during m. 9 mid-measure. During Hancock's final chorus (5:43), the left-hand harmonies express the ii–V–I progression (but now with m. 9 as A♭13 with added fourth, rather than A♭7alt). Again, the voice-leading here outlines the harmonic shift, with F6 of m. 8 yielding to E the following measure. Thus that m. 9 right-hand pitch material corresponds to A♭7alt, with the line paced to resolve to F (D♭Maj7♯11) on the downbeat of m. 10. However, notice that Hancock returns to E6 at m. 10, and he postpones a downward resolution to E♭6 until m. 11.

The isolated measures from Hancock's four choruses are meant to show how Hancock here calls upon voice-leading moves consistent with hard bop practice. He does this by transforming the G♭Maj7 E♭min9 D♭maj(♯11) harmonic progression in these three measures into a more functional ii V I harmonic progression. At mm. 9–10, the voice-leading of Choruses 1, 2, and 4 expresses the resolution of the altered dominant harmony into D♭Maj13. At mm. 8–9, the voice-leading of Chorus 4 reflects the motion from the ii chord to the altered dominant harmony (F–E). Thus despite the metric complexity and the relative absence of functional harmonic progressions in "Black Comedy," Hancock nevertheless roots this portion of his improvisation in more traditional practice.

"STUFF"

Commentary on "Stuff" focuses on its rhythm-and-blues based rhythms. Chambers derides Williams's "infectious, toe-tapping, and trite" boogaloo rhythms. His use of the term boogaloo, a mid-1960s dance craze, seems intended as pejorative. Belden describes it as a soul-jazz composition, comparing its groove to the pop-soul grooves heard on the Motown recording label, but highlighting its combination of pop music harmonies along with more modal ("Phrygian-mode sound") harmonies.[13] Belden further notes this is Hancock's initial recording on Fender Rhodes electric piano. Both Chambers and Belden consider "Stuff" as a harbinger, representing Davis's imminent move to rock- and R&B-based rhythms and electric instruments.

"Stuff" also reveals evident postproduction activities. The released master is from two takes: the first statement of the melody to "Stuff" is then spliced (at 1:50) into a complete take that lasts the remainder of the composition.[14] A careful listen reveals the overt splice. The initial portion is slightly faster than the later portion and the splice appears mid-measure, with the new material appearing after an abruptly truncated 2/4 bar.

The Real Book includes a lead sheet to "Stuff." In it, the transcribed melody lasts 40½ bars, containing the curious 2/4 bar that arises from the splice at 1:50.[15] The lead sheet gives no evidence that "Stuff" consists of anything but a standard repeated chorus structure, whose melody would be played relatively consistently. This implies a fixed definitive version of the composition from the standpoint of melody and form.

The Real Book also indicates the feel of the composition as "rock," linking with Chambers's and Belden's focus on "Stuff's" R&B rhythms.[16] But absent from *The Real Book*, from Chambers's observations, and from Belden's comments is perhaps the most arresting aspect to "Stuff." The melody consists of a series of brief aphoristic fragments of typically three to five pitches, yet each head chorus places these melodic fragments in differing metric positions. The effect is startling, one akin to viewing similar objects from multiple viewpoints or perspectives. Rather than head statements with relatively consistent placement of melody and harmony, each head chorus is unique from the standpoint of melody and harmony. Since Davis and Shorter play the head in unison, it is extremely likely that each varied head statement was written in advance.

Given the alterations between each head statement, it is clear why those statements last as long as the improvisations. The group states the

---

13 Chambers, *Milestones*, 128; Belden, Liner notes, 98–99.

14 Belden, Liner notes, 99.

15 The location of the 2/4 bar in *The Real Book* lead sheet to "Stuff" changed once published by Hal Leonard. The original versions placed it correctly at m. 41, the Leonard version at m. 35. See *The Real Book*, 6th ed. (Milwaukee, Wisc.: Hal Leonard, n.d.), 390–91.

16 This designation was removed from the Hal Leonard, *The Real Book*, 6th ed.

melody four times prior to the improvisations, and once more following the solos. The improvisations do not begin until six minutes into the track. With "Stuff," then—like "Nefertiti" (discussed in chapter 6)—the group advances melodic statements as a principal element of the recording. And with "Stuff" the melody statements vary to an unprecedented extent.

In order to show these melodic variations, example 7.2 aligns the melody for mm. 1–12 of each of the five head statements. For the first chorus, the transcription also numbers each of the brief melodic fragments 1–8. Fragments 1 and 6, which begin and end the first 8-bar section, appear consistently each chorus. However, all other fragments shift. Relative to the first chorus, Fragment 2 appears a beat earlier during Choruses 2–4, and two beats earlier during Chorus 5. Fragment 3 shifts two beats earlier during all the latter choruses. Relative to the first chorus, Fragment 4 appears two beats earlier during Choruses 2–3, and three beats earlier during Choruses 4–5—there the final pitch now appears on the downbeat of m. 4. And Fragment 5 shifts consistently, appearing one beat earlier (Chorus 2), two beats earlier (Chorus 3 and 5), and a full measure earlier (Chorus 4). Fragment 6, completing the 8-bar section, appears consistently with each chorus. And Fragments 7–8 also undergo revision.

EXAMPLE 7.2   Mm 1–12 of Head Statements on "Stuff"

This technique of shifting the melodic fragments each head statement poses a fascinating and drastic means for reinterpreting chorus structure. This reinterpretation is furthered by the harmonic environment, which likewise alters from chorus to chorus. The opening 12 measures use all the dominant harmonies that appear chromatically between B♭7 and D7 (B♭7, B7, C7, D♭7, D7), but the harmonizations in each instance differ. As with the melodic fragments, the harmonic alterations between choruses show "Stuff" challenging the notion of a definitive overarching chorus structure.

And not only do the melodic fragments and the harmonizations change from chorus to chorus: the length of each chorus changes with each of the five statements of the melody, and the constituent sections of "Stuff" each time differ. The first chorus (transcribed in *The Real Book*) consists of 40 bars (up through the 2/4 bar at the splice). If we acknowledge these 40 bars as consisting of five 8-bar sections (Sections A–E), the latter head statements organize according to table 7.1.

Thus not only are the melodic fragments shifted and the harmonic progressions altered during head statements, the length of each chorus and the internal sections constantly evolve. Far from a trite boogaloo, "Stuff" puts forth a consistently shifting form whose constants are the ordering of the melodic fragments, the general outlines of the harmonic progression, and the underlying pulse and meter. Here the sections expand and contract, and the 8-bar regularity of the first chorus is immediately abandoned and reconsidered with each subsequent chorus. This radically overturns the implications of a fixed chorus structure suggested by *The Real Book* lead sheet. While "Stuff" shares with "Nefertiti" the focus on repeated head statements, in many ways "Stuff" is the more radical composition. Its melodic, harmonic, and formal outlines are even more malleable, its challenges to conventions of chorus structure more severe.

TABLE 7.1   Organization of Head Statements in Sections A–E of "Stuff"

	Section				
	A	B	C	D	E
First head statement (:30) (40 bars + ½ bar before splice)	8 mm.	8	8	8	8 (+ ½)
Second head statement (1:58) (38 bars)	8	8	4	8	8 (+ 2-bar tag)
Third head statement (3:14) (38 bars)	8	7	5	6	10 (+2-bar tag)
Fourth head statement (4:29) (42 bars)	8	10	6	7	9 (+ 2-bar tag)
Fifth head statement (14:35) (41 bars)	8	7	6	7	11 (+ 2-bar tag)

"PETITS MACHINS"

The use of electric bass and electric piano, and the focus on a single tonal center during the improvisations of "Petits Machins," highlights Davis's interest in departing from a postbop orientation, and moving toward the sounds and textures he would explore on his later fusion recordings. *Miles Davis Quintet 1965-68* now lists Gil Evans as co-composer for the composition, along with Miles Davis. Evans later recorded it on his own album, *Svengali*, under the title "Eleven." (Evans's trumpeter Johnny Coles also recorded it on one of his recordings for the Mainstream label.) The alternate title "Eleven" refers to the 11/4 meter heard during the first portion of the head (Section 1). On "Petits Machins" the group expresses the 11/4 meter with a repeating riff and chromatically ascending dominant harmonies. Section 2 moves to a contrasting 10-bar section in 4/4. The opening 6 bars of Section 2 rely on an F pedal point in the bass, above which occur shifting harmonies each measure.

The melody for the initial 4 bars of Section 2 resembles that of Davis's earlier composition "Nardis," both in terms of its opening interval and general shape. In addition, the collection of pitches in the melody throughout the opening 6 bars of Section 2 (F–G–A♭–B–C–D♭–E–F) contain two augmented seconds (A♭–B and D♭–E), which convey an exoticism shared by "Nardis," whose melody also projects a pair of augmented seconds at mm. 2 (D♯–C) and 7 (G♯–F). In Section 2 of "Petits Machins," the static F pedal section yields to a syncopated progression (mm. 7–8) and a change of bass in mm. 9–10.

Perhaps due to the metric complexity of Section 1, the improvisations omit that section and take place only over Section 2. But while the improvisations for the later Gil Evans version also use solely the 10-bar cycle of Section 2, the Davis quintet makes one alteration to Section 2 during the improvisations. This is Davis's—by now—well-worn practice of metric deletion. Throughout the trumpet solo, the quintet maintains a repeated 9-bar cycle, rather than the 10 bars of Section 2 heard during the head. The quintet merely omits m. 10 of Section 2 during the solos and maintains the harmonic progression of mm. 1–9. As in the head, the syncopated progression occurs in m. 7. Unlike the head, Carter usually does not participate in playing the mm. 7–8 syncopation during the improvisations, and here Hancock interprets this progression more freely. The quintet does not return to the head following the improvisations. Instead, like "Filles de Kilimanjaro," the recording concludes with a second Davis improvisation.

David Baker transcribed and provided a brief analysis of Davis's solo in a 1969 issue of *Down Beat*. Ian Carr's biography also contains a transcription, and an annotated transcription of a portion of the solo likewise appears in a 2004 publication entitled *The Music of Miles Davis*.[17] There is much to commend Baker's transcription, with its sensitivity to bent notes, slides, smears, and Davis's technique of playing behind the beat.[18] Baker points out Davis's use of a single motive that furnishes the material for the solo. This motive is based on pitch and consists of two forms, Ab–G–F and A–G–F, heard initially in the second and fourth measures of Davis's solo.[19] This motive is also the focus of Carr's commentary and the Giel 2004 transcription. While Baker's claim that the motive furnishes the material for the *entire* solo is perhaps overstated, it certainly is one of its principal features.

Baker highlights the difference in the two forms of the motive, which revolves around the use of the pitch Ab or A natural. He writes, "The simple device of alternating Ab and A gives the illusion that the solo vacillates between F major and F minor…although the rhythm section suggests F minor throughout."[20] His point regarding the motive is significant because it underscores how the motive provides a crucial aspect of pacing, conveys a sense of voice-leading distinguished by its variants formed by Ab or A natural, and how those two pitches create focal arrival points.

The comments about the harmonic accompaniment in both the Baker and the later *Music of Miles Davis* transcription are less compelling, however. Baker notes the dominance of F in the bass during the trumpet improvisation, but suggests a single harmonic orientation—an extended vamp on F minor. The later Giel transcription instead regards the

---

17 David Baker, "Miles Davis—'Petits Machins' Solo," *Down Beat* 36/26 (December 25, 1969): 46–47, Ian Carr, *Miles Davis: The Definitive Biography* (New York: Thunder's Mouth Press, 1998), 590–91; and Lex Giel, *The Music of Miles Davis* (Milwaukee, Wisc.: Hal Leonard, 2004), 306–8.

18 The transcription does stray from accuracy, however, during mm. 49–77. Baker adds two extra beats of silence in the transcription at m. 49, placing the notation off by a half-measure for the next twenty measures. Subsequent measures shift the notation of the solo by yet another beat (m. 71ff.), and the transcription finally returns to accurate metrical notation by m. 78. The Giel transcription also departs from accuracy at m. 49.

19 Baker's analysis and transcription are written up a step, notated for Bb trumpet. Thus he describes the motive as Bb–A–G and B–A–G.

20 Baker, "Miles Davis," 46. I have changed the identification of key here to reflect the concert key, rather than the Bb trumpet key.

orientation as "F mixolydian with emphasis on the I chord throughout."[21] Both regard the improvisation as an open form over an extended pedal point of F. The improvisations do rely on F as a focal pedal point. But absent from both analyses is the fact that throughout the solo the quintet preserves the underlying 9-bar chorus structure and the harmonic progression of Section 2. And the opening harmony of each 9-bar cycle is F major (usually with added sixth, ninth, or major seventh), rather than F minor or F7. It is here that Davis relies on the major form of the motive (A–G–F). Example 7.3 transcribes the opening 19 bars of Davis's solo (:28) to show the use of the major form at the top of each of the choruses.[22]

EXAMPLE 7.3   Measures 1–19 of Davis's Solo on "Petits Machines" (:28)

21 Giel, *Music of Miles Davis*, 306.
22 The harmonies of the syncopated progression are indicated in the transcription (mm. 7 and 16) as fourth chords built on F, G♭, A♭, and A. Hancock plays those harmonies quite loosely throughout the performance.

Therefore, not only does Davis use the major form of the motive, but its role is a formal one. The overall motivic strategy—the sense of pacing, arrival, and voice-leading conveyed by the major form of the motive—is directly tied to and motivated by the underlying 9-bar form, whose first measure corresponds to F major. Its use often follows the minor form of the motive (A♭–G–F, mm. 7–9), or precedes the minor form (mm. 11–13). While the major form of the motive also occurs elsewhere (m. 4), Davis most frequently uses the major form of the motive as a means to mark the top of the form. During choruses 2–5, in particular, the pitch A5 of this motive forms the registral high point of the solo and coincides with the beginning of the 9-bar chorus.

"TOUT DE SUITE"

The quintet recorded both an alternate take and a released track to "Tout de Suite." The head constitutes an elaborate 70-bar form, an unprecedented formal length and design for the quintet's studio compositions. The melody and harmonic structure during the head is relatively consistent between both takes. However, the improvisational sections differ extensively between the two. The alternate take adheres to the 70-bar chorus structure and retains the triple meter and harmonic progression of the head during the improvisations. In contrast, the released track moves to a rock-based accompaniment, and the improvisations take place primarily over a bass pedal point of F while the keyboard accompaniment cycles through the harmonies of Sections D and E (mm. 41–70). On this released take, the role of Tony Williams during the improvisations is notable since his accompaniment suppresses any commitment to the 3/4 meter, in favor of the pulse and its eighth-note subdivision.

The extended 70-bar head of "Tout de Suite" consists of five sections (Sections A–E).

FORM OF HEAD TO "TOUT DE SUITE"

Intro: 16 bars (first time only)
Section A: 8 bars (rhythm section only): mm. 1–8
Section B: 16 bars, mm. 9–24
Section C: 16 bars, mm. 25–40
Section D: 14 bars, mm. 41–54
Section E: 16 bars, mm. 55–70

Despite the length of the form, the voice-leading connections within the slowly unfolding melody create an astonishing degree of continuity.

The following analysis discusses how these voice-leading connections operate and how the melodic lines create a series of beautifully wrought arch-shaped structures in Sections B, C, and D. Example 7.4 contains a transcription of the melody without rhythmic values. Since the horns play the melody flexibly, there are differences among the different head statements and between the two takes. The example is drawn from the first statement of the alternate take.

EXAMPLE 7.4 "Tout de Suite": Melodic Organization (transcribed from alternate take)

The melody follows a 16-bar introductory section and Section A. (The group does not repeat again the introductory 16 measures.) The two harmonies of Section A (mm. 1–8) appear in stark juxtaposition. Hancock usually leads in to the opening F harmony with an R & B–based keyboard formula, while the following dissonant harmony is G major stated with an F♯ in the bass.

The melody of Section B (mm. 9–24; :49 from alternate take) forms a series of four four-measure ideas, all related by the opening rhythmic motive of upbeat (beat 3) to downbeat that links the first and second measures of each 4-bar idea. This rhythmic motive in the melody relates very clearly to the accompanimental rhythm stated by the rhythm section throughout the head statements. These 16 bars of Section B also form a gradually ascending arch shape that progresses stepwise until the crest of the arch at m. 18. (Example 7.4 provides stems to the pitches that participate in this arch motion, and dotted slurs to show the rise and fall of those arches.) The line indirectly connects C5 to D5 in the first four-measure section (mm. 9–12), and E5 to F in the second (mm. 13–16). The apex of the arch takes place with a leap to A5 at m. 18. During this third 4-bar section (mm. 17–20), the melody winds down to return to C5, the original beginning point of the melody. And during the fourth 4-bar section, the melody progresses downward further, here moving to E4.

Measures 21–24 in many ways provide a convincing close to the entire 16-bar Section B. These bars complete the 16-bar design of the four phrases, they conclude the arch shape, and the final melodic pitches here all correspond to an evident evocation of C major, corresponding to the C heard in the bass at mm. 23–24. Yet one detail inhibits a sense of closure at mm. 23–24: the additional A♭ pitch added to the C major harmony. While likely more efficient to label the harmony as A♭Maj7♯5/C here, perhaps it is more accurate to describe the harmony as a C triad with the additional pitch of A♭. This captures more precisely the harmonic arrival on C major, with the additional pitch of A♭ adding a particular piquancy. And this piquancy works against the other musical dimensions (four phrases and arch form) that work to create a sense of closure. This is a subtle point, but one worth hearing, since the following Section C concludes with a related procedure.

The melody at Section C (1:22) initiates another arch shape. It begins with the same pitch of E that concluded Section B, before ascending stepwise to B (m. 30). Like the uppermost pitch of the earlier arch-form melody of Section B (at m. 18), the high point of this Section C arch likewise culminates with a leap, now from B4 to G5 (mm. 30–31). They also set up an answering six measures (mm. 31–36) that changes the direction of the line downward, from G to E to D, with a repetition of E to D (mm. 34–35).

Example 7.5 transcribes the trumpet and bass parts to Section C (taken from the first head statement of the alternate take) with rhythmic values to show additional details. It begins with an evident metrical conflict created by the bass, which stratifies quarter note triplets across the opening 2 bars, creating the perception of an accelerated meter. (This metrical conflict is heightened further on the released track as Tony Williams maintains a straight eighth note feel in the original meter.) There are some evident correspondences between the horn melody, which remains in the original meter, and the bass riff in this passage. The opening two pitches of both ascend to F♯, the following G–F♯–G design in the bass (mm. 25–26) is echoed by the horns (indicated by brackets in the transcription). Both parts ascend to A, the bass at m. 26, and the melody at m. 29. But the ascent to A happens more lazily in the melody, as it decorates a chromatic ascent through G, G♯, and A.

EXAMPLE 7.5   Section C from "Tout de Suite" (transcribed from alternate take, 1:22)

And the effect of mm. 28–30 is magical. The bass moves to F in these measures and returns to the underlying triple meter. Yet the decorated G♯ in the melody at m. 28 sounds out of phase with the harmony, an out-of-focus moment that comes into focus the following measures as the melody pitches A–G–A–B in the melody at mm. 29–30 now substantiate the underlying F major harmony. The opening metrical conflict and the move out and into harmonic focus at m. 25–30 create an astonishing six measures, which further set up the ascent of the arch that culminates at m. 31.

This section closes with a 4-bar phrase (mm. 37–40) that recalls the upbeat (beat 3) to downbeat rhythm of each 4-bar phrase of Section B.

And this phrase rounds off Section C, whose 16 bars rhyme with the 16 bars heard in Section B. Yet the regular 4 by 4 phrasing of Section B is absent in Section C. Only the final phrase of Section C occupies 4 bars, its rhythm an evident recollection of Section B. The arch design supports a grouping of 6 bars, with mm. 25–30 forming the ascent, and mm. 31–36 the descent. The harmonic rhythm in these measures likewise supports this 6-bar grouping since the harmonic rhythm accelerates to one change per measure at mm. 31–36. (However, there is a notable harmonic anticipation of the following E♭ in the bass the last beat of m. 35.)

The discussion of Section B called attention to the closing harmony, whose A♭ added to the C major harmony worked against the other musical dimensions that contributed to closure. A related technique arises at the end of Section C. The long-held pitch of A at mm. 39–40 creates a sense of stasis and ending. Yet the countermelody played by saxophone and keyboard disrupts the sense of closure, since that countermelody continues across into the next section.

And another factor creates continuity between Sections C and D. As the dotted slurs in Example 7.4 show, three arch-form melodies appear over Sections B, C, and D. But while the arch-form melodies of Sections B and C are initiated at the beginning of these sections, that of Section D begins earlier, with the melodic move from G to A the end of Section C. These pitches launch the ensuing long-range melody that gradually ascends to its highest point F5 at mm. 51–52. G and A thus not only conclude Section C but provide a link into the following section.

The final two sections, Section D and E, begin at m. 41. Clearly the group considered these last two sections as somewhat self-contained: Hancock's comping during the improvisations on the released take omit the harmonies of Sections A–C, and cycle through only the harmonies of Sections D and E heard at mm. 41–70. At the onset of Section D (1:55), the melody continues by returning to A, the final pitch of Section C, and the opening four measures (mm. 41–44) depart from and return to that A. The ensuing four measures carve out an elaborated chromatic ascent, first to B♭ (mm. 45–6) before moving to B (mm. 47–48). Here the elaborations of those primary pitches (A–B♭–B) include upper embellishments, indicated with asterisks in example 7.4.

The ascent through Section D crests through two waves, both creating a series of whole-step ascents. The first wave appears as A–B–C♯ (mm. 48–50), the second as C♯/D♭–E♭–F (mm. 51–52). The rhythmic orientation of those two waves is not identical, but does form a rhyme through the use of rhythmic values that mildly conflict with the underlying triple meter. The first wave (A–B–C♯) appears with its first two pitches as afterbeat quarter-note triplets (over beats 2 and 3, m. 48), with the upper pitch C♯ appearing on the downbeat of m. 49. The second wave (D♭–E♭–F) appears as afterbeat groupings of 4 quarter notes over the triple meter at m. 51, with the upper pitch F anticipating the downbeat of m. 52. Following the ascent to F, the melody returns downward in a brief descent from E♭5 to C5 to conclude this arch-form melody.

In contrast to Sections B–D, the final Section E (2:25) does not involve an elaborated arch-form melody. Instead, the entire section forms a long-range response to the E♭–C descent that concluded Section D. In the trumpet, the melody initially transposes and reverses those pitches to C♯–E, repeated each measure between 56 and 59. During the ensuing measures the saxophone now responds to that plaintive upward minor-third inquiry with a downward gesture, from B to G♯ (mm. 60–63) as the trumpet either remains on E (mm. 60–61) or restates the C♯–E inquiry (m. 62). Measures 64–66 alternate the minor third motion between parts, as one part holds and the other restates their motive, and the melody converges on B/D for the final three measures of the form. The horn players play this section loosely and freely during each of the individual versions. (This transcription draws from the opening head of the alternate take performance.)

There is one other intriguing aspect to Section E. This is the decidedly out-of-phase aspect to these 16 bars. The harmonies shift every 4 bars, at mm. 55, 59, 63, and 67. Yet the melodic organization is out of phase with these 4-bar shifts, shown by the slurs in example 7.4. The C♯–E trumpet melody (above the tenor saxophone A) repeats for 4 bars at mm. 56–59, setting up a 4-bar pattern out of phase with the harmonic rhythm. Similarly, the B–G♯ descent in the saxophone appears as a 4-bar pattern mm. 60–63, occurring one measure after the harmonic shift. (Shorter once plays the pattern as B–A, at m. 62.) Measures 64–67 alternate the two patterns, and the final B/D harmony appears at mm. 68–70, again 1 bar after the harmonic shift. Throughout Section E, the 4-bar melodic design in the horns remains unaligned with the 4-bar harmonic shifts.

"Tout de Suite" is a stunning achievement. The 70-bar form shows the group's ongoing concern with challenging conventional relationships between head statements and improvisation. Rather than an episodic series of disconnected sections, the voice-leading connections link the distinct sections. Sections C and D both begin with the melodic pitch that concluded the previous section, and Section E begins with C♯–E, transposing and reversing the E♭–C that concluded Section D. Moreover, the elaborate arch shape of the melodies at Sections B–D creates a focused internal relationship among those three sections.

Harmonically, the work is a hybrid. It uses the extended harmonies and pedal point construction of the earlier quintet compositions (see the harmonies of the introduction, for example). With those harmonies also appear simpler triadic structures above the bass. The following includes the harmonies supplied by Hancock during the improvisations. These harmonies are derived from Sections D–E (mm. 41–70): during the improvisations, they occur over an F pedal point in the bass.[23]

HARMONIES DURING IMPROVISATIONS OVER F PEDAL, RELEASED TAKE (DERIVED FROM MM. 41–70)

From Section D: Fmaj7(♯11) Dtriad E♭triad Btriad Atriad E♭min9(A♭triad)
From Section E: G°9 G(♭9) Gmin9 G(♭9)

"FILLES DE KILIMANJARO"

The sunny affect of the opening to "Filles de Kilimanjaro" contrasts starkly with the brooding or mysterious disposition of many of the second quintet compositions. It begins with a bright major mode diatonic melody, stated over a pedal point: Harvey Pekar described it as resembling a Latin American folk tune.[24] The head to "Filles de Kilimanjaro" consists of melodic fragments that appear in consistent order. These create seven brief sections (Sections A–G). A bass riff (often doubled by electric piano) formed by a stepwise descent from C to G links most of the sections. The group states the melody to "Filles de Kilimanjaro" three times prior to the improvisations, interlaces sections A, B, and C during Hancock's solo, and ends with a second improvisation by Davis. The recording concludes with a fade rather than with a return to the head.

The melody pitches for the seven sections appear in example 7.6 (the example contains pitches without rhythmic values, taken from the opening head statement). With few exceptions (Section E of the first head statement, discussed below), they all appear over a G pedal point in the bass. Similar to the melody to several of the sections of "Tout de Suite,"

23 The rhythm section cycles through these harmonies once before Davis begins his solo. He begins prior to the end of the cycle (3:10) on the Gmin9 harmony, and Hancock then links from it to the second harmony Dtriad/F and continues the progression. The four harmonies from Section E bear some resemblance to the four harmonies heard during the introduction. Example 7.4 includes those introductory harmonies.

24 Harvey Pekar, "Miles Davis 1964–69 Recordings," *Coda* 147 (May 1976):11

Sections A, B, and F are arch-form melodies, although here they rise and fall much more quickly than those of "Tout de Suite." The melody to Sections A and B both end with the same pitch of A, and both are diatonic to G major (although Hancock's accompaniment moves outside the diatonicism in Section B). The final three pitches of Section B outline an A minor harmony. The use of diatonic triadic harmonies over a fixed bass pedal point was to be a technique explored by a number of fusion composers in the following decade.[25] Section F, in contrast, outlines an A major triad over the G pedal point.

EXAMPLE 7.6   Melodic Sections (A–G) from "Filles de Kilimanjaro" (transcribed from opening head statement)

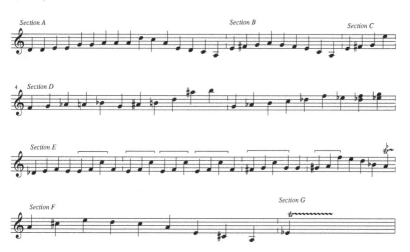

In addition to the three arch-form melodies, there are four others. Section C consists of a single ascent. The horns play Section D loosely each time, but here the melody moves outside the largely diatonic field of the first three sections. The first portion elaborates the motion from B♭ to B natural in two octaves, and the second portion ends by expressing a shift from D♭ to E♭ major (D/F to E♭/G) in the horns. (The example provides the pitches from the first head statement.) Section E—the longest of the seven sections—likewise departs from the diatonicism of the earlier

---

25 Chick Corea's "Sometime Ago" and Chuck Mangione's "Land of Make Believe" are two such examples.

melodies. It elaborates an ascending chromatic melody, one masked by the melodic pedal point of C. Following the initial D♭, the line progresses E–F–F♯–G–G♯–A. Brackets in the example are included to indicate that chromatic ascent. The final section is a brief decoration of E♭.

The use to which meter is put during head statements of the head is remarkable.[26] During the first head statement, there is a calculated ambiguity between triple (3/4) and quadruple (4/4) meter. Central to this 3/4 versus 4/4 ambiguity is Williams's drumming, which does not provide significant metrical cues either way.[27] The bass accompaniment changes during each statement of the head, and these changes each time realign the relationship of melody to accompaniment. As with "Stuff," the result is one of shifting perspectives, allowing the listener to regard the same (or related) melodic material through differing viewpoints.

Example 7.7 shows how this applies in each head statement of Section A. It includes the repeated melody, and the bass accompaniment for each of the three statements of the head appears beneath it.[28] This initial section (like the following B section) lasts 6 bars, consisting of 4 bars of melody, and followed by a descending bass/keyboard riff that decorates a descent from C to G.

EXAMPLE 7.7   Shifting Metrical Perspectives on Section A of "Filles de Kilimanjaro"

26 Chambers inexplicably describes the meter of "Filles de Kilimanjaro" as 5/4; see Chambers, *Milestones* 2, 130.

27 This metrical ambiguity is similar to Williams's accompaniment to the improvisations in "Tout de Suite," which similarly does not provide metrical cues to the underlying triple meter.

28 There are a few discrepancies in the performance of the melody among these three initial head statements. For visual ease, the transcribed melody provides only the opening head statement in order to highlight differences in bass accompaniment during the initial three-head statements.

Example 7.7 indicates that during the first head statement (:00) the group juxtaposes the 4/4 melody with a bass ostinato that repeats in cycles of 3 beats. In the opening two measures, the melody very clearly sounds in 4/4 meter, particularly with its repeated rhythmic pattern of dotted quarter and eighth note. And while the bass ostinato supports a layer of 3/4, it sounds as an interesting syncopation but one that does not override the larger 4/4 meter. The metric identity of the melody at mm. 3–4 sounds, to my ears at least, still in 4/4, but it is more ambiguous since the longer held pitches of E (m. 3) and A (m. 4) appear every three beats. Thus while at mm. 3–4 the melody implies—very slightly—a level of 3/4, the 4/4 meter still remains, a meter that the beginning of the bass/keyboard riff at m. 5 supports. Yet even that riff causes some metric uncertainty since it lasts five beats before the bass resumes the (G–D–D) ostinato riff at m. 6. The bass/keyboard riff at mm. 5–6 suggests a grouping of 5 + 3 quarter notes.

Thus we can regard the relationship of bass to melody at mm. 1–4, in particular, as one that superimposes a layer of 3/4 that syncopates against the 4/4 of the melody. The example also shows that the bass shifts to a 4/4 accompanimental figure for the second head statement (1:15) and aligns with the 4/4 melody stated by the horns. Note the difference in bass accompaniment during the second and third head statements shown in the example, however. (The horns here interpret the m. 3 melody differently from the first head statement by anticipating the measure.) While the bass plays the same figure, the figure appears metrically changed during the third head statement (2:52). (The third head statement begins slightly askew, as the horns begin early and the horns and rhythm gradually adjust during those opening measures.) For all three head statements, the relationship of melody to bass accompaniment shifts, shifting the metrical perspective of the melody each time.

Beyond the statements of Section A, the entire first head statement plays out some of the implications of the 3/4 and 4/4 meters. During Sections A–C the bass remains in 3/4, and the horn statements are in 4/4. But by Section D (of this initial head statement at :26), the melodic fragments are largely resistant to any underlying meter, and thus take on the 3/4 metric identity of the bass accompaniment. Example 7.8 provides the melody and bass to the following Section E (:35), in order to show how 3/4 co-opts the 4/4 meter. Here the slowly ascending horn lines take on the metric identity of the 3/4 bass accompaniment.

Note too that the bass accompaniment here moves away from the G pedal that dominated all the earlier sections, and its pitch material is

EXAMPLE 7.8   Section E of Opening Head Statement to "Filles de Kilimanjaro" (:35)
(triple meter; bass accompaniment derived from melody)

intimately related to that stated by the horns. For the initial eight measures, Carter uses solely three pitches—D♭–E–F—the same three pitches stated by the horns during the first measure of this section. Particularly at the third and fifth measures of this section, the D♭–E–F–E bass motion closely mirrors that heard by the horns at the first measure. Carter's accompaniment freely interprets the melodic motion that opens this section.

By Section G of the first head statement, both horns and bass seamlessly return to 4/4. And during the second and third head statements, both horns and bass remain in 4/4, leaving behind the triple/quadruple conflicts of the initial head statement. In contrast to the first head statement shown in example 7.8, the two latter head statements of Section E are brought into the sphere of the 4/4 meter and the underlying G pedal.

The solos primarily take place over a G pedal point, and Carter refers to the C–G stepwise descent from the head throughout. There are only a few departures from the G tonal center, to E♭ (4:39 and 6:11) and A♭ (5:29 and 9:00). Davis, in particular, seems comfortably committed to improvising by alluding to the melodies of Sections A–G (as well as the stepwise C–G descent). He also seems committed to using as a template their large-scale shifts between G major diatonicism and more remote D♭ and E♭ harmonies implied by the melody at the end of Section D (he implies E♭ at 4:34 and D♭ at 5:51).

Since Davis's initial trumpet solo begins four minutes into the composition, the recording exhibits the quintet's ongoing concern with highlighting the composition's melody and readdressing the relationship between compositional melody and improvisation. There is a stripping away of much of the harmonic complexity and detail of the earlier quintet compositions, although the seven melodic fragments seem calculated to move in and out of harmonic focus with the G pedal point. With the absence of an evident harmonic progression, the composition becomes more or less melodically determined and Davis's improvisation, in particular, seems to celebrate the opportunity to rely on melodic paraphrase. Even the piano and bass accompanimental figures heard between head statements make use of the C–G melodic stepwise descent as a way of adding color to the largely static pedal point.

With the generally monochromatic harmonic canvas of "Filles de Kilimanjaro," the compositional focus shifts to the placement of recurring melodic segments in different frameworks. Its overarching compositional principles are similar to that heard in "Stuff"—a series of ordered melodic statements and fragments return altered and recast. This is particularly true between the opening head—which cultivates a deliberate metric ambiguity, shifting seamlessly between 4/4 and 3/4—and later head statements. The shifting metrical perspectives create a kaleidoscopic effect, rearranging the perspective on the same melodic objects.

THERE IS A DEFINITE ALLURE in considering these final two recordings through their relationship to postbop jazz, avant-garde jazz, and fusion. Without denying those relationships, it is important to acknowledge their other innovations. Much of this had to do with the clear departures from chorus structures and their attendant head–solos–head frameworks. Many of the compositions shifted the balance, as protracted repetitions of the head or extended formal frameworks submerged individual improvisations until later in each performance. The discussion of "Filles de Kilimanjaro" and "Stuff" above called attention to the abstraction and reworking of melodic fragments throughout the performances. Even the use of rock rhythms is highly abstracted on several of these compositions—the accompaniment patterns for the improvisations on "Tout de Suite" (released track), as well as on the opening head to "Filles de Kilimanjaro" provide pulse but avoid any commitment to a larger metric framework.

Davis's turn to fusion would have significant consequences. While still controversial, it nevertheless indicated the trumpeter's commitment to change and it offered some alternatives to postbop jazz that became strongly influential the following decade. But Davis's eventual move to fusion has provided a yardstick to measure the final two quintet recordings in a way that eclipses their other innovative but less influential features. While transitional, with their use of rock rhythms, electric instruments, and extended tonal centers, these recordings also pivot away from—if not critique—many of the principles of small group improvisation and the traditions from which the quintet members had emerged.

CHAPTER 8

THE QUINTET AND ITS LEGACIES

THROUGHOUT THE BOOK I HAVE attempted to present the ways in which the studio albums of Davis's second quintet were seminal, through their compositional, melodic, harmonic, formal, improvisational, and participatory strategies. I also regard the ways their contents were *not* seminal, since many of their techniques lavishly explored common features of jazz traditions in which the players were steeped. Further, while recorded within a period of only 3½ years, each album differs in significant ways from the others; each offers different innovations and responses. Their chronological organization here is not necessarily intended to suggest an overall evolutionary process, and we might instead regard the differences among them as offering shifts in musical priorities. They reflect the wide musical interests, expansive musical curiosity, and sympathetic collaboration brought by all five musicians. They also acknowledge the intense musical and cultural ferment taking place in the second half of the 1960s.

The degree of Davis's role versus the role of the other members in shaping the direction of the quintet, like many collaborative endeavors, is probably impossible to pinpoint. Ron Carter described their relation: "Sixty per cent of this was the band taking a new direction and forty per cent was Miles recognizing this, and, while not being able to predict it would go a certain way, understanding that it was definitely taking a turn. I think he was happy to take a back seat and be an inspiration but not hold the reins too tight, and give the horses their head knowing that it would work out all right."[1] Whatever the proportion, certainly the final two quintet studio recordings reflected a decision on the part of Davis to grab the reins more tightly and control the direction of the quintet further by providing most of the compositions, altering instrumentation, and reshaping attitudes toward composition and improvisation.

REPERTORY

The group's longevity helped the players develop a striking level of musical rapport, enhanced by the individual players' own separate recording and performance projects, which frequently included each other. But the players were undoubtedly aware that the Davis recordings largely required a particular and different repertory from their own. Until the later release of Davis's *Water Babies*, "Footprints" remained the only Shorter composition common to both Shorter's own recordings and Davis's quintet. Hancock himself made this acknowledgment: "I had other tunes on my own recordings that really didn't lend themselves to Miles's band."[2] In Hancock's case, Bob Belden has speculated that the harmonic complexity of Hancock's compositions challenged Davis in a way that brought out some weaknesses in the trumpeter's playing, explaining why the quintet rehearsed but did not record some of Hancock's compositions.[3] Another more positive viewpoint might propose that the members appropriately customized their compositions for the quintet recordings, and that the quintet compositions required a specific and unique personality distinct from the original compositions the players recorded elsewhere. And the discussion of studio processes in this book further called attention to Davis's role in enhancing the specific

1 *Milestones: The Music and Times of Miles Davis* 2 (New York: Da Capo, 1998), 82. Originally publ. University of Toronto Press, 1983 and 1985.
2 Stephen Pond, *Head Hunters: The Making of Jazz's First Platinum Album* (Ann Arbor: University of Michigan, 2005), 152.
3 Bob Belden, Liner notes to *Miles Davis Quintet 1965–68* (Columbia/Sony 67398), 93.

personality of those compositions, not only through melodic, harmonic, or metric alterations and instrumentation, but also by proposing specific roles for rhythm section accompaniment, especially during head statements.

In what ways do any of the second quintet studio compositions form part of the jazz standard repertory? The very idea of jazz standards constitutes a form of historicism: standards enshrine older compositions, composers, or jazz styles. At the same time, standards arise because they offer players a richness that permits multiple reworkings, alternate reinterpretations that cut across the grain of earlier performances. Naturally, answers to the question of what constitutes a jazz standard differ, subject to any number of factors: different jazz communities, musical taste, presence of multiple recordings or performances of particular compositions, ease of availability in the form of lead sheets, and so forth. As discussed in the introduction to this book, widely circulated lead sheets, particularly in collections such as *The Real Book,* offer a type of reception history for the second quintet recordings since they made available for players written versions of a number of them: "E.S.P.," "Eighty-One," "Iris," "Orbits," "Dolores," "Freedom Jazz Dance," "Footprints," "The Sorcerer," "Prince of Darkness," "Pee Wee," "Nefertiti," "Fall," "Pinocchio," and "Stuff." Presence in such sources virtually guaranteed a wider circulation among jazz musicians.[4]

The second quintet players themselves continued to rerecord those studio compositions after the quintet disbanded. Carter's "R.J." appeared on his 1970 recording *Uptown Conversation* in a performance with Hancock that eliminated the tentative or problematic elements brought on by the 19-bar form heard on *E.S.P.* The formation of the V.S.O.P. ("Very Special Onetime Performance") Quintet, consisting of Davis's second quintet members (along with trumpeter Freddie Hubbard in place of Davis) was itself an act of self-conscious historicism, initially part of a 1976 Newport Jazz Festival retrospective of Hancock's career. The V.S.O.P quintet recorded a live version of "Dolores" on a 1977 recording (*V.S.O.P.: The Quintet*), and two version of "Pee Wee" from a 1979 performance (rereleased in 2004 as *V.S.O.P. Live under the Sky*). Their live performance of "Dolores" differs from that of the *Miles Smiles* version in particular ways. Unlike the earlier version, all the musicians adhere loosely to an 8 + 8 + 6 + 8 formal structure, but the length of the sections

---

4 For a history of fake books in America, including the genesis of *The Real Book,* see Barry Kernfeld, *The Story of Fake Books: Bootlegging Songs to Musicians* (Lanham, Md.: Scarecrow Press, 2006).

occasionally expand and contract during the performance, and the players—especially Shorter—rely on melodic paraphrase to reorient the players. And although most of these later recreations of second quintet compositions by those players took place in acoustic settings, Shorter did record "Pinocchio" with the fusion group Weather Report. It appeared on their 1978 album, *Mr. Gone*, an album that for many critics made too many Faustian bargains with pop and disco. (*Down Beat* awarded the album merely one star.)

The 1994 recording *A Tribute to Miles* appeared three years after Davis's death, involving the remaining second quintet members with trumpeter Wallace Roney taking the place of Davis. (Roney had participated with Davis on the 1991 Montreux Jazz retrospective of Gil Evans's arrangements. Roney was there to fill in for Davis or play some of his parts, since it wasn't clear how much or whether Davis would be available to play, due to both failing health and tardiness. Davis was there, and died two months after the Montreux performance.) The group performed four of the second quintet compositions on the recording, "R.J.," "Little One," "Pinocchio," and "Eighty-One." More recently, Hancock and Shorter rerecorded "Nefertiti" on Hancock's recording *The Joni Letters*, the recipient of a Grammy award in 2008 for Album of the Year.

Or does the status of these compositions as jazz standards rely more specifically on performances by other musicians who were not quintet members? "Nefertiti" and "Footprints" remain the most recorded of the second quintet compositions. "Nefertiti" appears on recordings by players and groups as diverse as Ray Drummond, Larry Coryell, Joanne Brackeen, Chick Corea, Lee Konitz, Michel Camilo, Frank Morgan, Clark Terry's Big BAD Band, and J. J. Johnson. "Footprints" received treatments by Ahmad Jamal, Larry Coryell, Frank Morgan, James Williams, Kenny Barron and Regina Carter, and Toots Thielemans. Other quintet compositions appear less frequently: Chet Baker recorded "E.S.P." in 1977; Peter Erskine recorded "E.S.P." in a 1982 version with pianist Kenny Kirkland playing a solo remarkably indebted to Hancock; pianist Denny Zeitlin recorded it in 2004. Drummer Cindy Blackman recorded "Prince of Darkness" (1997); Roy Hargrove, "Pinocchio" (1992); Chick Corea, "Masqualero" (1972); Fred Hersch, "Iris" (2006).

Second quintet compositions also appear mingled within entire recordings dedicated to the compositions of Hancock or Shorter. "The Sorcerer" appears on *Fingerpainting*, a tribute to Hancock's compositions in a trio collaboration of Christian McBride, Nicholas Payton, and Mark Whitfield. Ricky Ford's *Shorter Ideas* includes "Pinocchio." *Shorter by Two* was a two-piano recording of Shorter compositions with versions of "Dolores," "Pinocchio," "Iris," and "Nefertiti" played by Kirk Lightsey and Harold Danko.

Danko indicated that the complexities of Shorter's compositions, especially as vehicles for duo piano improvisation, made them particularly demanding. About the recording of "Dolores" and "Pinocchio" on *Shorter by Two* he acknowledged, "The elusiveness of the harmony coupled with the varied phrase lengths posed many musical challenges." Danko also recorded "E.S.P." with Chet Baker, and he stated the following: "During that same time (on a mission of some kind) I tried to get Lee Konitz to include 'E.S.P.' in his repertoire after he sight read it on a gig at Strykers once and played amazingly, pretty much by instinct off the melody. The more we studied and rehearsed it, the more 'inside' he played, and we ended up abandoning the tune."[5] Danko's comments draw attention to the provisional status of some of the second quintet compositions as standards, since the harmonic progressions and formal organization often require players to bypass more conventional improvisational paths and reveal the inadequacy of those more conventional paths.

Beyond the view of the second quintet compositions as jazz standards, their influence extends more generally to contemporary jazz composition. Their legacy extends into formal structure (single-section forms), metrical structure (exploration of nonquadruple or nonduple hypermeter), harmonic structure and progression (sus chords, maj7$\sharp$5 chords, slash chords, pedal point harmonies, hexatonic/augmented scale harmonies), melodic structure (fourth-based melodic ideas, expanding/collapsing motives). Yet it is essential to point out that these quintet compositions are inseparable from a broader compositional tradition that includes other jazz composers of the 1960s, such as Booker Little, Eric Dolphy, John Coltrane, Joe Henderson, Chick Corea, Andrew Hill, and others.[6] All sought to expand formal, metrical, harmonic, and melodic dimensions within small group improvisation.

OTHER LEGACIES: FUSION AND RETURNS TO TRADITION

Davis and most of the other quintet members, particularly Williams, Shorter, and Hancock (and their groups Lifetime, Weather Report, and Headhunters), were key to the development of fusion music of the late 1960s and 1970s. (Ron Carter played a less visible role, but his studio

---

5 Both quotations from Danko taken from private communication, August 23, 2009.
6 See Ron Miller, *Modal Jazz: Composition and Harmony* (Rottenburg, Germany: Advance Music, 1996), esp. vol. 1.

recordings of the late 1960s included recordings with pop artists such as Aretha Franklin and covers of Beatles compositions with Wes Montgomery.) The previous chapter discussed how Davis's search for new material and formal solutions arose with the final second quintet recordings of 1968, during which he began using electronic instruments, funk and rock rhythms, extended pedal point and ostinato figures, and sparer harmonic textures, often taking place in contexts that rethought earlier ideas of musical form. It also suggested that many of the impulses of fusion were already present in funky jazz (or, as it was later labeled, soul jazz) of the 1960s, with the use of R & B rhythms, electric instruments, popular music covers, and guitar effects of distortion and feedback.

It is possible and illustrative to hear retentions of the second quintet studio recordings in some of the players' later fusion recordings, in terms of both compositional and improvisational elements. On *In a Silent Way*, Davis's first complete studio recording following the disbanding of the second quintet, his composition "It's About That Time" consists of two alternating sections, an E♭ neighbor-note figure heard beneath a 3-bar harmonic progression, and a 2-bar groove riff. The group determines spontaneously the length of the two sections, recalling a similar technique heard in "Agitation" (*E.S.P.*), which also freely alternated two distinct sections. The title track to Tony Williams's 1969 Lifetime recording *Emergency* alternates rock rhythms with walking bass (played by organist Larry Young) swing rhythms, much like the rock/swing juxtapositions heard in Davis's "Country Son" (*Miles in the Sky*). During Hancock's solo on "Sly" (from his 1973 recording *Head Hunters*) the group alternates two loose harmonic centers, related to the organization of "Riot" (*Nefertiti*), and the "Sly" improvisation adopts similar techniques of harmonic superimposition, creating the effect of an enhanced harmonic progression within a relatively static harmonic frame. Weather Report's first two recordings clearly took "Nefertiti" as an important departure point for using mood and color in place of a series of individual improvisations. And it is likely that the second quintet studio recordings helped the musicians conceptualize ways for building compositional structures that avoided chorus structure improvisation.

Davis's motivations—the extent to which Davis's fusion music involved a sincere artistic response to surrounding musical and cultural forces, or was merely crass commercialism—are all beyond the scope of this study. Speculation on such motivations, the influence of musicians and groups (such as Jimi Hendrix, Sly and the Family Stone, and James Brown) as well as the role of other individuals (such as Columbia Records executive Clive Davis and Davis's second wife Betty Mabry) have been presented

argument

elsewhere in some detail.[7] Discussion of motivations fuels the polemics of fusion more generally. Due to its purported *(purpose)* commercialism, simplicity, and departures from key principles of earlier forms of jazz, fusion remains a controversial and problematic facet of many jazz historical narratives. Fusion music opened up deep fissures within communities of musicians, critics, and historians, usually arising through competing or conflicting views of jazz (as well as the role of artistic versus commercial success), and they continue to linger.[8] Whatever the relation of fusion to earlier jazz traditions, the success of many of the early fusion groups created a drastically enhanced audience, and also provided this audience with a receptive entry point for more traditional forms of jazz.[9]

The hard bop resurgence *(revive)* of the 1980s engaged features of hard bop and postbop jazz through instrumentation, accompanimental techniques, and harmonic language. It formed part of a larger neotraditional historicist stance that also included the jazz repertory movement (Lincoln Center Jazz Orchestra, Smithsonian Jazz Masterworks Orchestra, and Carnegie Hall Jazz Band) and recreations of earlier works of Armstrong, Morton, Ellington, Monk, and others. Naturally, even while fusion posed alternative paths, hard bop ensembles such as Art Blakey's Jazz Messengers remained committed to quartet and quintet ensembles with acoustic bass and piano, standard 4/4 walking bass textures, and chorus structure improvisation. Blakey himself played a crucial role in the 1980s hard bop resurgence, as his group served as training ground for a number of significant instrumentalists. This set of players, that Stuart Nicholson refers to as "Blakey's class of 1980–89,"[10] included, among others, Terence Blanchard, Donald Harrison, Mulgrew Miller, Wallace Roney, Bobby Watson, and Branford and Wynton Marsalis, many of whom were indebted to the improvisational approaches of the Davis second quintet members.

---

7 See, for example Jack Chambers, *Milestones 2*, and John Szwed, *So What: The Life and Times of Miles Davis* (New York: Simon & Schuster, 2002).

8 Chambers, *Milestones*; Szwed, *So What*; Pond, *Head Hunters*; Stanley Crouch, "Play the Right Thing," *New Republic* (February 12, 1990): 30–37. For a thorough consideration of fusion, see Stuart Nicholson, *Jazz-Rock: A History* (New York: Schirmer, 1998).

9 In the liner notes to *V.S.O.P.: The Quintet* (1977), Conrad Silvert wrote, "The fact that more than 100,000 people turned out in just one month to see the V.S.O.P. Quintet shows not only that jazz remains as vital as any American art form, but that five musicians, by playing (with their individual bands) music so many purists claim is destroying jazz, have actually helped to broaden the 'pure jazz' audience." (Columbia C2 34976).

10 Stuart Nicholson, *Jazz: The 1980s Resurgence* (New York: Da Capo, 1995), 227.

Wynton Marsalis is probably the principal spokesperson for a larger neotraditionalist view, both in terms of his work as artistic director of Jazz at Lincoln Center, and his latter compositions and recordings, which clearly fused historical influences such as Armstrong and Ellington. Yet his early career aligned in significant ways with Davis's second quintet. More than half the compositions on his first recording as leader (1981) included the Davis rhythm section of Hancock, Carter, and Williams, with the group recording a version of the second quintet composition "R.J." on it. Marsalis subsequently recorded again with the Davis rhythm section (*Herbie Hancock Quartet*, 1982), now including performances of second quintet compositions "The Sorcerer" and "Pee Wee." Along with his brother Branford, Marsalis toured in 1983 with the Davis rhythm section as V.S.O.P II. Marsalis's own quintet with Branford was modeled in significant ways on the Davis second quintet.[11] According to Marsalis, it was only around 1987 that his compositional and aesthetic priorities shifted and he began incorporating earlier jazz traditions in earnest.[12]

CODA

Others may wish to explore more deeply implications and questions raised by some of the quintet's techniques discussed within the book. Some of these questions arise when considering the degrees of congruence between different instruments within a performance in situations such as "time, no changes," when different players maintain simultaneous different underlying forms ("Dolores"), or when different players use distinct pitch collections simultaneously over a bass pedal point ("Freedom Jazz Dance"). All these questions, of course, bring up further questions about perception—for example, are the different underlying formal or pitch strategies audible or analytically meaningful? Different listeners may have different answers. My own position here is that the role of analysis is to provide further, alternative, or nuanced ways into hearing the music, to consider how the moment-to-moment flow of improvisation resonates with or creates frictions with aspects of jazz traditions in which the players were so firmly rooted, and to regard how the recordings themselves participated in shaping that jazz tradition.

Davis remains an elusive figure. He exhibited a keen ability to conceptualize musical dimensions, and he seems to have thought about them in terms of exchanges of musical space and density. His own celebrated

11 Scott DeVeaux and Gary Giddins, *Jazz* (New York: W. W. Norton, 2009), 525.
12 Howard Reich, "Wynton Marsalis," *Down Beat* (December 1997): 34.

use of musical space through melodic pacing was complemented in his first quintet by the denser melodic pacing of saxophonist Coltrane. The move to slower harmonic pacing of his compositions of the late 1950s opened up musical spaces to be complemented by denser harmonic accompaniment.[13] Davis's requests for Hancock to cease accompanying behind soloists on the second quintet recordings created enhanced musical spaces that frequently supported denser musical dialogues between the soloists and drummer Tony Williams. And Davis's use of guitar or electric keyboard to double bass lines on his late 1967 and early 1968 recordings (such as "Filles de Kilimanjaro") created a denser bottom texture, complementing the move to a more spacious and sparer harmonic language.

Davis's work goes beyond his participation in shaping many of the significant jazz styles of the second half of the twentieth century. It also extends to his role as leader, his reliance on other players to provide creative foils, and his use of an infinite palette of expressive timbres. Davis was restless and eager to change, quick to use his own musical tastes to capitalize and expand on existing musical directions, and in search of musical challenges that required unique and sometimes transcendent solutions.

13   See the interview with pianist René Urtreger in Andrea Pejrolo, "The Origins of Modal Jazz in the Music of Miles Davis: A Complete Transcription and a Linear/Harmonic Analysis of *Ascenseur pour l'échafaud* (*Lift to the Scaffold*)—1957" (Ph.D. diss., New York University, 2001), 239. Utreger discussed Davis's suggestions for accompaniment to the slow harmonic rhythm of the D minor compositions on the soundtrack, recalling that "Davis liked chords with as many notes as possible and with very close voicings, based on second or third intervals, particularly seconds. For instance, he would put his hands on the piano and [on a D-7 chord] play D, E, F, G, and A at the same time."

DISCOGRAPHY OF RECORDINGS

(COMPILED BY MICHAEL CONKLIN)

Sort By Record Date

Drummer

Blakey, Art, *Meet You at the Jazz Corner of the World* (BLUE NOTE BLP 4055, rec. September 1960, reissued 2004 Blue Note Records).

Blakey, Art, *Pisces* (BLUE NOTE (J) GXF 3060, rec. February and May 1961, April 1964).

Blakey, Art, *The Witch Doctor* (BLUE NOTE BST 84258, rec. March 1961, reissued 1999 Blue Note Records, with 1 bonus track).

Blakey, Art, *The Freedom Rider* (BLUE NOTE BLP 4156, rec. February and May 1961, reissued 1998 Blue Note Records, with 4 bonus tracks).

Blakey, Art, *Root and Herbs* (BLUE NOTE BST 84347, rec. February and May 1961, reissued 1999 Blue Note Records, with 4 bonus tracks).

Blakey, Art, *Ugetsu* (RIVERSIDE RLP 464, rec. June 1963, reissued 1989 Concord Music Group, with 3 bonus tracks).

Burton, Gary, *The Time Machine* (RCA RECORDS 3642, rec. April 1965).

Byrd, Donald, *Free Form* (BLUE NOTE BST 84118, rec. December 1961, reissued 2004 Blue Note with 1 bonus track).

Carter, Ron, *Uptown Conversation* (EMBRYO RECORDS SD 521, rec. October 1969, reissued 1992 Atlantic Records, with 2 bonus tracks).

Coleman, Ornette, *The Shape of Jazz to Come* (ATLANTIC LP 1317, rec. May 1959, reissued 1990 Atlantic Records).

Coleman, Ornette, *Change of the Century* (ATLANTIC LP 1327, rec. October 1959, reissued 1992 Atlantic Records).

Coleman, Ornette, *Free Jazz* (ATLANTIC LP 1364, rec. December 1960, reissued 1990 Atlantic Records).

Coltrane, John, *A Love Supreme* (IMPULSE A 77, rec. December 1964, reissued 1995 Impulse).

Coltrane, John, *Ascension* (IMPULSE A 95, rec. June 1965, reissued 1996 Aris/GRP).

Davis, Miles, *Birth of the Cool* (CAPITOL T 792, rec. January and April 1949, March 1950, reissued 1989 Capitol Records, with 1 bonus track).

Davis, Miles, *Round About Midnight* (COLUMBIA CL 949, rec. October 1955, June and September 1956, reissued 2001 Columbia Records, with 4 bonus tracks).

Davis, Miles, *Circle in the Round* (COLUMBIA/LEGACY KC2 36278, rec. October 1955, March 1961, December 1967, January, February, and November 1968, January 1970, reissued 1991 Columbia Records).

Davis, Miles, *Ascenseur pour l'échafaud* (FONTANA (F) 662 213 TR, rec. December 1957, reissued 2007 Verve Records).

Davis, Miles, *Porgy and Bess* (COLUMBIA CL 1274, rec. July and August 1958, reissued 1997 Columbia Records, with 2 bonus tracks).

Davis, Miles, *Kind of Blue* (COLUMBIA CL 1355, rec. March and April 1959, reissued 1992 Columbia Records).

Davis, Miles, *Sketches of Spain* (COLUMBIA CL 1480, rec. November 1959 and March 1960, reissued 1991 Columbia Records).

Davis, Miles, *Directions* (COLUMBIA KC2 36472, rec. March 1960, April 1963, May and December 1967, January and November 1968, February and May 1970).

Davis, Miles, *Someday My Prince Will Come* (COLUMBIA CL 1656, rec. March 1961, reissued 1997 Columbia Records, with 2 bonus tracks).

Davis, Miles, *Seven Steps to Heaven* (COLUMBIA/LEGACY CL 2051, rec. April and May 1963, reissued 2005 Columbia Records, with 2 bonus tracks).

Davis, Miles, *Miles Davis in Europe* (COLUMBIA CL 2183, rec. July 1963, reissued 2005 Columbia/Legacy, with 2 bonus tracks).

Davis, Miles, *Live at the 1963 Monterey Jazz Festival* (MONTEREY JAZZ FESTIVAL RECORDS, rec. September 1963, issued 2007 Monterey Jazz Festival Records).

Davis, Miles, *My Funny Valentine* (COLUMBIA CL 2306, rec. February 1964, reissued 2005 Sony Music Entertainment, Inc.).

Davis, Miles, *Four and More* (COLUMBIA C2K48821, rec. February 1964, reissued Columbia 1992, with 7 bonus tracks).

Davis, Miles, *Miles in Berlin* (CBS (G) SBPG 62976, rec. September 1964, reissued 2006 Columbia, with 1 bonus track).

Davis, Miles, *The Complete Quintet Recordings 1965–1968* (COLUMBIA/LEGACY C6K 67398, and C6K 67398, rec. between January 20, 1965, and June 21, 1968).

Davis, Miles, *E.S.P.* (COLUMBIA CL 2350, rec. January 1965, reissued 1998 Legacy).

Davis, Miles, *Live at the Plugged Nickel* (COLUMBIA/LEGACY BL 38267, rec. December 1965).

Davis, Miles, *Miles Smiles* (COLUMBIA CL 2601, rec. October 1966, reissued 1992 Columbia/Legacy).

Davis, Miles, *Sorcerer* (COLUMBIA CL 2732, rec. August 1962 and May 1967, reissued 1998 Sony Music Entertainment Inc., with 2 bonus tracks).

Davis, Miles, *Nefertiti* (COLUMBIA CS 9594, rec. June 1967, reissued 1998 Columbia Records, with 4 bonus tracks).

Davis, Miles, *Water Babies* (COLUMBIA PC 34396, rec. June 1967 and November 1968, reissued 2002 Columbia Records, with 1 bonus track).

Davis, Miles, *Miles in the Sky* (COLUMBIA CS 9628, rec. January and May 1968, reissued 1998 Sony Music Entertainment Inc., with 2 bonus tracks).

Davis, Miles, *Filles de Kilimanjaro* (COLUMBIA CS 9750, rec. June and September 1968, reissued 2002 Columbia/Legacy, with 1 bonus track).

Davis, Miles, *In a Silent Way* (COLUMBIA CS 9875, rec. February 1969, reissued 2002 Columbia, with 1 bonus track).

Davis, Miles, *Bitches Brew* (COLUMBIA GP 26, rec. August 1969, reissued 1999 Columbia/Legacy, with 1 bonus track).

Danko, Harold, *Shorter by Two* (SUNNYSIDE RECORDS SSC 1004, rec. July 1983).

Dolphy, Eric, *Out There* (NEW JAZZ NJLP 8252, rec. August 1960, reissued 2006 Prestige).

Dolphy, Eric, *Far Cry* (NEW JAZZ NJLP 8270, rec. December 1960, reissued 1992 New Jazz/OJC, with 1 bonus track).

Dolphy, Eric, *Live at the Gaslight Inn* (INGO (Italy) 14 rec. October 1962, reissued 2007 Get Back).

Dolphy, Eric, *Illinois Concert* (BLUE NOTE CDP 7243 4 99826-2, rec. March 1963, reissued 1999 Blue Note, with 1 bonus track).

Dolphy, Eric, *Out to Lunch* (BLUE NOTE BLP 4163, rec. February 1964, reissued 1999 Blue Note).

Dorham, Kenny, *Una Mas* (BLUE NOTE BLP 4127, rec. April 1963, reissued 1993 Blue Note, with 1 bonus track).

Ellis, Don, *New Ideas* (NEW JAZZ NJLP 8257, rec. May 1961, reissued 1992 New Jazz).

Evans, Gil, *Svengali* (ATLANTIC SD 1643, rec. May 1973, reissued 1999 Koch Records, with 1 bonus track).

Ford, Ricky, *Shorter Ideas* (MUSE MR 5314, rec. August 1984).

Hancock, Herbie, *Takin' Off* (BLUE NOTE BST 84109, rec. May 1962, reissued 1987 Blue Note, with 3 bonus tracks).

Hancock, Herbie, *My Point of View* (BLUE NOTE BST 84126, rec. March 1963, reissued 1987 Blue Note, with 1 bonus track).

Hancock, Herbie, *Inventions and Dimensions* (BLUE NOTE BLP 4147, rec. August 1963, reissued 1988 Blue Note, with 1 bonus track).

Hancock, Herbie, *Empyrean Isles* (BLUE NOTE BLP 4175, rec. June 1964, reissued 1999 Blue Note, with 6 bonus tracks).

Hancock, Herbie, *Maiden Voyage* (BLUE NOTE BST 84195, rec. March 1965, reissued 1986 Blue Note).

Hancock, Herbie, *Speak Like a Child* (BLUE NOTE BST 84279, rec. March 1968, reissued 1987 Blue Note, with 3 bonus tracks).

Hancock, Herbie, *The Prisoner* (BLUE NOTE BST 84321, rec. April 1969, reissued 1987 Blue Note, with 2 bonus tracks).

Hancock, Herbie,, *V.S.O.P. The Quintet* (COLUMBIA LSP 982152-1, rec. July 1977, reissued 2001 Sony Music Entertainment Inc., with 4 bonus tracks).

Hancock, Herbie, *V.S.O.P Live under the Sky* (COLUMBIA (J) 30AP 1036, rec. July 1979, reissued 2004 Columbia, with 11 bonus tracks).

Hancock, Herbie, *Quartet* (COLUMBIA C2 38275, rec. July 1981, reissued 2009 Sony Music Group).

Hancock, Herbie, *A Tribute to Miles* (QWEST RECORDS 9362 45059-2, rec. September 1992).

Hancock, Herbie, *River: The Joni Letters* (VERVE RECORDS B0010063–02, rec. 2007).

Harris, Eddie, *Plug Me In* (ATLANTIC SD 1506, rec. March 1968).

Hill, Andrew, *Point of Departure* (BLUE NOTE BST 84167, rec. March 1964, reissued 1999 Blue Note, with 3 bonus tracks).

Hubbard, Freddie, *Ready for Freddie* (BLUE NOTE BST 84085, rec. August 1961, reissued 2003 Blue Note, with 2 bonus tracks).

Lloyd, Charles, *Of Course, Of Course* (COLUMBIA CS 9212, rec. March 1964 and October 1965, reissued 2007 Columbia, with 3 bonus tracks).

Lloyd, Charles, *Nirvana* (COLUMBIA CS-9609, rec. May 1964).

McBride, Christian, *Fingerpainting* (VERVE, rec. April 1997).

McLean, Jackie, *Vertigo* (BLUE NOTE LT 1085, rec. May 1959 and February 1963, reissued 2000 Blue Note, with 5 bonus tracks).

Moncur III, Grachan, *Evolution* (BLUE NOTE BLP 4153, rec. November 1963, reissued 2008 Blue Note).

Moncur III, Grachan, *Some Other Stuff* (TOSHIBA EMI TOCJ 4177, rec. July 1964, reissued 2009 Blue Note).

Morgan, Lee, *Minor Strain* (ROULETTE RECORDS B2–94574, rec. May and July 1960, reissued 1990 Capitol).

Shorter, Wayne, *Introducing Wayne Shorter* (VEE-JAY VJLP 3006, rec. November 1959, reissued 2004 Vee-jay, with 5 bonus tracks).

Shorter, Wayne, *Second Genesis* (VEE-JAY VJS 3057, rec. October 1960, reissued 2002 Collectables).

Shorter, Wayne, *Wayning Moments* (VEE-JAY VJ LP 3029, rec. 1962, reissued 2000 Koch, with 8 bonus tracks).

Shorter, Wayne, *Juju* (BLUE NOTE BST 84182, rec. August 1963, reissued 1987 Blue Note).

Shorter, Wayne, *Night Dreamer* (BLUE NOTE BLP 4173, rec. April 1964, reissued 1987 Blue Note, with 1 bonus track).

Shorter, Wayne, *Speak No Evil* (BLUE NOTE BST 84194, rec. December 1964, reissued 1987 Blue Note).

Shorter, Wayne, *The Soothsayer* (BLUE NOTE LT 988, rec. March 1965, reissued 1990 Blue Note, with 1 bonus track).

Shorter, Wayne, *Etcetera* (BLUE NOTE LT 1056, rec. June 1965).

Shorter, Wayne, *The All Seeing Eye* (BLUE NOTE BLP 4219, rec. October 1965, reissued 1999 Blue Note).

Shorter, Wayne, *Adam's Apple* (BLUE NOTE BLP 4232, rec. February 1966, reissued 1987 Blue Note, with 1 bonus track).

Shorter, Wayne, *Schizophrenia* (BLUE NOTE BST 84297, rec. March 1967).

Weather Report, *Mr. Gone* (COLUMBIA PC 35358, rec. May 1978, reissued 1991 Columbia).

Williams, Tony, *Life Time* (BLUE NOTE BLP 4180, rec. August 1964).

Williams, Tony, *Spring* (BLUE NOTE BST 84216, rec. August 1965, reissued 1990 Blue Note).

Williams, Tony, *Emergency* (POLYDOR/POLYGRAM 24–4017, rec. 1969, reissued 1991 Polydor).

BIBLIOGRAPHY

Adams, Kurtis. "Ornette Coleman and *The Shape of Jazz to Come.*" D.M.A. thesis, University of Colorado at Boulder, 2008.

Alkyer, Frank, Ed Enright, and Jason Koransky, eds. *The Miles Davis Reader.* New York: Hal Leonard Books, 2007.

Baker, David. "Miles Davis: 'Petits Machins' Solo." *Down Beat* 36/26 (December 25, 1969): 46–47.

Baker, David, Lida Belt, and Herman Hudson, eds. *The Black Composer Speaks.* Bloomington, Ind.: Afro-American Arts Institute, 1978.

Bashour, Frederick. "A Different View: 'On Miles and the Modes.'" *College Music Symposium 39* (1999): 124–29.

Belden, Bob. Liner notes to *Miles Davis Quintet, 1965–68.* Columbia 4–67398.

Berliner, Paul. *Thinking in Jazz: The Infinite Art of Improvisation.* Chicago: University of Chicago Press, 1994.

Brofsky, Howard. "Miles Davis and 'My Funny Valentine': The Evolution of a Solo." *Black Music Research Journal* 3 (1983): 23–45.

Brownell, John. "Analytical Models of Jazz Improvisation." *Jazzforschung/Jazz Research* 26 (1994): 9–29.

Buium, Greg. "Interview: Gary Peacock, Pts. 1 and 2." *Cadence* (September 2001): 9–15 and *Cadence* (October 2001): 5–13.

Carr, Ian. *Miles Davis: The Definitive Biography.* Revised ed. New York: Thunder's Mouth Press, 1998.

Chambers, J. *Milestones: The Music and Times of Miles Davis.* New York: Da Capo Press, 1998. Originally pub. University of Toronto, 1983 and 1985.

Charry, Eric. "Freedom and Form in Ornette Coleman's Early Atlantic Recordings." *Annual Review of Jazz Studies* 9 (1997): 261–94.

Cogswell, Michael. "Melodic Organization in Two Solos by Ornette Coleman." *Annual Review of Jazz Studies* 7 (1994–95): 101–44.

Collier, James. *The Making of Jazz: A Comprehensive History*. Boston: Houghton Mifflin, 1978.

Coolman, Todd. "The Miles Davis Quintet of the Mid-1960s: Synthesis of Improvisational and Compositional Elements." Ph.D. diss., New York University, 1997.

Crouch, Stanley. "Play the Right Thing." *The New Republic* (February 12, 1990): 30–37.

Davis, Miles. *Miles Davis Originals, Vol. 1*. Milwaukee, Wisc.: Hal Leonard, ca. 2001.

Davis, Miles, and Quincy Troupe. *Miles: The Autobiography*. New York: Touchstone, 1989.

de Barros, Paul. "Tony Williams: Two Decades of Drum Innovation." *Down Beat* 50/11 (November 1983): 14–16.

DeMotta, David. "An Analysis of Herbie Hancock's Accompanying in the Miles Davis Quintet on the 1967 Album *No Blues*." M.Mus. thesis, William Paterson University, 2006.

Deveaux, Scott. *The Birth of Bebop: A Social and Musical History*. Berkeley: University of California Press, 1997.

Deveaux, Scott, and Gary Giddins. *Jazz*. New York: W. W. Norton, 2009.

Dobbins, Bill. *Chick Corea Piano Improvisations*. Rottenburg, Germany: Advance Music, 1990.

———. *Herbie Hancock: Classic Jazz Compositions and Piano Solos*. Rottenburg, Germany: Advance Music, 1992.

Dorham, Kenny. "Review: *E.S.P.*" *Down Beat* 32/27 (December 30, 1965): 34.

"Drum Talk: Coast to Coast." *Down Beat* 31/8 (March 26, 1964): 13–19ff.

Dybo, Tor. "Analyzing Interaction during Jazz Improvisation." *Jazzforschung/Jazz Research* 31 (1999): 51–64.

Early, Gerald, ed. *Miles Davis and American Culture*. St. Louis: Missouri Historical Society Press, 2001.

Feather, Leonard. "Miles Davis: Blindfold Test Pt. 1." *Down Beat* 35/12 (June 13, 1968): 34.

Ferriter, Gene. "The Learned Man." *Rhythm* (January 1990): 34–39.

Giel, Lex. *The Music of Miles Davis: A Study and Analysis of Compositions and Solo Transcriptions from the Great Jazz Composer and Improviser*. Milwaukee, Wisc.: Hal Leonard, 2004.

Gridley, Mark. *Jazz Styles: History and Analysis*. 10th ed. Upper Saddle River, N.J.: Pearson Prentice Hall, 2009.

Hamilton, Andy. *Lee Konitz: Conversations on the Improviser's Art*. Ann Arbor: University of Michigan Press, 2007.

Harris, Eddie. *The Eddie Harris Interverlistic Concept, For All Single Line Wind Instruments*. Chicago: Author, 1971. 2nd ed. republished by Seventh House, 2006.

Heckman, Don. "Ron Carter." *Down Beat* 31/9 (April 9, 1964): 18–19.

Helzer, Rick. "Two Compositions by Wayne Shorter: 'Pinocchio' and 'Dolores.'" *Jazz Improv* 2/3 (1999): 210–11.

Hodson, Robert. *Interaction, Improvisation, and Interplay in Jazz*. New York: Routledge, 2007.

Jones, LeRoi. "Introducing Wayne Shorter." *The Jazz Review* 2/10 (November 1959): 22–24.

Jost, Ekkehard. *Free Jazz*. New York: Da Capo Press, 1981.

———. "Über einige Probleme Jazzmusikalischer Analyse." *Jazzforschung/Jazz Research* 31 (1999): 11–18.

Julien, Patricia. *The Structural Function of Harmonic Relations in Wayne Shorter's Early Compositions, 1959–1963*. Ph.D. diss., University of Maryland, 2003.

Kahn, Ashley. *Kind of Blue: The Making of the Miles Davis Masterpiece*. New York: Da Capo Press, 2001.

Kart, Lawrence (Larry). *Jazz in Search of Itself*. New Haven: Yale University Press, 2004.

——. "Review: *Miles in the Sky*." *Down Beat* 35/20 (October 3, 1968): 24.

Kernfeld, Barry. "Adderley, Coltrane, and Davis at the Twilight of Bebop: The Search for Melodic Coherence (1958–1959)." Ph.D. diss., Cornell University, 1981.

——. *The Story of Fake Books: Bootlegging Songs to Musicians*. Lanham, Md.: Scarecrow Press, 2006.

——. *What to Listen for in Jazz*. New Haven: Yale University Press, 1995.

Kernfeld, Barry, ed. *The New Grove Dictionary of Jazz*. 2nd ed. New York: Grove, 2002.

Kerschbaumer, Franz. "Der Einfluss des Free Jazz auf die Music von Miles Davis." *Jazzforschung/Jazz Research* 34 (2002): 109–13.

——. "Miles Davis: Stillkritische Untersuchungen zur Musikalischen Entwicklung seines Personalstils." *Jazzforschung/Jazz Research* 5 (1978).

Kirchner, Bill, ed. *A Miles Davis Reader*. Washington, D.C.: Smithsonian Institution Press, 1997.

Krieger, Franz. "Herbie Hancock in seiner Zeit bei Miles Davis: Transkription und Analyse ausgewählter 'My Funny Valentine'-soli." *Jazzforschung/Jazz Research* 30 (1998): 101–56.

Levine, Mark. *The Jazz Theory Book*. Petaluma, Calif.: Sher Music, 1995.

Logan, T. "Wayne Shorter: Doubletake." *Down Beat* 41/12 (June 20, 1974): 16–17ff.

Lyons, Leonard. *The Great Jazz Pianists: Speaking of Their Lives and Music*. New York: W. Morrow, 1983.

Magee, Jeffrey. "Kinds of Blue: Miles Davis, Afro-Modernism, and the Blues." *Jazz Perspectives* 1/1 (May 2007): 5–27.

Maher, Paul, and Michael K. Dorr. *Miles on Miles: Interviews and Encounters with Miles Davis*. Chicago: Lawrence Hill Books, 2009.

Martin, Henry. "The Nature of Recomposition: Miles Davis and 'Stella By Starlight.'" *Annual Review of Jazz Studies* 9 (1997): 77–92.

Martin, Henry, and Keith Waters. *Jazz: The First 100 Years*. 2nd ed. Belmont, Calif.:Thomson Schirmer, 2006.

Mattingly, Rich. "Tony Williams." *Modern Drummer* (June 1984): 8–13ff.

Mauleón, Rebeca. *101 Montunos*. Petaluma, Calif.: Sher Music, 1999.

Mercer, Michelle. *Footprints: The Life and Work of Wayne Shorter*. New York: J. P. Tarcher/Penguin, 2004.

Milkowski, Bill. "Tony Williams: A Master's Perspective." *Modern Drummer* (July 1992): 20–25ff.

Miller, Ron. *Modal Jazz Composition & Harmony*. Rottenburg, Germany: Advance Music, 1996.

Milner, Greg. *Perfecting Sound Forever: An Aural History of Recorded Music*. New York: Faber and Faber, 2009.

Monson, Ingrid. *Freedom Sounds: Civil Rights Call out to Jazz and Africa*. New York: Oxford University Press, 2007.

———. *Saying Something: Jazz Improvisation and Interaction.* Chicago: University of Chicago Press, 1996.

Morgan, David. "Superimposition in the Improvisations of Herbie Hancock." *Annual Review of Jazz Studies* 11 (2000): 69–90.

Morgenstern, Dan. "Review: *Miles Smiles.*" *Down Beat* 34/13 (June 29, 1967): 28.

Nemeyer, Eric. "The Magical Journey: An Interview with Wayne Shorter." *Jazz Improv* 2/3 (1999): 72–82.

Nicholson, Stuart. *Jazz: The 1980s Resurgence.* New York: Da Capo Press, 1995.

———. *Jazz Rock: A History.* New York: Schirmer Books, 1998.

Pejrolo, Andrea. The Origins of Modal Jazz in the Music of Miles Davis: A Complete Transcription and a Linear/Harmonic Analysis of *Ascenseur pour l'échafaud* (*Lift to the Scaffold*), 1957. Ph.D. diss., New York University, 2001.

Point, Michael. "Tony Williams: The Final Interview." *Down Beat* 64/4 (April 1997): 22–24.

Pond, Stephen. *Head Hunters: The Making of Jazz's First Platinum Album.* Ann Arbor: University of Michigan Press, 2005.

Porter, Lewis. *John Coltrane: His Life and Music.* Ann Arbor: University of Michigan Press, 1998.

———. "John Coltrane's *A Love Supreme:* Jazz Improvisation as Composition." *Journal of the American Musicological Society* 38/3 (Fall 1985): 593–621.

Quinn, Bill. "Review: *Sorcerer.*" *Down Beat* 35/2 (January 25, 1968): 29.

The Real Book. 6th ed. Milwaukee, Wisc.: Hal Leonard, ca. 2006.

Reeves, Scott. *Creative Jazz Improvisation.* Englewood Cliffs, N.J.: Prentice Hall, 1989.

Russell, George. *The Lydian Chromatic Concept of Tonal Organization for Improvisation.* 2nd ed. New York: Concept, 1959.

Sagee, Alona. "Miles Davis's Improvised Solos in Recordings of 'Walkin': 1954–67." *Annual Review of Jazz Studies* 13 (2003): 27–47.

Schoenberg, Arnold. *Fundamentals of Musical Composition.* London: Faber and Faber, 1967.

Schuller, Gunther. *A Collection of the Compositions of Ornette Coleman.* New York: MJQ Music, 1961.

———. *Musings: The Musical Worlds of Gunther Schuller.* New York: Oxford University Press, 1986.

Shorter, Wayne. *The New Best of Wayne Shorter.* Milwaukee, Wisc.: Hal Leonard, ca. 2004.

Siders, Harvey. "Review: Miles Davis, *My Funny Valentine.*" *Down Beat* 32/12 (June 3, 1965): 27.

Sidran, Ben. *Talking Jazz: An Oral History.* Expanded ed. New York: Da Capo Press, 1995.

Silvert, Conrad. "Herbie Hancock: Revamping the Past, Creating the Future." *Down Beat* 44/15 (September 8, 1977): 16–17ff.

———. "Wayne Shorter: Imagination Unlimited." *Down Beat* 44/13 (July 14, 1977): 15–16ff.

Simons, David. *Studio Stories: How the Great New York Records Were Made: From Miles to Madonna.* San Francisco: Backbeat Books, 2004.

Stewart, Zan. "Miles Lives!" *Down Beat* 59/9 (September 1992): 16–21.

Strunk, Steven. "The Harmony of Early Bop: A Layered Approach." *Journal of Jazz Studies* 6 (1979): 4–53.

———. "Notes on Harmony in Wayne Shorter's Early Compositions: 1959–63." *Journal of Music Theory* 49/2 (Fall 2005): 301–32.

Szwed, John. *So What: The Life of Miles Davis*. New York: Simon & Schuster, 2002.

Taylor, Arthur. *Notes and Tones: Musician-To-Musician Interviews*. Expanded ed. New York: Da Capo, 1993.

Taylor, Billy. *Jazz Piano: A Jazz History*. Dubuque, Iowa: Brown, 1983.

Thomson, William. "On Miles and the Modes." *College Music Symposium* 38 (1998): 17–32.

Tirro, Frank. *Jazz: A History*. 2nd ed. New York: W. W. Norton, 1993.

Townley, Ray. "Hancock Plugs In." *Down Beat* 41/17 (October 24, 1974): 13–15ff.

Ulanov, Barry. *A History of Jazz in America*. New York: Viking Press, 1952.

Underwood, Lee. "Aspiring to a Lifetime of Leadership." *Down Beat* 46/12 (June 21, 1979): 20–21ff.

Wald, Aran. "Tony Williams." *Modern Drummer* 2/1 (January 1978): 6–7ff.

Walser, Robert. "Deep Jazz: Notes on Interiority, Race, and Criticism." Essay in *Inventing the Psychological: Toward a Cultural History of Emotional Life in America*. Ed. by Joel Pfister and Nancy Schnog. New Haven: Yale University Press, 1997.

———. " 'Out of Notes': Signification, Interpretation, and the Problem of Miles Davis." *Musical Quarterly* 77/2 (1993): 343–65.

Waters, Keith. "Blurring the Barline: Metric Displacement in the Piano Solos of Herbie Hancock." *Annual Review of Jazz Studies* 8 (1996): 19–37.

———. "Modes, Scales, Functional Harmony, and Non-Functional Harmony in the Compositions of Herbie Hancock." *Journal of Music Theory* 49/2 (2005): 333–57.

———. "Motivic and Formal Improvisation in the Miles Davis Quintet 1965–1968." *Tijdschrift voor Muziektheorie* 8/1 (February 2003): 25–39.

———. "Outside Forces: 'Autumn Leaves' in the 1960s." *Current Musicology* 71–73 (2001): 276–302.

Waters, Keith, and David Diamond. "Out Front: The Art of Booker Little." *Annual Review of Jazz Studies* 11 (2000–2001): 1–38.

Weidenmüller, Johannes. "The Use of Metric Modulation and Superimposition in the Music of the Miles Davis Quintet from 1963 to 1968." M.Mus. thesis, University of Colorado at Boulder, 2007.

Weiskopf, Walt, and Ramon Ricker. *The Augmented Scale in Jazz*. New Albany, Ind.: Jamey Aebersold Jazz, 1993.

Welding, Pete. "Review: Wayne Shorter, *Night Dreamer*." *Down Beat* 31/13 (December 3, 1964): 26–27.

Williams, Martin. "Recording Miles Davis." Essay in *Jazz Masters in Transition: 1957–69*. New York: Da Capo Press, 1980.

Wong, Herb. "World Class Drummer: Tony Williams." *Jazz Times* (September 1988): 17–19.

Woodson, Craig. "Solo Jazz Drumming: An Analytic Study of the Improvisation Techniques of Anthony Williams." Ph.D. diss., University of California–Los Angeles, 1973.

Yudkin, Jeremy. *Miles Davis, Miles Smiles, and the Invention of Post Bop*. Bloomington: Indiana University Press, 2008.

INDEX

CPSIA information can be obtained
at www.ICGtesting.com
Printed in the USA
BVHW080215060122
624997BV00003B/6